TENNIS

Strokes,
Strategy,
and Programs

TENNIS

Strokes, Strategy, and Programs

Jim Brown
McNeese State University

PRENTICE-HALL, INC., Englewood Cliffs, New Jersey 07632

Library of Congress Cataloging in Publication Data

BROWN, JIM (date)
    Tennis, strokes, strategy, and programs.

    Bibliography: p.
    Includes index.
    1. Tennis. I. Title.
GV995.B6925   796.34'22   79-23982
ISBN 0-13-903351-3

Editorial/production supervision and
   interior design by Frank J. Hubert
Cover design by R L Communications
Manufacturing buyer: Harry P. Baisley

Printed in the United States of America

10 9 8 7 6 5 4 3 2 1

PRENTICE-HALL INTERNATIONAL, INC., *London*
PRENTICE-HALL OF AUSTRALIA PTY. LIMITED, *Sydney*
PRENTICE-HALL OF CANADA, LTD., *Toronto*
PRENTICE-HALL OF INDIA PRIVATE LIMITED, *New Delhi*
PRENTICE-HALL OF JAPAN, INC., *Tokyo*
PRENTICE-HALL OF SOUTHEAST ASIA PTE. LTD., *Singapore*
WHITEHALL BOOKS LIMITED, *Wellington, New Zealand*

CONTENTS

Preface

This book is two books. The first is for players, teachers, and coaches, but especially for players. The second is for teachers, coaches, parents, program directors, club professionals, and volunteer workers. Together, the two books in one were written to provide a comprehensive tennis guide.

Each chapter has a one word title. These eight words are meant to be descriptive and to emphasize the style of the book—practical, complete, and efficient. Every sentence should have an idea or a piece of information helpful to someone. Throw-away words, phrases, and sentences were thrown away.

The first chapter, **Background,** lays the foundation for the rest of the book. There is some history, advice on buying equipment, a one hundred and thirty-one word glossary, and answers to sixty questions about rules.

Strokes has three features: fundamentals for eight strokes, instruction and pictures for righthanders and lefthanders, and common problems and their corrections.

The strength of **Strategy** is one hundred and eighty-three strategy tips which are numbered, boldfaced, explained, and grouped according to strokes, singles, doubles, and special situations.

Thinking goes beyond strategy to more intangible areas of the game such as concentration, anticipation, psychological factors, and developing a personal philosophy of the game.

Teaching is for those already in the field as well as those learning to be tennis instructors and teaching pros. Suggestions are given for teaching everyone from children to adults, from private lessons to physical education classes. The range between those extremes is considerable.

The **Coaching** chapter covers recruiting, scheduling, buying supplies, practicing, scouting, publicizing teams, taking care of injuries, and developing coaching and teaching skills.

Conducting competition may not be as much fun as playing, but someone has to do it. If that person is you, **Competition** tells how to set up and run eight kinds of tournaments and matches.

Drills is exactly what the title says. There are more than eighty drills and their variations for beginners, intermediates, and advanced players. All of them are explained and grouped by strokes, and most of them are diagrammed.

Throughout the book there are comments set apart from the text. You may not agree with what is said, but reading them might make you examine your own attitudes about tennis. There are also review questions for you or your students.

Steve Haller and Ann Chamberlain took the pictures for this book. Tennis playing friends from Southwest Louisiana posed for the pictures. The Bancroft Sporting Goods Company provided rackets, balls, and some of the clothes. *Scholastic Coach, The Woman,* and Prentice-Hall, Inc., released previously written material for use in this book. Arlene and Matthew Brown helped in special ways.

Jim Brown
Lake Charles, La.

Chapter 1

Background

A RECENT HISTORY OF CHANGES

When Walter Wingfield received a British patent for lawn tennis in 1874, he could not have predicted what the game would be like today. He did not plan on point penalties, feed-in consolations, team tennis, rackets that cost hundreds of dollars, and millionaire players. There are people who think his idea of the game was better than ours. Tennis, perhaps more than any sport, has changed drastically in a relatively short period of time. Most of those changes have occurred recently.

PUBLIC COURT TENNIS

Not long ago, tennis was a game played primarily by rich men who belonged to exclusive clubs. Although club tennis is stronger than ever, people of all classes now play. In the United States and Australia most of them play on public courts. In Latin America, Asia, and parts of Europe, most players still belong to clubs.

WOMEN PLAYERS

When the United States National Lawn Tennis Association (now the United States Tennis Association) "extended its protective wing" to women players in 1889, tennis became a respectable if not popular sport for both sexes. By the mid-1970s, as many women were playing tennis as men.

PLAYERS OF ALL AGES

The ages of people playing tennis have also changed. At the tournament level, once dominated by young and middle aged men, players now range from the eight and under group to the over seventy division.

THE NUMBER OF PEOPLE PLAYING

The cumulative effect of more women, more men, more young people, more older people, and more people from the middle and lower classes has been an enormous increase in the total number of people who play tennis. Surveys have estimated that about thirty million Americans play tennis regularly.

STYLE OF PLAY

With the increase in the number of people playing tennis has come changes in the style of play. Good players in the 1930's, 1940's, and 1950's generally used classic strokes to achieve success. These strokes were copied by younger players. Now there are great players who use a variety of grips and swings to become champions. When several million television viewers see a champion with unorthodox strokes, the influence on beginning and intermediate players is tremendous. Traditional and unorthodox styles of play are imitated by today's young players with varying degrees of success.

OPEN TENNIS

Tennis was once played only by amateurs. One of the most dramatic changes has been the rise of professional tennis. The world's greatest players once performed in one night stands across the world. Now world class players turn professional during their teens or early twenties, play before thousands of spectators in the stands and millions on television, and compete for hundreds of thousands of dollars. Open tennis was a development of the 1960's, and tennis remains one of the few sports in which pros compete regularly with amateurs.

TELEVISED TENNIS

More than any other factor, the influence of television may be responsible for change. The increase in the number of players happened almost simultaneously with the increase in tennis events shown on television. Tennis players became celebrities equal to baseball, basketball, and football stars. When the tennis boom of the 1970's occurred, television fed the national tennis appetite with advertisements for hundreds of tennis-related products.

TENNIS TECHNOLOGY

Technology has also changed tennis. Courts used to be made of grass, clay, or concrete. Now there are courts made of colorful synthetic products with made-to-order slow, fast, or medium surfaces. The new interest in tennis has produced more public courts, more school courts, more tennis clubs, and more indoor facilities than ever before.

Tennis players have survived a technological blitz of rackets. Although metal rackets made an uneventful debut earlier in the century, most players used wooden rackets until the late 1960s and early 1970s. Since that time, a barrage of rackets made of steel, aluminum, fiberglass, graphite, and other space age products has hit the market. About 40 percent of all tennis players now use something other than wood rackets. No one has invented a racket that will enable us to beat someone who is better than we are, but manufacturers keep trying.

The line of new tennis products goes far beyond courts and rackets. The tennis accessory industry provides thousands of things which may or may not do anything to help us play better, but probably do make us look and feel better.

Tennis Instruction

Tennis instruction has gone from not enough to too much. During the first two-thirds of the century there was not enough interest to support many teaching professionals. The only teachers, other than a few club pros in metropolitan areas, were physical education teachers and ex-players trying to earn extra money. Now there are tennis pros, camps, courses, and clinics throughout the world. Since the profession is still young, there are some teachers who are not very good at teaching the game. But they are getting better, and now there are organizations which train and certify pros.

Future Changes

If tennis changes as much during the second one hundred years as during the first one hundred, we will not be able to predict its future any better than Major Wingfield could have. But because of the changes, or in spite of them, it is safe to say that millions of people will continue to enjoy playing the game. They will play because tennis is good for physical fitness, because at most levels it is a very sociable game, because it is a lifetime sport, because it is relatively inexpensive, and most of all, because tennis is fun.

EQUIPMENT

Rackets

If you have to buy a racket, do not spend a lot of money for one until you have decided to play tennis regularly. Many people buy a racket, play once or twice, then decide tennis is not their game. New rackets range in price from a few dollars to hundreds of dollars. Although it is possible to get a racket for a few dollars, at that price you should not expect much in quality or durability. For a little more, you can find a racket that is adequate for getting started. Most of the major sporting goods companies sell rackets within the entire price range, so the brand name is not that important for a beginner. As you improve your game, you will be able to decide on a racket with a feel that suits you. Before buying an expensive one, try to borrow different rackets from players you know or from stores that loan demonstrators so you can see how each one hits. Picking up and swinging a racket in a store or specialty shop is not sufficient to get a racket's feel. The only way to do that is to play with one.

There are several ways to determine if you are getting a quality racket. One way is to look on the side of the shaft (the part between the strings and the grip) for markings indicating the racket's grip size and weight. On quality rackets you will see something like 4½ L, 4⅝ M, or similar letters and numbers (See Figure 1-1). The number refers to the circumference of the grip in inches and the letter means either a light, medium, or heavy racket. If there are no markings, you are looking at a cheap racket.

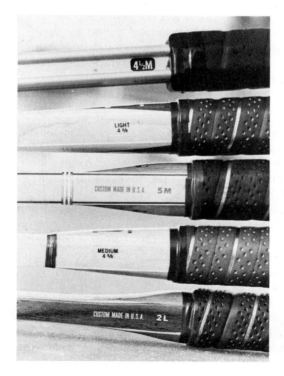

Figure 1–1 The numbers and letters on the shaft indicate the size of the grip and weight of the racket.

However, there are some inferior rackets with these markings, so this is not the only method of determining the quality of a racket.

A second way to judge the quality of some wooden rackets is to look for separate laminated wood strips that form the racket head or bow (the part where the strings are). Generally, good rackets will have five to twelve strips of wood pressed together. On some good rackets the laminations may not be visible because of the outer finish. Cheaper rackets may have fewer wood strips or a one-piece top.

Once you reach a certain price range in rackets, the difference is one of personal preference, not quality. A two hundred dollar racket is not necessarily better for you than a racket that costs one hundred dollars or less. Every racket on the market will give you something and take something away. A cheap racket will give you more money in your pocket, but will take away things like durability and a smooth feel when you hit. A racket that is very resilient will give you more power than you've ever had, but may take away some touch shots and consistency. A two hundred dollar racket gives you something to talk about at a party, but it will not win matches for you. Somewhere out there is a racket that is best suited for your style of play. When you find it, quit looking. You cannot buy your way into tennis heaven. Sooner or later you have to hit the ball over the net and the racket will be just about as good as you are.

A third method of determining racket quality is to observe the general workmanship of the racket. Does it look cheap or is it well-designed? Is the material used to make the grip thick, durable looking leather? Are the laminated strips put together smoothly on a wooden racket? On metal rackets, is the welding or riveting secure?

Finally, it is a good idea to ask the opinions of other tennis players and to observe which rackets are being used in your area. Experienced players have usually played with a variety of rackets, and they can give you sound advice. The most popular rackets are frequently the best, so if you see a lot of people playing with a particular kind, it is probably of high quality.

You will have to decide whether to buy a racket made of wood, metal, or some other product such as fiberglass or graphite. There are many differences among rackets, but generally speaking wooden rackets usually have stiffer frames and give the player more control and less power. Steel, aluminum, composite, fiberglass, and graphite rackets provide more power but less control. There is a wide range of racket flexibility and resiliency within each category, so again it is best if you test various rackets before making a choice. Since accuracy will be a problem during the first few months of play, it may be best to begin playing with a wooden racket or with an aluminum model. After you have played for a while, you may decide to buy a more expensive racket. By then you will be in a better position to make a decision regarding a racket to suit your style of play.

Two other decisions you will have to make before buying a racket involve the size of the grip and the weight of the racket. Grip sizes range from 4 to 5 inches. The most common size for men is 4⅝ inches; women tend to use rackets with a slightly smaller grip. If the grip size is too small or too large, the racket may turn in your hand when you hit. One way to determine the proper grip size for you is to shake hands with the racket handle. As your fingers curl around the grip, the end of your thumb should touch the first joint of your middle finger, as shown in Figure 1-2.

If the thumb does not reach that point, the grip is too large; if the thumb overlaps the joint, the grip is too small. A second way to determine the right grip size is to measure the distance from the tip of your ring finger to the second line that runs across your palm. That distance should be very close to the proper grip circumference for you. A third way to know if a racket's grip is the right size is simply by feel. It should feel comfortable and maneuverable in your hand. The shape of the grip should not be overlooked. It is important that you choose a racket that fits the contour of your hand. Also remember that racket grips can be replaced and that many of them can be reduced or increased in circumference by the person who strings your racket.

Unstrung tennis rackets vary in weight from 12 to 15 ounces. The light, medium, and heavy designations mentioned earlier may vary from brand to brand, but light rackets usually weigh 12 to 13 ounces, mediums from 13 to 14, and heavies weigh 14 ounces or more. The light rackets are easier to handle, but supply less power; the heavy ones enable you to hit with more force, but the added weight makes the racket more difficult to maneuver and may tire your arm before a match is finished. The medium

Figure 1–2 The end of the thumb usually meets the first joint of the middle finger when the grip is the right size.

weight rackets are sold most often to adults and are a compromise between power and handling ease. Rackets for children should be on the light side, with smaller than average grip sizes. Rackets a few inches shorter than standard sizes are also available and are effective for children and some adults just beginning to play.

Cheap rackets will last less than a year if you play regularly. Quality rackets should last several years if you take care of them. If a racket breaks shortly after you have purchased it, take it back to the dealer and ask for a replacement. Several companies guarantee rackets for up to one year. Do not waste money buying a racket press. Good rackets should not warp and bad ones will, press or no press. A racket cover is more attractive and useful than a press. A cover protects frame and strings from moisture and can be used to hold keys, wallets, and coin purses while you play. It also helps you identify your racket when not in use.

Beginners need only one racket; intermediates and advanced players frequently own two or more so they will have an alternate if the strings in one break during play or if the grip on one becomes too slick because of moisture.

Strings   Department stores and many sporting goods stores sell rackets already strung. Pro shops and specialty shops often sell unstrung frames and give you the choice of the kind of strings to be used. Beginners and intermediates should ask for nylon strings because they are cheap, reasonably durable, and replaceable with more expensive strings later. There are several kinds of nylon strings and many brand names. Ask your instructor, tennis pro, or stringer what your options are. Many advanced players also use rackets strung with nylon. Others prefer gut, a crude but graphic description of beef or sheep muscle tissue processed for racket string. Gut is expensive and must be kept dry, but it is an extremely resilient and sensitive stringing material. If money is not a consideration, you may want to use gut. If you do not care to pay twenty to forty dollars for each restringing job, use nylon.

Rackets can be strung from pressure in the 40 pound range to nearly 70 pounds. A reasonable average is 51 to 56 pounds. Beginners should have their rackets strung at about 50 to 53 pounds for more effective ball control. Local advanced players prefer the 54 to 60 pound range, and some world class players may have their rackets strung at more than 60 pounds. Players using oversized rackets also get stringing jobs at more than 60 pounds. Tight strings are more likely to break and more likely to warp the racket than looser strings.

It is difficult to predict how long racket strings will last. Many beginners and intermediates can play for months with the same set of strings. Advanced players may wear out or break strings in a matter of weeks or even days. Durability depends on the quality of the string, how the person plays, the style of game, and how well the player takes care of his or her rackets. There are products available that can be applied to strings to make them last longer.

Grips   When you get ready to change grips on a racket, you will have three choices: expensive or inexpensive, holes or no holes in the leather, and a flat or raised grip. Changing grips should cost no more than a few dollars. The work can be done in a few minutes. Some grips have small perforations which presumably allow the leather to get more air for quick drying. Flat grips have small grooves at the seams, and raised grips have ridges instead of grooves. Which one you decide on is strictly a matter of personal preference; one is not better than the other.

Taking Care of Your Rackets

1. Do not store your rackets in car trunks, near windows, in utility rooms, or other extremely hot or cold places. Find a safe place at home where room temperatures are moderate.
2. Keep racket covers on rackets when they are not being used. The covers prevent accidental breaks and protect the strings from moisture.
3. Avoid spinning the racket on the court to determine who serves and receives. The daily routine of spinning can wear away the top of the frame and the friction may eventually break any exposed strings. Spin the racket in your hands instead of letting it fall to the court.
4. Keep the grip clean by using alcohol, steel wool, or by lightly washing the leather with soap and water. Washing will dry the leather, which is bad for durability but good for preventing slippage in hot weather.
5. Don't throw your racket. Sounds ridiculous, but people do it.

BALLS

Tennis balls come in almost as many varieties as rackets. Here you cannot afford to start out with cheap ones and then graduate to better quality balls as you improve. It is important to always play with good balls, so buy the best ones available the first time out. Brand names can be deceiving but Bancroft, Dunlop, Penn, Slazenger, Spalding, and Wilson are some of the companies that make good tennis balls. You can save money by watching for sales, shopping at discount stores, and buying a dozen or more balls at a time.

The balls packaged in cans are packed under pressure. When you open the can, you should hear a hissing sound which is the pressurized air being released. If you do not hear that sound, return the can to the dealer for a refund or a new can. If a ball breaks within the first two or three sets, all three balls should be returned for replacement.

You cannot play with one can of balls forever. Three balls may last two or three outings for beginners and some intermediates, but after that they will begin to lose pressure and bounce, or the fuzz will wear off. When that happens use them for practice only. You can extend the life of balls by keeping them in the original cans and by storing them in a cool place.

Some tennis balls (Tretorns, for example) are not packaged under pressure. They are sold in a box. These balls are not as bouncy as those that are pressurized, but they never go dead. They will eventually lose their fuzz and that will affect the bounce of the ball. Nonpressurized tennis balls are popular at high altitudes where the thin air off-sets the built-in heaviness of the ball.

Ask for heavy duty balls if you are going to play on hard surfaces like concrete. Regular championship balls are used on softer surfaces because they do not wear out as quickly. You can also buy balls in a can made specifically for play in high altitudes.

SHOES

In choosing tennis shoes the four factors to consider are cost, durability, comfort, and weight. Shoes vary widely in price. Frequency of play, style of play, and the type of court surface will determine how much wear you will get from your shoes. People who play often on hard surfaces may wear out a pair of shoes within a few weeks. Those who play on softer surfaces may get several months out of their shoes. It is not unusual for the toe of one shoe to wear out completely while the rest of the shoe is still in perfect condition. Single shoes are available from some companies. Leather topped tennis shoes are more comfortable and more expensive than canvas topped shoes. But if you are the kind of player who wears out the sole or toe quickly, the comfort may not be worth the expense.

Buy the lightest shoe possible if you are satisfied with the cost, comfort, and durability. A difference of a few ounces will seem like pounds during the third set of a match.[1]

[1] Jim and Arlene Brown, "A Woman's Guide to Beginning Tennis," *The Woman*, 10, no. 6 (June 1975), 110–15.

GLOSSARY

ace   a serve which the receiver cannot touch with the racket

ad   advantage; refers to the point after the score is deuce

ad court   the left half of a player's court as that player faces the net from the baseline

ad in   a reference to the score when the player serving has won the point after the score was deuce

ad out   a reference to the score when the player receiving the serve has won the point after the score was deuce

all   a tie score; for example, 30 all means that the score is 30–30

alley   the 4½ foot wide lane running parallel to and on both sides of the singles court; the alleys are in play for all shots after the serve in doubles

amateur   a person who does not accept money for playing or teaching tennis

American twist   a type of serve in which the spin imparted by the racket is the opposite of what it would normally be; a righthander's American twist serve has left-to-right spin on the ball

angle shot   a shot which crosses the net at a severe angle

approach shot   a shot which the hitter follows to the net

Association of Tennis Professionals (A.T.P.)   an organization composed of most of the leading male players in the world

Australian doubles   a doubles formation in which the player at net (the server's partner) lines up on the same half of the doubles court as the server

back court   that part of the court between the service line and the baseline

backhand   a stroke which a righthanded player hits by reaching across the body to the left side; a lefthanded player reaches across to the right side to hit a backhand

backspin   reverse spin on the ball, like a car wheel in reverse

backswing   the preparation for a stroke in which the racket is drawn back before being swung forward

baseline   the boundary line that runs parallel to and 39 feet from the net

block   the return of a ball with a very short swinging motion

carry   a shot which is carried on the racket strings, slung, or hit twice as the ball is returned; carries are illegal and may be called by the umpire or the player who hits the shot on which the violation occurs

center mark   a line dividing the baseline at the center; the server may not legally step on the center mark before striking the ball

center service line   the line in the middle of the court that divides the two service courts

chip   a groundstroke hit with a short backswing and with backspin on the ball; the chip is usually meant to be a shallow shot (not very deep into the opponent's court)

choke   to play poorly because of the pressure of competition

choke up   to hold the racket at a point away from the base of the grip

chop   a shot hit with backspin to any part of the court

circuit   a series of tournaments at the state, sectional, national, or international level

closed stance   a position in which the toes of both feet form a line parallel to either sideline

closed tournament   an event open only to players in a particular geographical area

composite   a reference to tennis rackets made from a combination of two or more materials; for example, one made from wood and fiberglass

Continental grip   a way of holding the racket so that the player does not have to change grips between the forehand and backhand strokes; a more complete description is presented in the chapter on strokes

crosscourt   a shot hit diagonally from one corner of the court to the opposite corner

Davis Cup   an international team tennis event for male players; a match or "tie" between the teams representing two countries consists of four singles matches and one doubles match

deep   a reference to the area near the baseline

default   the awarding of a match to one player or team because an opponent fails to appear or is not able to complete the match

deuce   a tie score at 40–40 and each tie thereafter in the same game

deuce court   the right half of a player's court as that player faces the net from the baseline

dink   a shot hit with very little pace or depth

double fault   failure on both attempts to serve into the proper court

doubles   a match played with four players; also, an informal expression sometimes used to indicate a double fault

down the line   a shot hit parallel to either sideline

drive   a groundstroke hit forcefully and deeply into an opponent's backcourt

drop shot   a softly hit shot, usually having backspin, which barely clears the net and bounces within 2 or 3 feet of the net

error   a point lost as a result of one player's mistake rather than the other player's good shot

fast   a reference to a tennis court surface on which the ball bounces low and moves rapidly toward the hitter

fault   failure on an attempt to serve into the proper court

feed-in consolation   a tournament in which players who lose through the quarterfinal round re-enter the championship draw and may finish as high as fifth

finals   the match played to determine the winner of a tournament

flat   a reference to a shot hit with little or no spin

follow through   that part of the swinging motion after the ball has been hit

forehand   a stroke which a righthanded player hits on the right side of the body and which a lefthander hits on the left side

forfeit   synonym for default

grip   the manner in which a racket is held; also, that part of the racket where it is held

groove   to hit shots in a patterned, disciplined, and consistent manner

groundstroke   a shot which is hit after the ball has bounced on the court

hacker   a person who does not play tennis well

half volley   a shot hit just after the ball has bounced on the court; contact is made below the level of the knees

hold serve   a game won by the server

hook   a slang term meaning to cheat

International Tennis Federation (I.T.F.)   an organization which governs international amateur competition and which has some jurisdiction over professional tennis

invitational tournament   a tournament open only to players who have been invited to participate

junior   a player eighteen years old or younger

junior veteran   a player between 35 and 45 years old

ladder tournament   a type of competition in which the names of participants are placed in a column, players may advance up the column or ladder by challenging and defeating players whose names appear above their own

let   a serve that hits the top of the net and bounces in the proper service court; also an expression used to indicate that a point should be replayed for a number of other reasons

linesperson   an official who is responsible for calling balls out at either the baseline, service line, sideline, or center service line

lob   a high, arching shot

lob volley   a lob hit with a volley

long   an informal expression used to indicate that a shot is out

love   an archaic but commonly used word meaning zero in the tennis scoring system

match   a contest between two players in singles, four players in doubles, or between two teams, as when two school teams compete against each other

match point   the stage of a match when a player can win the match by winning the next point; the term is used by spectators and television commentators during a match and by players after a match; it is not used by the umpire or players in calling out the score

mixed doubles   competition between a man and woman on one team against a man and woman on the other team

net umpire   an official who is responsible for calling let serves

no   an expression which some players use to call shots out

no-ad   a scoring system in which a maximum of seven points constitutes a game; if the score is tied at three points for each player, the next player to win a point wins the game

not up   an expression used to indicate that a ball has bounced twice on the same side before being hit

no man's land   the area of the court between the service line and the baseline; this area is usually considered a poor part of the court to stand in during a rally

open tennis   competition open to amateur and professional players

out   a call indicating that a shot has bounced outside the boundary line

overhead smash   a hard, powerful stroke hit from an over-the-head racket position

pace   the velocity with which a ball is hit

passing shot   a groundstroke hit out of the reach of an opponent at the net

percentage shot   the safest, most effective shot hit in a particular situation

placement   a winning shot hit to an open area of the court

poach   movement of a player at the net in front of a partner to hit a volley

point penalty   a system in which a player may be penalized points in a game for improper behavior

pro set   a match which is completed when one player or team has won at least eight games and is ahead by at least two games

pusher   a type of player who is consistent, but who hits with very little pace

put-away   a reference to a shot that is literally put away (out of reach) from an opponent

qualifying round   a series of matches played to determine which players will be added to a tournament field

rally   an exchange of shots

racket head   the part of the racket where the strings are attached

ready position   the position in which a player stands while waiting for a shot

receiver   the player who will return a serve

referee   an official who is responsible for supervising all competition during a tournament

retriever   a type of player, much like the pusher, who gets everything back but does not play aggressively

round robin   a type of competition in which all participants compete against all other participants in a series of matches; the player or team finishing the competition with the best win—loss percentage is the winner

rush   to move toward the net

second   an informal expression used by some players to indicate that the first serve was out

senior   a player over forty-five years old

serve   the shot used to put the ball into play at the beginning of a point

service break   the loss of a game by the player serving

service court   the area into which the ball must be served; its boundaries are the net, the center line, the service line, and the singles sideline; the server tries to serve into the service court diagonally across the net from where he or she stands

service line   the line that is parallel to and 21 feet from the net

set   that part of a match which is completed when a player or team has won at least six games and is ahead by at least two games; the set may continue until one player has a two game advantage, or a tie breaker may be played when each player has won six games

set point   the stage of a set when a player can win the set by winning the next point

sideline   the boundary line that runs from the net to the baseline; the singles sidelines are closer to the center of the court than the doubles sidelines

single elimination tournament   a type of competition in which players' names are drawn and placed on lines in a tournament bracket; matches are played between players whose names appear on connected bracket lines; players who win advance to the next round of competition; those who lose a match are eliminated

slice   to hit a ball with sidespin, like the spin of a top

slow   a reference to a court surface on which the ball bounces and slows down after the bounce

split   an expression used to indicate that two players or teams have each won a set

straight sets   a reference to winning a match without losing a set

stroke   a manner in which a ball is hit

sudden death   a tie breaker method of completing a set when both players have won six games

take two   an expression meaning that the server should repeat both service attempts

teaching pro   a person who teaches people to play tennis and is paid for the service; teaching pros are usually distinguished from playing pros, although some professionals teach and play for money

throat   the part of the racket just below the head

tie breaker   a method of completing a set when both players or teams have won six games

topspin   the bottom to top rotation imparted to a ball by a racket, like a car wheel going forward

touch   the ability to hit a variety of precision shots

umpire   a person who is responsible for officiating a match between two players or two doubles teams

unforced error   a point lost with absolutely no pressure having been exerted by the opponent

United States Tennis Association (U.S.T.A.)   a national, noncommercial membership organization which promotes tennis in a variety of ways; those ways are described in the chapter entitled "Coaching"

VASSS   Van Alen Simplified Scoring System; a system in which 21 or 31 points constitute a set

volley   a shot hit before the ball bounces on the court

Western grip   a way of holding the racket in which the wrist is positioned directly behind the handle as the ball is hit

wide   an expression used by some players to indicate a shot was outside of a sideline

Wightman Cup   competition for women players representing the United States and England

Wimbledon   a tournament held in England; generally considered to be the most prestigious in the world

World Tennis Association (W.T.A.)   an organization consisting of the world's leading female professional players[2]

[2] Jim Brown, *Tennis Without Lessons* (Englewood Cliffs, N.J.: Prentice-Hall, Inc., 1978), pp. 22–28.

RULES

In this section, the most frequently asked questions about the rules of tennis will be answered. These questions and answers are separated into categories which have been indicated with subtitles. Some of the questions will seem simple to the intermediate and advanced players, but those questions are perfectly reasonable and proper for beginning players. The answers include comments about some of the unwritten rules of tennis.

SCORING

How do you keep score?   The server's score is always given first, and the same player serves a complete game. Points are: love (meaning zero); 15 (the first point won by either player or team); 30 (the second point); 40 (third point); and game (fourth point). If the players are tied at four or more points during a game, the score is called "deuce." When one player goes ahead by one point after the score is deuce, the score is called "ad in" or "advantage server" if the server is ahead. It is called "ad out" or "advantage receiver" if the receiver is ahead. A player must win two consecutive points after the score is deuce in order to win that game. If not, the score reverts to deuce.

What is a set?   A set has been completed when one player or team has won at least six games and is ahead by at least two games (6–0, 6–1, 6–2, 6–3, or 6–4). If a player wins at least six games but is not ahead by at least two games, the set continues until one player is ahead by two games (7–5, 8–6, 9–7, etc.). This procedure is followed unless a tie breaker is used to complete a set.

What is a match?   A match is whatever the tournament director says it is in formal competition or whatever two or four players decide it is in informal competition. A match usually consists of two out of three sets, but it can be three out of five sets or a pro set. A match may also refer to competition between two tennis teams.

What is a pro set?   A pro set has been completed when one player wins at least eight games and is ahead by at least two games (8–0, 8–1, 8–2, etc.).

What is no-ad scoring?   In no-ad scoring, the first player to win four points wins the game. Points are called 1, 2, 3, and game, instead of 15, 30, 40, and game. There is no deuce or ad. When the score is tied at 3–3, the next point

17

determines that game. At 3–3, the receiver may choose to receive the serve from the left or right side.

Who keeps score? In some tournament competition, there may be an umpire assigned to a match and he or she will call out the score. In most cases, however, the players keep their own score, and the server should call out the score before each point is played.

How is a point won? Most often a player wins a point when the opponent does not serve or return a ball over the net and into the proper court. Players must hit the ball before it bounces or after the first bounce.

Are balls that hit the lines good? Yes.

Tie Breaker

What is a tie breaker? A tie breaker is commonly used to complete a set when the score is 6–6 in games. Instead of playing until one player gains a two game lead, the players or teams play a series of points, the winner of which wins that set. The most popular tie breaker consists of the best of nine points (the first player to win five points wins the set, 7–6). To begin a nine point tie breaker, Smith, whose turn it is to serve after the twelfth game, serves a point from the right side of the court and then serves the second point from the left side. Then the opponent, Jones, serves the next two points, first from the right side and then from the left. The players then change ends of the court without taking a break. The first server, Smith, serves two more points first from the right, then from the left. If neither player has won five points, the serve goes back to the second player, Jones, who serves the last three points. On the ninth point of a tie breaker, the receiver, Smith, has the choice of receiving the serve from either the left or right side of the court. The winner of the tie breaker wins the set, 7–6. Figures 1-3 and 1-4 illustrate no-ad scoring.

What is the order of serves when a tie breaker is necessary in doubles? Teams use the order of serves just described for singles play. The players on both teams serve from the sides established during the preceding set. When a ninth point is necessary, the receiving team decides which partner (and thus which side) will receive the serve.

How does the next set after a tie breaker begin? The players stay on the ends of the court where the tie breaker was completed. The player or team who served second in the tie breaker serves the first game of the next set. The players play one game, then change ends of the court.

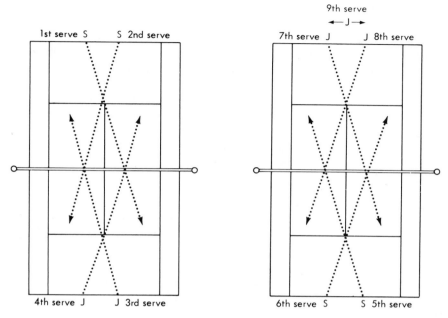

Nine Point Tie-Breaker

Players change ends after 4 points.

Figure 1–3   **Figure 1–4**

SERVING

Are balls that hit the top of the net in play?   Serves that hit the top of the net and fall into the proper court are repeated without any penalty. This is called a "let." Other shots that hit the top of the net and fall into the proper court are in play. If a serve hits the net and bounces outside of the service court, the serve is a fault.

Where do you stand if you are the server?   To begin a game, stand anywhere behind the baseline and between the center mark and the singles sideline. On the second point, move to the left side of the center mark as you face the net. Alternate serving from the right and left sides on each point for the remainder of the game. Remember that the same person serves the entire game. In doubles, the rule is the same except that you can stand as far over as the doubles sideline.

How many times can the server have to put the ball into play?   Two chances on each point, not counting lets.

How many times can the server serve a let on the same point? There is no limit.

What is a foot fault? A foot fault is committed when the server touches the court on or beyond the baseline before striking the ball. The player who commits a foot fault loses that chance to serve the ball into play.

Who calls foot faults? In tournaments where linespersons are available, they call the violations. In informal competition the rule is seldom enforced. You are on your honor not to foot fault and you should politely complain to your opponent if you know he or she is foot faulting. Be sure that you are not guilty of the same offense before complaining about someone else.

How do you determine who serves first? Spin a racket or flip a coin. The winner of the spin may choose to serve the first game, to receive serve the first game, to begin play on either end of the court, or ask the other player to choose one of these three options.

Do doubles partners have to maintain the order of serve during the entire match? No. The order of serve can be changed at the beginning of each set.

When a ball bounces so close to a line you don't know whether it was in or out, it should be played as a good shot. Do not ask to replay the point. Either have the courage to call it out or the decency to assume it was in. Don't ask spectators what they think. If you ask your opponent's opinion, accept it. It is better not to ask. It is your responsibility to call shots on your side of the net.

What happens if a player serves from the wrong side of the court? The point stands, and the players play the next point from the proper court, depending on what the score is.

Can a player serve with an underhand motion? Yes.

Can a player let the ball bounce and then put it into play as a serve? No.

Can the server toss the ball and catch it rather than serve it? Yes, but it is a fault if the server swings and misses.

In doubles, does the server's partner have to stand at the net while the serve is being delivered? No, the partner can stand anywhere.

In a match without linespersons, can the receiver's partner call a serve out? Yes.

RECEIVING SERVE

What determines if the receiver is ready to return a serve? If the receiver attempts to return a serve, he or she is ready. If you are not ready, make no attempt to hit the ball. Ask the server to take two.

In doubles, can partners change sides of the court on which they receive the serve during a set? No. They can change at the beginning of the next set.

What happens when doubles partners play a point after having lined up on the wrong side of their court? The point stands, and the correction is made at the end of that game.

Where must the receiver stand to return serve? Anywhere.

If a serve hits a receiver or receiver's partner before bouncing, what happens? The person who gets hit loses the point.

FORFEIT TIMES, DELAYS, WAITING PERIODS

How much time should a player be allowed after the announced starting time of a match before a forfeit is declared? Each tournament director establishes the rules regarding forfeits, but fifteen minutes is usually the maximum time allowed.

How much time should a player be allowed between matches in a tournament? At least fifteen minutes, but more if possible.

How much time is allowed if a player cannot continue to play because of an injury? If the injury is a temporary one caused by an accident, such as running into a fence or falling on the court, the umpire should give that player a reasonable amount of time to recover (a few seconds, or at the most, a couple of minutes). If the player cannot continue because of "natural loss of physical condition," such as cramps or illness, no time for recovery is allowed.

Is there any rest period in a two out of three set match?   In men's competition, no; in women's play there may be a ten minute rest period after the second set.

If a match is delayed by rain, are the players allowed a warmup period when play resumes?   Yes.

CHANGING ENDS

When do players change ends of the court?   When the total number of games in a set equals an odd number.

How much time is a player allowed between games when players change ends of the court?   Ninety seconds.

CALLING SHOTS

Who calls shots in or out?   If there are no linespersons, each player is responsible for calling shots out on his or her side of the court. If the shot is in, do not say anything. If the shot is out, shout "out" whether or not you swing at or hit the ball.

What if you are not sure if a ball is in or out?   If the shot was that close, you should play the ball as if it were in. If the shot was the last in a rally and you are not sure, ask for your opponent's opinion and accept the decision. If your opponent does not know, it is your call and you should give the other player the benefit of the doubt.

What if you think your opponent is cheating you?   Complain. If that does not work, stop the match and ask for an umpire.

SHOTS NEAR THE NET

Can a player reach over the net to hit a ball?   Not unless the ball has bounced on that player's side of the net and is carried back across the net by the wind or spin.

Can a player touch the net?   Not while the point is in progress.

Does the ball have to clear the top of the net?   No, a ball can be returned around the sides of the net posts.

COACHING

Can a coach talk with a player for the purpose of giving instructions during a match? Most conferences, leagues, and tournaments have their own rules regarding coaching during a match. The United States Tennis Association has ruled that it is not permissible unless a local rule has been made.

DIMENSIONS

How high is the net? Three feet at the center; three feet, six inches at the net posts.

What are the dimensions of a tennis court? Seventy-eight feet long and twenty-seven feet wide for a singles court; seventy-eight by thirty-six for a doubles court.

How wide are the alleys? Four and one-half feet.

How wide should the lines be painted? Two inches.

How much distance should there be between the baseline and the fence? Twenty-one feet.

How much distance should there be between the doubles sidelines and the fence or next court? Twelve feet.

SPECIAL SITUATIONS

What happens if a ball rolls onto the court while a point is in progress? A let is in order if either player calls for a let before the point is completed. In this case, playing a let means replaying the point entirely. This does not mean that you or the other player should delay the call until you see that you may lose the point. Neither should you call a let if your opponent is about to put away a shot when the ball rolls onto the court. Before returning the ball to another court, make sure that returning it will not interrupt a point in progress.

What happens if a ball rolls onto the court between the first and second serves? Technically, nothing. In social tennis, if there is an unusual delay, it is common to give the server two more attempts.

What happens if a ball in play strikes a ball lying on the court?   The player or team on whose side the ball is lying loses the point unless the ball in play can be returned.

Can a player touch the ball with any part of the body during a point?   No.

Should a point be replayed if the ball breaks during the point?   Yes.

What happens if you are standing outside the boundary line and a ball that would have been out touches you first?   The player who catches or touches the ball loses the point.

What happens when a ball hits a permanent fixture near the court?   The player who last hit the ball loses the point.

Can you throw your racket at the ball and hit it?   Not legally.

Can you deliberately distract your opponent before or during a point?   No.

Who is the final authority in a tournament match?   The umpire.[3]

REVIEW QUESTIONS

1. What are some of the ways to determine the quality of a racket?

2. How can you decide on the proper grip size of a racket?

3. Suggest ways to extend the life of a tennis racket.

4. Compare nylon and gut strings in terms of cost, resiliency, and durability.

5. What are four factors to consider in purchasing tennis shoes?

6. What is the difference between traditional scoring, the VASSS system, and no-ad scoring?

7. Draw a tennis court and label the following areas: baseline, service line, backcourt, singles sideline, left service court, and center service line.

8. Identify and explain the primary function of these organizations: U.S.T.A., I.T.F., A.T.P., and W.T.A.

9. What is the difference between single elimination, feed-in consolation, ladder, and round robin forms of competition?

[3] Brown, *Tennis Without Lessons*, pp. 17–22.

10. What is the difference between open, closed, invitational, and qualifying tournaments?

11. Explain the nine point tie breaker system.

12. Define the following terms: umpire, let, foot fault, match, set, and pro set.

Chapter 2

STROKES

One of the most common expressions heard from spectators when they are watching advanced players is "They really make it look easy." The reason good players make it look easy is that while most spectators are watching the ball being hit by one player, they do not see that the other player is working very hard to get into position for the next shot. By the time they look, the hitter has prepared so well that there is nothing left to do but swing at the ball. Getting ready to hit a shot is as important as actually hitting the ball. The player who prepares well for each shot is always in a good tactical position on the court, is in a comfortable position to hit the ball, and is also positioned so that he or she can choose from a variety of alternatives on where and how to hit a return. The idea is to work hard in between shots so you can relax and concentrate during the shot.

PREPARING TO HIT

HITTING SHOTS THAT COME AT YOU

Although most players learn to hit from a stationary position, very few shots are hit in such a way that a simple ready-pivot-step-swing sequence of movements is practical. Most of the time you have to run, shuffle, or move in some manner to be in a position to pivot, step, and swing. One of the few times when little lateral, forward, or backward movement is necessary is on the return of serve. Here are some suggestions on getting ready to hit that shot and others that come to where you are on the court.

First decide how you are going to hold the racket while you wait. The choices are a forehand grip, a backhand grip, an in-between grip, and the Continental grip. The technique for using various grips is discussed in this chapter, but right now think about which grip is best for you in the ready position. Which grip is most comfortable for you? On which side do you expect most serves or other shots to come? Is the forehand more difficult to change to than the backhand, or vice versa? If you cannot decide what to do, do whatever comes naturally during play. Don't worry about it unless problems develop.

In the ready position, hold the racket out in front of your body with the racket pointing directly toward your opponent or slightly toward your backhand side. Use the nonracket hand to support the racket at the throat or on the shaft (the parts between the head and the handle). The racket should be far enough in front of you so that your weight is thrown forward a bit on service returns. On other shots you can carry the racket closer in to your body, but still in front. This position will force you to put your weight on your toes instead of your heels; a position that should help you react faster to any shot. Bend slightly at the knees and at the waist. If you are waiting for a serve, spread your feet a little wider than the width of your shoulders. Be ready to step forward and attack the ball before it attacks you. The players in Figure 2-1 are demonstrating the ready position.

MOVING TO HIT SHOTS

Most shots are hit on the run or after running to get into position. The latter is preferable. If you run first, set up second, and hit third, you are in a better position than most players. Ideally, you want to hit every groundstroke from approximately the same body position. The only way to achieve that goal is to get into position very quickly so you will have the luxury of hitting from a position in which you are comfortable.

There are a couple of ways to get to the ball. One way is to shuffle laterally. Instead of crossing your legs to move to one side, slide your feet alternately to the side where the ball is going. If you have to move to the

Figure 2–1   In the ready position, the players lean forward, bend slightly at the waist and knees, and point the racket forward.

right, first slide the right foot to the right and follow it by sliding the left foot. To do the same thing faster, use a skipping or hopping movement. The feet are still shuffling without crossing, but with a little bounce. If you really have to hurry to get to a ball in another part of the court, you simply have to turn and run. Use a crossover step as if you are going to pivot forward, and push off hard with the other foot.

Regardless of how you get to a ball, get there early and set up for the shot. Try to avoid arriving just in time to make contact with the ball. Pivot, shuffle, slide, or turn and run, but when you get there, plant the foot that is farther away from the net. Then shift your weight forward onto the other foot as you hit. If you have to get a short shot that bounces directly in front of you, move in to one side of the ball rather than going to it in a straight line. If you have to run wide for a ball, try to advance toward the ball instead of running parallel to the baseline. If you can move laterally and forward at the same time, you will have more power on the shot.

After each shot, start getting ready for the next one by (1) moving the racket back to the ready position in front of your body, and (2) positioning yourself in the best possible spot for the next return. For groundstrokes, that spot is usually at the center of the baseline, although it may change as the point progresses. As soon as you see where the next shot is coming, adjust your grip, get your racket back, and start moving toward the ball again.

FOREHAND

FUNDAMENTALS

- Use the Eastern forehand grip.
- Prepare early.
- Turn your side to the net and step forward.
- Swing in a slightly upward motion.
- Keep the wrist firmly in place.
- Follow through out, across, and up.

USE THE EASTERN FOREHAND GRIP

With one edge of the racket pointing toward the court, shake hands with the racket as if you were going to shake hands with another person. Curl your fingers around the grip near the base. Holding the racket out to your right side (for righthanders), your palm should be slightly behind the

Figure 2–2   From the front, the Eastern forehand grip looks like this.

racket handle, your wrist should be slightly to the right of the top of the handle, and the "V" formed by the thumb and index finger should be above but slightly toward the back part of the grip. The Eastern grip is shown from the front in Figure 2-2, from the top in Figure 2-3, and from the back in Figure 2-4. Lefthanders should hold the racket so that the wrist is slightly to the left of the top of the grip as you look down over the top.

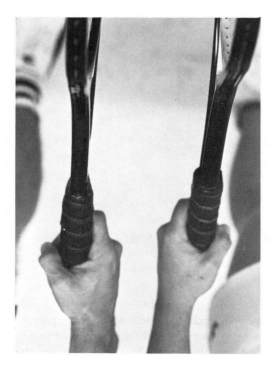

Figure 2–3   Looking from the top, the righthander's wrist is slightly to the right of the top of the handle. The lefthander's wrist is to the left.

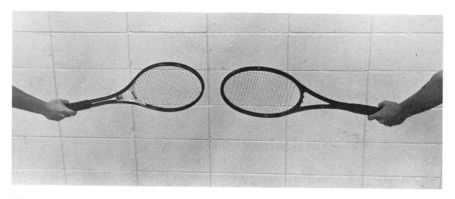

Figure 2–4 From the back, the racket head is cocked up slightly, and there is a curve formed by the back of the hand and the forearm.

PREPARE EARLY

As soon as you know the ball is going to your forehand side, begin your backswing. The backswing is made by bringing the racket back either in a straight line parallel to the court or in a slight up, then down loop to a position where the racket is a bit lower than waist high and pointing to the fence or wall behind your baseline (Figure 2-5). If the racket head can be

Figure 2–5 Take the racket back so that it points to the wall or fence behind you. Your feet should be parallel to the sidelines on many forehand shots.

seen behind your body by a person standing in front of you, it is probably too far back. If you wait until you arrive at the ball to start your backswing, you will not have time to adjust to unexpected bounces, spin, or velocity. If the racket is already back there when you move into position, all you have to worry about is hitting.

Turn Your Side to the Net and Step Forward

As the ball comes to your forehand, move into a position so that your left shoulder points to the ball and your feet form a line approximately parallel to the sideline (Figure 2-5). If you are lefthanded, your right shoulder should point to the ball and your right foot will move forward to form the line parallel to the sideline (Figure 2-5). Use the foot farther away from the net to push off and transfer your weight forward as you begin to swing at the ball. As you hit, make sure that your weight moves forward. Some players take a small step forward with the foot closest to the net just before they hit the ball.

The forward weight transfer is one of the most important parts of any groundstroke. If you do not or cannot put it into your stroke, you will be hitting only with the power provided by your arm instead of with the entire weight of your body. That causes a lack of power and a very tired arm before the match or practice session is completed. One way to determine if your weight is on the foot closest to the net is to be aware of the position of the shoulder closest to the net. If that shoulder is on a more or less even plane with the other shoulder or is in a downward posture, your weight is forward. If the shoulder is pointing up, your weight is still on the rear foot.

Swing in a Slightly Upward Motion

As you swing at the ball, the racket should travel in a slightly upward trajectory. This upward and forward action of the racket allows you to hit with a slight amount of topspin, which is good for safety and consistency, and causes a high bounce on the other side of the net. Make contact with the ball just before it reaches a point even with the midsection of your body (Figure 2-6). You will not be able to do that on every shot, but you should try.

Keep the Wrist Firmly in Place

The wrist should be firm and in a position that forms a curve with the top of your forearm. Hold your wrist firmly in place throughout the stroke. Think of sweeping something off of a table or ironing board. Extend your arm comfortably but not completely as you swing. Try to carry the ball on

Figure 2–6 Try to make contact while the ball is rising and before it gets even with the middle of your body.

your racket strings. Hold the racket tightly enough so it will not turn in your hand on impact, but not so tightly that you lose the feel of the racket.

FOLLOW THROUGH OUT, ACROSS, AND UP

After the hit, follow the ball with your racket. Try to reach out and touch the net with your racket. When it cannot go any further forward, it should cross the front of your body and finish high on the opposite side from which you started (Figure 2-7).

Every time you hit a forehand, the total action involved in the swing should be about the same. If the ball comes at you lower than the waist, bend your knees, keep your back straight, and use the same swinging motion. Do not stand straight up and golf at the ball. If you get caught in a position where the ball is going to bounce deeply in your back court and high to your forehand, retreat quickly, plant the back foot, and move your weight forward as you swing. If the ball falls short in your court, move up, plant, step, swing, and follow through.

FOREHAND PROBLEMS AND CORRECTIONS

While there are a few major points to remember in hitting any stroke, there are probably fifty things that can go wrong. The average player should not be worrying about or even thinking about all of these potential

Figure 2–7 Follow through, staying high, across the front of your body.

problems. If you are a teaching pro, a coach, or an instructor, you should be aware of them and point them out only when necessary. Avoid overloading your own brain or those of your players with too much information. Here are some of the more common problems players have with the forehand and what to do about them.

1.   Facing the net while you hit—Work hard between shots to get your feet lined up properly. If you do not step in the right direction (which is the direction you want to hit), it is impossible to transfer your weight forward with the shot. If your feet are parallel to the baseline when you hit, they are in the wrong place.

2.   Wrong grip—The wrist should be in a position to push the racket forward with the stroke. That means it should be slightly to the right of top for righthanders and a bit to the left for lefthanders. Beginners may want to put the wrist too far back, resulting in a Western grip. If you put the racket on the court, then reach down and pick it up like a frying pan, that is a Western grip (Figure 2-8). Some players use it effectively, but it is best to hold the Eastern forehand grip. If you decide to change from the Western to the Eastern, do it gradually.

3.   Floppy wrist—Keep the wrist almost rigid during the swing. If it flexes (bends forward) during the swing, your stroke will be inconsistent. At

Figure 2–8 The wrist is directly behind the racket handle with a Western grip.

the same time you are keeping it firm, also keep the wrist and racket head up. On most shots the racket head should be higher than the wrist. If you let it droop, you will lose power.

4. Tucked elbow—Your arm should be comfortably stretched out when you swing. Not stiff armed, but not tucked into your ribs, either. Keeping the elbow too close to your side will cause you to slap at the ball. That causes shallow, weak, or inconsistent shots (Figure 2-9).

5. Poor racket angle—In any shot, your strings have to reflect the ball in the direction you want to hit. If they are pointing to the sky on contact, your shots will go high. When they are facing downward, your shots will go into the net. You must have a mental picture of where your strings are directing the ball. The arrow in the racket in Figure 2-10 may help you get that picture.

6. Swinging too hard—A smooth, controlled swing is more effective than the all out swing. Hold the racket tightly, but relax as you swing. Think about how you look. Good technique is more important than hitting hard. Placement wins more points than power.

7. Hitting late—Make contact with the ball just before it gets even with you. If you are not doing that, you may be taking too big a windup or starting the backswing too late. Your racket should be back by the time the ball bounces in front of you.

35

Figure 2–9 Tucking the elbow causes you to slap at the ball.

8. **Crossing your body too soon with the racket**—Reach out toward the net with your swing. If you let the racket cut across in front of your chest too early, you will pull the ball out of the court.

9. **No follow through**—If you know you are going to stop your swing as soon as you make contact with the ball, the preceding part of your swing will be affected by slowing down too soon. Carry the ball on your strings as long as possible.

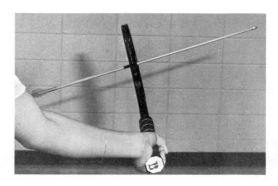

Figure 2–10 In most cases, the ball goes where the strings (and the arrow) point.

1.   Drop the ball with your left hand, simulate the forehand swing, and catch the ball with your right hand. If you can do that easily, drop the ball, swing with the forehand motion, and hit the ball with the open hand. This exercise helps you develop the swinging motion and also requires you to watch the ball as you hit.

2.   Drop a ball to your forehand side and hit it over the net with a forehand stroke. Turn your side to the net, extend your left arm and hand holding the ball, and drop the ball. Do not bounce it; just let it fall to the court. As it bounces up, lean forward and swing smoothly, aiming for a spot on the other side of the net.

3.   Holding the racket with a forehand grip, practice dribbling a tennis ball on the floor or court. Beginners frequently have difficulty in getting used to the distance from the hand to the racket head. Dribbling the ball fifty to a hundred times a day not only helps you adjust to the distance, it also makes the forehand grip seem like an automatic grip, and you may develop better racket control.

4.   With a forehand grip, turn your palm up and bounce the ball off the strings into the air as many times as you can without letting it touch the ground. This drill improves ball control and strengthens the wrist. You should be able to hit at least one hundred consecutive air dribbles without a miss.

5.   Mark a court or open area at home with X's spaced several feet apart and to the right of a starting point. Practice getting into position by moving to a spot and executing a forehand swing. Start from a central position, move alternately to each spot you have marked, plant your right foot, lean forward, and imagine you are swinging at and hitting a shot. After each shot, return to the starting point.

6.   Practice the forehand swing in front of a mirror. Say to yourself, "Ready, pivot, swing," or "Ready, pivot, step, swing." Concentrate on watching each part of the stroke by itself, then watch the total movement. Attempt to develop a smooth, coordinated series of movements as you pretend to hit.

7.   Practice changing back and forth between the forehand and backhand grips. You might also do this drill in front of a mirror. Repeat the grip changes so many times that you can change without looking at the racket. If you do not know how to hold the backhand grip, read the next part of this chapter before practicing this drill.

8.   Practice hitting forehands against a wall. Stand very close to the wall at first and work on accuracy as well as form. Set goals for the number of consecutive hits without a miss. As you become more consistent, move progressively further away from the wall until you are finally at the distance from the baseline to the net (39 feet).

9.   Get a friend to throw balls to your forehand. Take a basket of balls to the courts; have your friend stand about 20 feet away and use an underhanded toss that bounces easily about waist high. Begin your preparation from the ready position and pivot forward on each shot. As you get better, let the thrower toss balls away from where you are so you have to move, set up, then hit the shot. Return to a central position after every shot. This is another drill that can be used on any hard surface where there is enough open space in which to move and where there is a backstop to keep balls from getting away.

10.   Play a game with a friend using only the service courts. Stand on or behind the service line and put the ball into play by dropping it and softly hitting to your practice partner. Use short strokes. All shots must fall within the boundaries of the two service boxes. Keep score by counting the number of consecutive shots or by actually playing games using the conventional method of scoring.

11.   From a position near the baseline, practice hitting forehands against a friend. If both of you are righthanded, all shots will be hit crosscourt, from your forehand side to your opponent's. Set goals or count the number of consecutive shots played.

12.   Hit down-the-line forehand shots only. If your partner is good enough to keep the ball to your forehand side, hit fifty to one hundred shots with a forehand stroke so the ball travels parallel to the sideline. Concentrate on setting up early and hitting the ball deeply in your opponent's backcourt. If your friend is not good enough to hit all shots to your forehand, take turns throwing balls to the forehand.

13.   Practice forehand strokes using only the alley on one side of the court. All shots are directed toward the alley on the opposite side of the net. If you and your partner are both righthanded, he or she will have to either hit backhands on the return or move to the side of the court in order to practice forehand returns.

14.   Practice forehand approach shots. Ask your partner to throw or hit shots that bounce near the service line on your forehand side. Start from the center of the baseline, move in toward the ball, set up, and hit a forehand down the line on that side of the court.

15.   Practice the forehand swing with a cover on the racket. The added resistance will help improve your forearm and wrist strength.

16.   Squeeze a tennis ball. When you have some extra moments around the house or when your hands are free, hold an old tennis ball and squeeze it as hard as you can. Repeat 25 times and increase the number of consecutive squeezes by five each day. Your grip strength will improve significantly if you are conscientious about doing this exercise every day.

BACKHAND

The backhand is one of the most difficult shots for many tennis players to master. There are people who give detailed arguments why the backhand is a more natural stroke and should be easier to learn than the forehand. Don't you believe it. The arguments look good on paper, but on the courts it is another matter. People who have played other sports have had practice throwing, reaching, catching, pushing, hitting, and so on, but most of these movements are on the forehand side of the body. Very few sports involve the across-the-body action necessary to hit a backhand. Nevertheless, it is a shot that can be learned and that can become a consistent offensive weapon to add to your arsenal of strokes.

FUNDAMENTALS

- Use the Eastern, Continental, or two handed grip.
- Prepare early.
- Turn your side to the net and step forward.
- Swing parallel to the court.
- Follow through out, across, and up.

USE THE EASTERN, CONTINENTAL, OR TWO HANDED GRIP

There are at least three acceptable ways to hold the racket on the backhand. The most common grip is the Eastern backhand. With this grip, the righthander's wrist should be slightly to the left of the top of the racket handle as you look down on the racket. The lefthander's wrist will be slightly to the right of the top. Both grips are shown in Figure 2-11. Think of your thumb as having a top, bottom, outside, and inside. The inside part of your thumb should be in contact with the back, flat part of the racket handle. There are several ways in which the thumb might be aligned along that part of the grip, but it is essential that the inside part be in contact with the racket. During a point the thumb's position may change, but the part

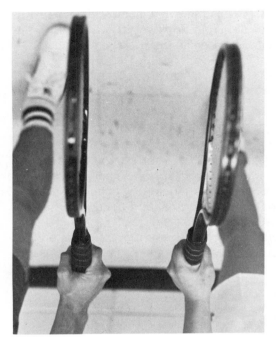

Figure 2–11 From the top, the righthander's wrist is to the left of the handle top and the lefthander's wrist is to the right with an Eastern backhand.

touching the grip should not. The Eastern grip from the rear is shown in Figure 2-12.

Players with strong forearms may want to use the Continental grip. Here the wrist is directly on top of the racket handle as you look down from the top. The thumb has to provide more support from the rear since the wrist is not positioned behind the racket. Again, avoid placing the bottom

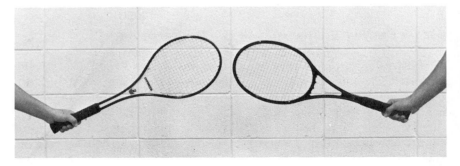

Figure 2–12 From the back, notice that the wrist is cocked up and the inside part of the thumb is in contact with the back panel of the racket handle.

part of the thumb on the back side of the grip. Extend it along the back so that the inside part of the thumb is in contact, pushing against the racket handle during the stroke. The Continental grip is shown in Figure 2-13. The advantage of holding the racket this way is that you do not have to change grips from the forehand to the backhand. The disadvantage is that some players do not feel entirely comfortable with shots on either side since the Continental is halfway between conventional forehand and backhand grips.

The two handed backhand has become a popular and effective stroke for many players. It has the advantages of giving added power, a more controlled swing, and a better racket position to hit with topspin. Its disadvantages are (1) that you may not be able to reach as far on wide shots as with a one hand stroke; (2) you may have problems on shots coming directly at you; and (3) using two hands might keep you from developing strength in your dominant arm.

There are two ways to hold the racket. One is to hold it with the right hand (righthanders) or the left hand (lefthanders) as you would for the one handed backhand. The other hand is placed on the handle in contact with the strong hand with a grip similar to the Eastern forehand. Both hands should be in place as the backswing begins (Figure 2-14).

Some players use two forehand grips to hit the two handed shot. The strongest hand holds the Eastern forehand grip at the base, and the opposite hand holds another forehand grip next to it. The advantage of this method is

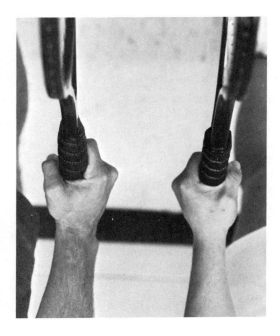

Figure 2–13 The wrist is directly over the top panel of the handle with a Continental grip.

Figure 2–14 One way to hold a two-handed backhand is to use a conventional backhand grip with the strong hand and an Eastern forehand with the weaker hand.

that the player never has to change grips. He or she simply adds or takes away an additional forehand grip for backhand shots (Figure 2-15).

PREPARE EARLY

Regardless of the way you hold the racket, start taking it back as soon as you see the ball coming. Use the nonracket hand to cradle the racket at the shaft or throat and to help turn the racket as you change to the backhand grip. Leave that hand on the racket throat during the entire backswing. Drawing the racket back with both hands will keep everything in the proper plane for a smooth swing, and the second hand will be there to give you added support as you begin to move the racket forward. As you bring the racket back, rotate your shoulders far enough so that your opponent can see your back. The racket should come back in a line parallel with the court or slightly below the waist. Some teachers tell their students to think of drawing a sword out of their pockets on the backhand. As with the forehand, point the racket to the fence or wall when you take it back. Learn to prepare as you move to hit the ball. Do not wait until the last second.

Figure 2–15 A second way to hold the racket for a two-handed backhand is to use two Eastern forehand grips.

Turn Your Side to the Net and Step Forward

Turn before you hit so that your shoulder is pointing in the direction you want to hit. Bend your knees slightly. The foot closest to the net may be pointing toward the sideline or it may be at a forty-five degree angle to the net (Figure 2-16). For added power take a small step forward with the foot closest to the net just before you hit. Put your weight into the shot by leaning forward as you swing. Be aware of the position of the shoulder closest to the net. If it is up, your weight is on the rear foot; if it is down or level, your weight can be transferred forward.

Swing Parallel to the Court

Swing in a trajectory approximately parallel to the court. Players who want topspin on this shot may start the racket head lower and swing upward. Backspin can be imparted by starting with the racket a bit higher than the waist. You do not have to rotate your shoulders on the backhand as much as you do on the forehand. Keep the wrist firmly in place throughout

43

Figure 2–16 To prepare, take the racket back to the fence or wall and step in the direction you want to hit.

the swing. There may be some rotation of the forearm, but leave that to very advanced players for the time being. The racket head should remain higher than your wrist on all but very low shots. Make contact with the ball even with or in front of the foot closest to the net. Hitting the ball in front helps you to use the pace of the other player and lessens the stress on your forearm. Keep your elbow down and away from your body as you swing. Try to look like the players in Figure 2-17.

Follow Through Out, Across, and Up

Follow through out toward the net, across the front of your body, and up, in that order. Think of reaching out and touching the net with the back of your racket hand. When you have reached as far as you can in the direction of the net, bring the racket across the front of your body and upward, finishing the stroke with the racket high on the opposite side of the body from which you started (Figure 2-18).

Figure 2–17 Step in the direction you want to hit; lean into the ball; and make contact out in front on the backhand.

Figure 2–18 Follow through on the backhand across the front of your body and up with the racket.

BACKHAND PROBLEMS AND CORRECTIONS

1. **Poor footwork**—The first place to look in diagnosing a problem on almost any stroke is the feet. Get to the ball early, line your feet up with the sideline, and lean into the shot.

2. **Wrong grip**—People resist the proper backhand grip more than any other. The wrist has to be on top of the handle as you look down on it or slightly to the left if you are righthanded. If you are lefthanded, the wrist will be slightly to the right of the top. Any other placement will cause a variety of problems, including lack of power, inconsistency, and directing the racket strings too far up or down.

3. **Floppy wrist**—As with the forehand, keep the wrist firmly in place throughout the stroke.

4. **Leading with the elbow**—Keep your elbow down and away from the body. If you are looking over the top of your elbow or arm to hit the backhand, your weight is probably on the wrong foot and you will jab at the ball rather than stroking it.

5. **Getting the racket back late**—Get the racket back as you move into position with your feet. If the ball bounces and you have not started your backswing, you will either hit late and push the ball off to the side or hurry your swing to hit it on time.

6. **No follow through**—Again, carry the ball on the strings if you can. Punching the ball causes shallow, weak shots.

7. **Crowding the ball**—Stay almost at arm's length to hit the shot. If you let the ball get too close, the whole stroke can break down.

BACKHAND SELF-HELP DRILLS

Many of the methods used to teach yourself the forehand can also be used with the backhand. These methods will be listed without any additional comment, and other techniques for specifically developing the backhand will be given.

1. Practice up-in-the-air dribbles and dribbling against the court or floor with a backhand grip.
2. Mark an open area on the court with X's; move to each mark alternately, and swing through the backhand stroke.
3. Practice the backhand in front of a mirror.
4. Practice changing back and forth between the backhand and forehand grips.

5. Practice hitting backhands against a wall.

6. Get a friend to throw balls to your backhand.

7. Play the short game (service courts only) using backhands only.

8. Practice hitting only backhands against a friend.

9. Hit down-the-line backhand shots only.

10. Practice backhands using only one alley.

11. Practice backhand approach shots.

12. Practice the backhand swing with a cover on the racket.

13. Practice against a wall, hitting forehand and backhand strokes alternately. This "V" drill will help you develop both strokes and will also help you learn to change grips easily and quickly.

14. Attach a 3-pound weight to a cord; tie the cord to a stick; hold the stick, palms down with both hands; and roll the weight up. This exercise will strengthen your fingers, wrists, and forearms, making it easier for you to hit a backhand.

15. Get a friend to throw balls alternately to your backhand and forehand. The balls should be thrown far enough away from you so you have to run to get to each shot. As you hit one ball, the next one is thrown to the opposite side.

16. Practice an isometric backhand. At the point of probable contact with the ball on the backhand, push against an immovable object for three ten-second periods daily. Rest at least one minute between the exercise periods.

BEGINNER'S SERVE

FUNDAMENTALS

- Use the Eastern forehand grip.
- Stand at an angle to the baseline.
- Toss slightly higher than you can reach.
- Scratch your back, then reach high to hit.
- Follow through out, across, and down.

Figure 2–19   The foot closest to the baseline should be at about a forty-five degree angle.

Use the Eastern Forehand Grip

Use this grip because the grip used by intermediate and advanced players is very awkward for people just learning to play. The Eastern forehand grip is comfortable and allows a reasonable amount of control over the ball. As your serving motion becomes more fluid, the grip can be changed to accommodate the swing. As you graduate into an advanced service grip, you can hit the ball in a wider variety of ways.

Stand at an Angle to the Baseline

Stand at about a forty-five degree angle to the net so that you are facing one of the net posts (Figure 2-19). If you are righthanded, your left foot will be forward and positioned at the angle. Lefthanders will have the right foot closest to the baseline. The stance is quite similar to the one most people assume when they stand to carry on an informal conversation. The foot away from the baseline should be placed so that if a line were drawn from the toes of one foot to the toes of the other, that line would point in the direction you want to serve. This is also shown in Figure 2-19. Put your

48

weight on the foot away from the baseline and spread your feet a bit wider than the width of your shoulders.

Some beginners face the net squarely while they are learning to serve, and some advanced players change the position of their feet to achieve special effects on their serves. The forty-five degree angle is comfortable and effective for players at all levels. The position of the feet will change as the weight moves forward, but that will be discussed later.

TOSS THE BALL SLIGHTLY HIGHER THAN YOU CAN REACH

The toss for the serve is the same for all players. Some may change the toss slightly to execute a particular kind of serve, but the basics are the same. To measure the right height for your toss, extend your arm and the racket upward as high as you can comfortably reach. Now put the racket a little in front of you so that if something were to fall off the top of the racket it would fall about a foot inside the baseline. With the arm and racket fully extended and slightly in front of you and the baseline, the ball should be tossed so it reaches a peak at the top of or slightly higher than your racket. The toss has to be at that spot consistently. If it is not where you want it to be, catch the ball or let it drop to the court and start again. You can learn to toss the ball exactly to the right spot every time. If you do, that is one thing you do not have to worry about going wrong in your motion.

Tossing or lifting the ball for the serve also involves technique. Hold the ball at the base of your fingers in the tossing hand and extend your arm in the direction you want to hit. Now lift your arm without bending it very much at the elbow. As you lift, release the ball at about head height by extending your fingers. The ball should go up without much spin. If it comes off of your fingertips or if you flip your wrist as you toss, the ball will have spin.

SCRATCH YOUR BACK, THEN REACH HIGH TO HIT

Hold the racket with the Eastern forehand grip, stand at an angle to the baseline, and now scratch your back with the racket. From that starting position, swing up at the ball you have learned to toss. It is important that the serving motion goes up at first rather than forward. Do not let your elbow lead the stroke. Keep it high until after the hit. When you hit, reach as high as you can. Your arm and racket should be fully extended when you make contact. Figures 2-20 and 2-21 show the servers having tossed the ball and making contact, respectively.

Figure 2–20 Beginners, start with the racket behind your back, toss out in front, then reach high to hit.

FOLLOW THROUGH OUT, ACROSS, AND DOWN

As you hit, the racket will be moving up and forward. After you hit, the racket will continue forward (toward the net) as far as it will go. The rest of the follow through should be across the front of your body, ending low on the opposite side from which you started (Figure 2-22).

REVIEW

Put the ball out in front of your body with the nonracket hand, and at the same time position the racket behind your back or head. As the ball reaches a peak on the toss, bring the racket upward and forward to hit the ball with your arm and racket fully extended. If you toss the ball in front of where you are standing, you have to move forward to make contact. The foot closest to the baseline should not move, but the other foot may leave the court and move forward as you hit or follow through. Your momentum may carry that foot slightly inside the baseline after you have served. That is a good indication that you are transferring your weight into the ball.

Figure 2–21 Keep your head up, make contact in front, and don't worry about your feet.

Figure 2–22 Finish the serving motion with the racket going down and across the front of your body to the opposite side.

Now you know the fundamentals of the serve. The next problem is how to mold the grip, the stance, the toss, the weight transfer, the swing, and the follow through into an actual rhythmic, reliable pattern on the court. Here are some drills, exercises, and learning techniques to help you achieve that goal. Select the ones you enjoy doing and the ones that seem to help you improve the most. There is something here for almost every level of tennis player.

1. Play catch with someone. Get a tennis ball, softball, or baseball, and practice throwing back and forth with your wife, husband, children, or friends. Throw for at least ten minutes the first session and try to add to the practice period every day. Stand at least 10 yards from your partner, and work on developing a smooth, loose motion. Remember that the serving motion is like the throwing motion. If you do not feel comfortable, get advice from your throwing partner. As your strength increases and the motion becomes more fluid, increase the throwing distance until you can easily throw a tennis ball 60 feet. That is the distance from the baseline to the service line on the opposite side of the net. If you cannot throw that far, you are going to have difficulty developing a strong serve.

2. Throw a tennis ball from the baseline into the proper service court. Take lots of balls with you to the courts so you will not have to stop to collect the balls after every few throws. It would be even better if you could take a partner with you to catch throws after they have bounced and return them to you.

3. Practice the service toss by aiming for a target. Place a basket or a racket cover, or draw a circle at a point inside the baseline where a correct service toss would land if the ball is not hit. See how many times you can execute the toss so that it hits the target.

4. Serve from the service line. Use the technique described earlier and practice serving into the left and right service courts from the service line instead of the baseline. As your accuracy and strength improve, gradually move back toward the baseline.

5. Serve into the fence surrounding the court or into a wall outside your home. If you do not have a basket of balls, practice your service motion by serving into the fence so you will not have to waste time chasing balls.

6. Practice the service motion with the cover on the racket. The added weight and resistance will help strengthen your serving arm. You can increase the weight further by putting things into the racket cover and placing it on the racket head.

7. **Practice the service motion in front of a mirror.** If you do not have high ceilings where you live, choke up on the racket, use a paddle, or simulate the swing with the palm of your hand. If you know how the serve is supposed to be hit, you can perfect your swing by watching yourself go through the motion.

8. **Serve from a position several feet behind the baseline.** Take three steps back from your normal serving position and serve into the proper court. Now move back as far as you can from the baseline and practice your serve. The practice at long distance will increase your strength and make serving from the baseline much easier.

9. **Count the number of consecutive balls served into each service court.** Try to add to the total each practice session. Set goals of 10, 20, 30, 40, or 50 good serves. Compete with a partner to make practicing more interesting.

10. **Serve while holding the racket several inches from the bottom of the grip.** As your accuracy improves, move your hand gradually down toward the normal position near the base of the grip.

11. **Serve to targets in the service court.** Place a racket cover or tennis ball can in the prime target areas (the corners of the box) and try to hit the objects with your serves.

12. **Play a game with a friend using only the serve and the service return.** Every serve into the proper court earns one point. Every return of serve into the singles court also earns a point. Each point ends after the serve or after the serve and a return. The server gets two chances to get the serve into play.

Think of the serve as having component parts. When you put these parts together, a smooth continuous motion develops. The idea is to eliminate as many of the variables as possible when serving. If you stand at exactly the same place to serve each time, that is a variable you no longer have to worry about. If your toss goes to the right spot every time, that is one less component part that can go wrong. If you know how all of these parts are supposed to fit together, you can correct your own faults. Don't add to the problem by doing things differently on every serve.

INTERMEDIATE AND ADVANCED SERVE

FUNDAMENTALS

- Use the Continental or modified backhand grip.
- Stand at an angle to the baseline.
- Move the hands down at the same time, then up at the same time.
- Toss the ball slightly higher than you can reach.
- Reach high to hit.
- Follow through out, across, and down.

USE THE CONTINENTAL OR MODIFIED BACKHAND GRIP

Players with advanced serves usually hold the racket with a Continental grip. With it the wrist is directly over the top of the racket handle as you look down over the top. Some players move their wrists a little toward the backhand side. These grips enable you to hit the serve with control, pace, and spin. The beginner's Eastern forehand grip for the serve is mainly for control.

STAND AT AN ANGLE TO THE BASELINE

The position of the feet is very similar to that described for the beginner's serve. You should have your side partially to the net so you can twist into the ball as you hit. The angle at which you stand may vary a few degrees in either direction, depending on individual preferences.

MOVE THE HANDS DOWN AT THE SAME TIME, THEN UP AT THE SAME TIME

Begin with the racket out in front about chest high and with the nonracket hand holding the ball against the racket strings (Figure 2-23). As the racket begins to drop in a pendulum motion by the side of your leg, the opposite hand should also move slightly downward preliminary to the toss. Both hands move down at the same time. The racket arm will be moving down, then into the back scratching position while the other arm begins to move up to lift the ball for the toss. There should be a rhythmic feel to the serving motion.

Figure 2–23 Advanced and intermediate players should begin the serving motion with the ball on the strings and the racket in front.

Toss the Ball Slightly Higher Than You Can Reach

The toss has to be timed so that the ball will reach its highest point at the same time the arm and racket extend to make contact. If the timing is not right, stop everything and start over. The toss also has to be far enough in front of you to force you to lean forward and beyond the baseline as you hit. Keep your head up and look at the ball you are tossing (Figure 2-24).

Reach High to Hit

As you bring the racket up and behind your back, your arm should begin to bend at the elbow and move through the backscratching position. Fully extend your arm to make contact with the ball. When you serve, the body is almost in a straight line at the moment of impact (Figure 2-25).

To make the most of the weight transfer, your feet will change positions during the motion. As you lean forward the foot closest to the line stays in the same place, but the other foot goes forward. Some players prefer to take one step, starting with the rear foot several inches from the

55

Figure 2–24 Toss the ball slightly in front of where you are standing and keep your head up.

Figure 2–25 Fully extend your body and your racket to make contact on the serve.

baseline and finishing one step inside the line. Other players make a two step approach with the rear foot. The server brings the back foot forward to a point just behind the front foot prior to hitting. This movement results in a springboard effect into the service motion and may even give added height and leverage if the server goes up on the toes. After the ball has been hit, the foot continues forward, touching down one step inside the baseline (Figure 2-26). Regardless of which method you use, try to keep your knees slightly bent during the first part of the motion. As you hit, extending the knees will add to the springboard effect, giving you more power.

Follow Through Out, Across, and Down

Follow through just like the beginners do. Reach out toward the net, then let the racket cross in front, finishing the stroke down and on the opposite side (Figure 2-26).

Serving Problems and Corrections

1. **Wrong grip**—Intermediate players may revert to the forehand grip. Check to see that the wrist is on top of the handle. If not, the ball may sail deep, you may not be able to hit with side spin, and you will not be able to break your wrist sufficiently to add power.

2. **High toss**—A toss that is too high will cause you to break the rhythm of your serve. You will have to wait on the ball instead of using a smooth, continuous motion.

Figure 2–26 Follow through, down, and across. Let the foot that started out in back touch down one step inside the baseline.

3.   Low toss—Remember to reach high on contact. A low toss will force you to bend your elbow and probably slap down at the ball, causing it to go into the net.

4.   Leading with the elbow—As you swing, the elbow must go from the bent position behind your back to a position as high as it will go. If you let the elbow go forward instead of upward, you will lose the effect of the windup and again lose power (Figure 2-27).

5.   Looking out instead of up—Keep your head up during the serve. Some players look out to see where the ball is going, causing a mishit.

6.   Turning the shoulders too soon—Your shoulders should rotate toward the net as you hit, not before. If you turn too early, your weight will shift with your shoulders and you will have nothing left to hit with but your arm. The idea is to get everything into the serve simultaneously.

7.   No weight transfer—Start with your weight on the back foot and shift forward as you hit. You should end up the serving motion closer to the net than you started. If you fall, fall forward instead of to the side.

8.   Lack of racket speed—Gradually build speed with the head of the racket during the serving motion. By the time you hit, the head should be

Figure 2-27 This player is letting the elbow lead the serving motion. Don't let it go forward; make it go up to reach high for the ball.

moving fast enough to provide power. If you are getting the racket to the extended arm position slowly, your serve will be weak.

9. No follow through—Make sure that racket keeps on going after you hit. If you stop it too soon, it will slow down too soon.

VOLLEY

The volley is an easy shot to learn in practice, but it can be difficult to hit in a match. There is one grip for volleys no matter where the ball is hit and the shot does not require a full swing. This can be an advantage in that the less motion, the fewer chances there are for an error. However, the stroke can give you problems in a match because you have less time to react than you would on shots returned from the baseline. This shot is one of the most challenging and exciting strokes in tennis. If you are in a position to volley, you are probably playing offensive tennis, which is more fun than defensive tennis for many players. If you can volley, you can take charge of a point, put pressure on your opponent, and cut the court space in half.

FUNDAMENTALS

- Use the Continental grip.
- Take a short backswing.
- Block the ball in front of and to the side of where you are standing.
- Step forward if you have time.

USE THE CONTINENTAL GRIP

The Continental grip is held by placing your wrist directly over the top of the top panel of the racket handle. Look back at Figure 2-13 to see how to hold the racket for this shot. It is used for all volleys—high, low, right side, and left side. Beginners may change back and forth from the forehand to the backhand grip at the net until the Continental is comfortable. This grip is a compromise between the forehand and backhand grips. The reason you cannot effectively change grips is because you do not have time to change when you are at the net. Since you have to hold the racket with only one grip, good players have demonstrated that you can hit a forehand volley better with a near-backhand grip (the Continental) than you can hit a backhand volley with an Eastern forehand grip. It is the lesser of two evils. Trust the stroke. After it works for you, the theory behind the grip will not matter.

TAKE A SHORT BACKSWING

The backswing for the volley on either side is a short, restricted motion. The movement begins from a ready position in which you are carrying the racket up and in front. The racket is cradled at the shaft with one hand and is pointing toward your opponent or slightly to the backhand side. As you see the ball coming, take the racket back to a point not much further back than an imaginary line even with you and parallel to the net. Rotate your shoulders in the direction of the backswing. The idea is to take a short, quick, controlled backswing because you do not have time to take a full swing. The players in Figure 2-28 have taken the racket back prior to a volley.

BLOCK THE BALL IN FRONT OF AND TO THE SIDE OF WHERE YOU ARE STANDING

Throughout the volley motion, keep your wrist cocked so that the racket forms a near-ninety degree angle with your forearm. Lead the stroke with your hand and the racket head. Swing forward from the shoulder and

Figure 2–28 Take a short backswing prior to a volley. There is not enough time for a big one.

elbow, but keep the wrist relatively fixed. Make contact with the ball well in front of your body and out to one side. If the ball comes directly at you, slide out to the side before you hit. When you hit, tilt your racket face up a little bit, giving backspin to the ball. Try to hit the ball while it is rising. It is very important to attack the ball rather than letting it get even with or behind you. Try to keep your eyes level with the ball. If it goes low, bend your knees and get down with it. Don't stick your racket down there and hope. One object is to avoid volleying up on the ball. If you volley up, the other player will be able to hit down on the return. Follow through in the direction you want to hit, but the follow through does not have to be as full as with groundstrokes.

STEP FORWARD IF YOU HAVE TIME

Decide where to stand in relation to the net. You have more freedom to position yourself than on other strokes, and your position will depend on what is happening during each point. This freedom, or problem, depending on how you look at it, will be discussed in the section on strategy. If you are learning to volley, stand eight to ten feet from the net. At that distance you have time to volley with some force, but you will still be close enough to the net to allow for a few errors in pace or direction while keeping the ball in play.

Your feet should be spread wider than your shoulders and firmly placed so you can push off at an angle in the direction of the net. Your weight should be thrown forward so your heels are barely in contact with the court, if in contact at all. Bend your knees enough to get the feeling of hitting out of a crouch. Bend forward slightly at the waist. As the ball approaches you want to be able to spring forward for the shot.

If you have time, step toward the net with the foot opposite of the side where you will hit the ball. Righthanders will step toward the ball with the left foot on the forehand side, and lefthanders will step forward with the right foot (Figure 2-29). On the backhand, the opposite foot goes into the shot (Figure 2-30). There are times when you have to get to the ball the best way you can under the circumstances. In those situations, forget about footwork, but concentrate on moving forward instead of moving laterally, parallel to the net, or away from the net.

If the ball comes right at you, the footwork is different. You can move in either direction, but you have to slide to one side of the path of the ball. Push off with one foot and step at about a forty-five degree angle to the net with the other. Whether you take head on shots with a forehand or backhand is up to you, but most players prefer the backhand.

Figure 2–29 On the forehand volley, step forward if you have time and make contact in front.

VOLLEY PROBLEMS AND CORRECTIONS

1. Loose grip—Hold the racket tightly. Too many players stand at the net half prepared and when the ball is hit to them, their rackets spin on impact. Hold tight and expect something bad to happen.

2. Wrong grip—Keep the wrist on top of the handle. If you hold either a forehand or backhand, you will not have enough power when the

Figure 2–30 On the backhand volley, step forward with the opposite foot when you can.

ball has to be hit with the grip you are not holding. If you try to change, you will get caught in between. Learn to readjust your grip without looking down. Some players revert to bad habits during the point.

3. **Closed eyes**—Be brave. Try to see the print on the ball when you hit it. Flinching as you hit is a habit that can be broken by practicing for hours at the net.

4. **Big backswing**—You may be swinging at the ball. Remember that the volley is a punch or block. You may get lucky occasionally and hit a winner with a swinging volley, but most of the time over-swinging causes you to hit out.

5. **Hitting late**—Same problem. Shorten your backswing. There is no time to take a big backswing. Expect every shot to come right at you.

6. **Letting the racket head drop**—Try to keep the racket head higher than your hand on most shots. Be aware of the angle formed by the forearm and the racket. Your forearm should be tight when you hit. If not, you will dribble shots into the net or hit weakly to the other side.

VOLLEY SELF-HELP DRILLS

There are very few drills or exercises for the volley which can be done alone. Most of the time you will need a friend to throw or hit balls to you.

1. **Practice in front of a mirror.** As with any other shot, you may be able to perfect your volley motion by watching yourself swing. Look for one component at a time, then watch yourself move through the whole stroke several times on each side of your body.

2. **Practice catching a tossed ball with the racket.** Have a friend toss to you, and instead of hitting at the ball, just reach out with the racket and "catch" it. The ball will often rebound off your racket with enough force to cross the net. If not, you will at least get used to the distance between the hand and the racket head. The drill will also give you a good start toward punching at the ball rather than swinging at it.

3. **Return tossed balls with volleys.** Have your partner throw softly to the forehand side only, later switching to the backhand. Volley the shots back in order to avoid having to chase balls. After you have become comfortable in hitting at the net, ask the thrower to mix up the tosses between the forehand and backhand sides.

4. **Volley from a position near the fence or wall surrounding the court.** To force yourself to take short backswings on volleys, stand near the

fence or wall and have someone throw to you. If you take too big a back-swing, your racket will bump the fence. Shorten the swing if that happens.

5.   **Volley from a position in a doorway or gate opening.** This exercise forces you to step forward as you hit the volley. If you do not step into the ball, your racket will hit the sides of the door or gate.

6.   **Volley toward a target on the court.** Place tennis ball cans or racket covers in spots on the court and direct your volleys to those spots. Work on hitting crosscourt volleys.

7.   **Take a volleying position, have your partner hit shots at you, but call the balls "in" or "out" without hitting and before the balls bounce.** Many beginners have trouble judging whether or not shots are going to be in the court or out. This drill helps you to improve your judgment of shots. You will need a basket of balls to do this drill effectively.

8.   **Count the number of consecutive volleys you and a friend can hit.** You will have to reach an intermediate or advanced level before you can control the ball well enough to do this drill.

9.   **Volley against two friends who alternately hit shots to you at the net.** The two against one drill enables you to hit many volleys in a short period of time. Rotate so that each player gets a turn at the net.

10.   **Stand in the service court near the net and move as fast as you can back and forth from the singles sideline to the midcourt line ten times.** Swing through the volley motion every time you reach a line. Try to increase the number of repetitions each time you do the drill. This is a good conditioning exercise.

11.   **Hit volleys against a wall or rebound net.** This is not a drill for beginners. Intermediates may be able to keep the ball in play long enough to make the drill worthwhile.

12.   **Stand in one service court near the net, and defend that area with volleys.** Your practice partner will drop and hit or return your volleys with attempted passing shots. Your goal is to return any shot that would fall within the boundaries formed by the center service line and the singles sideline.

OVERHEAD SMASH

If you have been waiting to read about the one shot in which you can really let out and hit as hard as you want to every time, the overhead smash is *not* it, at least not most of the time. One of the problems beginners and intermediates have with the shot is knowing when to attempt a put-away and when to go for placement instead of power. The guideline to follow is determined by where you are when your opponent hits a lob. If the ball is going to be smashed from a position in the forecourt and you are in good court position, try the put-away. But if you are preparing to return a lob and you are standing close to or behind your baseline, a winning smash should seldom be attempted. The reasons are easy to understand, but some players cannot resist the temptation to blast every lob hit to them, even when the odds are slim that the shot will be successful. From the baseline, it is very difficult to hit an outright winner. The distance is too far, the angle is poor, and your opponent has too much time to react to your shot. So instead of hitting an all out smash, you should hit the overhead firmly and deeply to an open spot or to a weakness. If the shot is hit well, your next shot might be a winner.

FUNDAMENTALS

- Use the Continental grip.
- Take lots of steps to get ready.
- Take an abbreviated backswing.
- Keep the ball in front and reach high to hit.

USE THE CONTINENTAL GRIP

This grip is used for the same reason advanced players use it on the serve. It allows you to snap the wrist at the top of the swing and it also gives you some alternatives about what to do with the ball. Since this grip is similar to the one used to hit a backhand, and since the overhead is hit on the forehand side of the body, some adjustments have to be made as the ball is hit. The main adjustment is made by rotating the wrist outward just before contact. An outward rotation means that looking at the back of your hand, the thumb goes away from you, down, and across. This pronation type of movement allows the ball to be hit flat (with little spin) and with more force than is put on groundstrokes. The inward and downward snap of the thumb and forearm puts added zip on the ball. If you do not rotate the wrist, the shot will have too much spin and probably go off too far to the side. The ball will also be hit with less velocity, which is bad on the smash.

TAKE LOTS OF STEPS TO GET READY

Failure to move the feet during preparation for the overhead shot is one of the most common errors made by players at all levels. Too many players see a lob coming, dig in to a fixed position with both feet, then try to hit. The problem is that since lobs are in the air longer than other shots, all of the variables such as velocity, spin, and trajectory may change during the flight of the ball. If you get set too soon, you might misread some of the variables and not adjust accordingly. Take several short, half and quarter steps while preparing to hit. A lot of foot movement will help you to be in the perfect position to hit when the times comes.

As soon as you see that you will hit a smash, turn your side to the net so that one foot is forward and one back (as in the serve). Righthanders will put the right foot back and the left one forward; lefthanders, just the opposite (Figure 2-31). As you hit, push off of the back foot and transfer your weight forward.

TAKE AN ABBREVIATED BACKSWING

Bring the racket directly up in front of your body to a position behind your head as you prepare to hit. If you were to take a full swing, you would drop the racket down and bring it up behind your back in the pendulum-like motion. By eliminating the full swing, you can reduce the margin of error. If your position on the court is good enough, you should still have enough power to put the ball away or to hit a strong placement. The full backswing can give you a more powerful motion, but it will be less efficient and less accurate than the restricted backswing.

As you bring the racket behind your head, point to the ball with the opposite hand (Figure 2-31). Pointing to the ball can improve your concentration and it will make you more aware of your position in relation to the ball. If you are pointing to the ball, you should also be able to make contact at the spot where you are pointing. You want to do that because the point of contact will be in front, forcing you to move your weight forward into the ball.

KEEP THE BALL IN FRONT AND REACH HIGH TO HIT

The smashing motion is similar to a forceful punch serve. Bring the racket forward as if throwing your racket across the net, and reach as high as you can to make contact. As you swing, make your weight move into the ball. Hit the ball at a point in front of your body. As you hit, rotate the wrist outward and snap down with the thumb. If you are close to the net, hit the

Figure 2-31 Righthanders, step forward with the left foot on the smash. Lefthanders, put the right foot forward. Point at the ball, then make contact out in front where you are pointing.

ball with as little spin as you can to get maximum velocity. If you are at midcourt, use some spin to make the ball curve down and into the court. If you are in the backcourt, put even more spin on the shot because the distance between you and your opponent is too far for a flat shot to be effective.

Follow through down and across your body. Bring the racket through the stroke naturally, then return it to the ready position for the next shot.

Overhead Smash Problems and Corrections

1. **Wrong grip**—Use the Continental grip. If not, your smash may have either too much spin or not enough. Inexperienced players may want to hit with a forehand grip, but they should gradually change to the Continental, just as they should on the serve.

2. **Poor footwork**—Dance, using many small steps to get ready for the shot. When you hit, one foot should be forward and the other back.

3. **Hitting behind the body**—Make contact in front. Shift gears into the ball as you swing.

4. **Letting the ball drop**—Make contact at a point where your arm and racket are fully extended. If you let it drop, the ball will probably go into the net.

5. **Big windup**—If you try to take a full swing at the ball, you give yourself more chances to make errors. Reduce the motion by bringing the

racket up in front of you, then to the backscratch position. You still have enough room to swing hard and high at the ball.

6. **Looking down before hitting**—Keep your eyes up until after you hit. Looking down or out at the other court too soon causes too many mishits.

OVERHEAD SMASH SELF-HELP DRILLS

Very few tennis players take the time to perfect this shot in practice. Most people hit a few during the warmup before the match and then take their chances on hitting good smashes during the match. Only outstanding athletes are gifted enough to get by with such limited practice. Most of us should hit 25 to 50 overheads every time we go out to play. If you do not have the time to put in that kind of practice, do not expect to develop a strong overhead.

If you have a basket of balls and can get together with a friend, take turns lobbing to each other. Stand very close to the net at first and have your practice partner feed you very soft, easy lobs. Take your time, get set, and get the feel of hitting deep, crisp smashes at close range. When you feel comfortable and confident at the net, gradually move back to positions deeper in the court. At midcourt, you will get practice judging whether to play the ball in the air or after the bounce, as well as hitting smashes at longer distances. If your partner is good enough, use a lob and smash drill, in which you hit smashes and the other player lobs as long as you can keep the ball in play. Change roles after each player has hit ten to fifteen smashes. Also practice smashing to different spots on the court. Place racket covers or cans on the court and try to hit them. If you can do that, try smashing to a spot left open by your opponent. This drill will force you to hit with direction while being aware of the court position of your opponent.

LOB

Like the overhead smash, the lob is one of the game's most valuable shots, but one which players seldom take the time to practice and refine. This shot is effective as an offensive weapon, as a defensive technique, and as a way to keep your opponent off balance. The lob is not something you use only when you are in trouble. It should be used any time it will help you win a point, and that is usually more often than most players realize.

FUNDAMENTALS (OFFENSIVE LOB)

- Use a forehand or backhand grip.
- Disguise the shot.
- Open the racket face.
- Lift the ball.
- Complete the follow through.

USE A FOREHAND OR BACKHAND GRIP

Hold the racket as you would for any groundstroke. There is no special grip for the lob.

DISGUISE THE SHOT

The offensive lob is designed to win the point by using a shot your opponent does not expect. Make it look like any other shot in your groundstroke collection. If you give the shot a different look in your preparation, the other player will anticipate what you are up to and get into a position to smash your lob.

OPEN THE RACKET FACE

Just before you make contact with the ball, rotate your wrist so that the racket face opens slightly to the sky. Although some players occasionally hit a topspin lob, most of the time the shot will be hit flat or with backspin. The opened racket face allows for backspin. The point of contact may be further back than on other shots because you are returning a forcing shot and because if you can wait another fraction of a second, your opponent will be committed even further toward the net.

LIFT THE BALL

With the open racket face, lift the ball upward and aim it high enough to clear your opponent's outstretched racket. The ball should be hit high enough so that it cannot be reached before the bounce and low enough so that it cannot be reached after the bounce. Direct the ball to the backhand side of the opponent whenever possible. If you make a mistake, make it by hitting the ball too high or too deep, not by hitting too low or too short.

COMPLETE THE FOLLOW THROUGH

Follow through in the direction you are attempting to hit the ball. The follow through may not be as complete as on normal groundstrokes, but do not deliberately try to restrict this part of the stroke. Hold the racket firmly, keep your wrist steady, and try to carry the ball on the strings as long as possible. If you think of shortening the follow through too much, you may begin to slow down the racket before contact. When that happens, the lob falls short.

FUNDAMENTALS (DEFENSIVE LOB)

- Use a forehand or backhand grip.
- Prepare while you are moving to the ball.
- Shorten your backswing.
- Lift the ball.

USE THE FOREHAND OR BACKHAND GRIP

Again, there is nothing special about the way you hold the racket for a defensive lob. If you are moving to the forehand side, use the Eastern forehand grip. Change to the backhand grip that suits you for shots on the other side of your body.

PREPARE WHILE YOU ARE MOVING TO THE BALL

When you hit this shot you are probably either running, out of position, off balance, or generally in trouble. Technique is not quite as important when you are scrambling to stay alive in a rally, but technique should not be overlooked. Run with the racket back if you can. Now, more than on any other shot, you do not have time for stroke preparation at the last second. Get into a respectable hitting position as much as possible on the way to the ball.

SHORTEN YOUR BACKSWING

Any time you are in trouble on the tennis court, shorten your swing. There are times when the motion used in retrieving a ball that has been smashed or hit forcefully looks almost like a volley motion. So take a shorter backswing when you hit a defensive lob. If the other player has hit the ball hard enough, you may be able to just block the ball upward to get it back.

Lift the Ball

Again, the racket face will be a little open as you make contact. As you rotate your wrist to open the racket, lift the ball. Get it well into the air so you will have time to recover and get back into position for the next shot. If the smash is hard enough, you may not even have to lift the ball to get it back. Just getting your racket to the ball in time and opening it may be enough to send the ball back high and deep.

If you can, follow through completely, but don't worry about it unless you are having problems. The follow through will be upward, outward, and across your body, in that order. A full follow through will help you get the feel of gently lifting the ball up into the air and deep into the backcourt. However, if you are really in trouble, you may have to restrict the follow through on a lob as you would on any other stroke when you are trying to survive the point.

Lob Problems and Corrections

1. **Hitting tentatively**—Go for the back part of the court. If you are afraid something bad will happen, it will.

2. **Not hustling**—Fight for the point. You have to want to stay in the point worse than the other player wants to end it. Don't give up on a shot until it bounces twice on your side.

3. **Not following through**—On lobs in which you are in relatively good position, hit through the ball. Failing to complete the swing will cause you to hit short.

Lob Self-help Drills

You need someone to throw or hit balls to you to develop this stroke. Dropping a ball and hitting lobs does not simulate game conditions. At first, stay on or just behind the baseline and return the ball with lobs to get the feel of the shot and to get used to the height and distance needed to make the shot effective. Then practice the offensive lob by attempting to barely clear the player at the net. If you hit short, the net player can practice the overhead smash. There you have a three-shot drill: (1) net player hits a deep, forcing shot; (2) you return with a lob; (3) if the lob falls short, the drill ends with a smash; if your lob clears the net player, the drill begins again. After you have become accustomed to the feel and trajectory of the shot, work on placing the ball either to different spots on the court or to your opponent's backhand. The last stage is to learn to hit the lob while

71

running. Have your practice partner toss balls alternately to each corner of your backcourt. Retrieve the first ball with a forehand, hitting high and deep, then head for the opposite corner of the backcourt to hit the next ball with a backhand lob. This drill will improve your physical condition as well as your lob.

Finally, use game and match situations to practice lobbing. If you are playing an informal match, use the lob more often than you would normally, even if a groundstroke might be more appropriate. Losing a few points in friendly matches for the sake of practice might result in a point-winning stroke in a tournament.

DROP SHOT

Drop shots should be used from a position inside the service line. Shots hit from further back in the court look good when they are successful, but the odds are against those shots being successful very often. Use the shot when your opponent is too far out of position behind the baseline, when he or she is off to either side of the court, or when a forcing shot is expected. The shot is most effective against opponents who are either slow or out of shape. The slow ones may not be able to get to the ball, and the players in poor condition will tire if you make them run enough. Hit the drop shot often enough to make your opponents think about the possibility that you might use the shot regularly. If they have to worry about possible drop shots, your other shots from similar positions on the court may become even more effective.

FUNDAMENTALS

- Disguise the shot.
- Swing from high to low.
- Hit with backspin.

DISGUISE THE SHOT

The drop shot should look like any other shot you might hit from the forecourt. This means there should be no exaggerated backswing, no delay in the stroke, no change in footwork, and no difference in facial expression.

Swing from High to Low

Hold the racket firmly, and delicately slide the racket face under the ball as you make contact. To do that, start the racket head above the level of the waist and swing down behind the ball.

Hit with Backspin

The combination of swinging from high to low and opening the racket face should impart backspin to the ball. Shots played after the bounce require a full, smooth follow through. Drop volleys are more effective if the follow through is abbreviated.

Hit the drop shot so that the ball is falling in a downward direction as it clears the net. Barely clearing the net is effective, but not absolutely necessary. The thing to avoid is hitting the ball so that it travels too far in a horizontal plane after the bounce. Putting backspin on the ball should make it bite into the court and not travel far toward the baseline. Expect your opponent to reach the ball and return it. If it is not returned, you win the point; if it is, you should be near the net and ready to volley the ball for a winner. Hitting drop shots on consecutive points may be a good idea if the other player has to work hard to get to the ball on the first drop shot.

Drop Shot Problems and Corrections

1. **Telegraphing the shot**—Ask your practice partner if he or she knows when you are going to hit the drop. If so, try to identify the mannerisms you exhibit before the shot and work on eliminating them.

2. **Holding the racket loosely**—Hold the racket firmly to feel the shot. You want to "baby" the ball across the net, but you have to hold the racket tightly to hit a precision shot like this one. Get down with the ball before you hit and as you hit. Standing straight up and dropping the racket head down will cause problems.

3. **Swinging too hard**—Hit the shot as easily as you can and still clear the net. If you do not have enough touch to hit the shot effectively, use another shot.

Drop Shot Self-help Drills

Have your practice partner drop and hit baseline drives to you at the net. Get the feel of the shot at first and work on direction and placement second. Playing short games and drop shot games can also help you to improve this stroke. Short games are played with two, three, or four people who use the service line as the back boundary. If there are three people, play two against one. Anything hit deeper than midcourt is out. Drop shot games can be played with lines marked 6 feet from and parallel to the net on each side. All shots must be drop shots and all must fall on or within the marked lines. Keep score as you would in a regular match.

HALF VOLLEY

The half volley is a shot you don't want to hit unless you have to. It usually means that you are out of position, have prepared late, or your opponent has hit a forcing shot. But if you have to hit it, you might as well learn how to make it an offensive weapon rather than a defensive prayer. The older you get, the more you will be out of position, so start working on it now.

FUNDAMENTALS

- Turn your side to the net early.
- Take a short backswing.
- Stay low while you hit.
- Follow through completely.

TURN YOUR SIDE TO THE NET EARLY

You don't have much time to get ready for this shot, so turn your side or at least your shoulders as soon as you know on which side you will have to take the ball. If you can turn early, your racket will be drawn back early.

TAKE A SHORT BACKSWING

There is no time to take a big backswing, so severely restrict that part of the hitting motion. Also, if you take a big backswing there is a tendency to overhit the ball. All you need to do is block this shot; big swings are not only time consuming, they are counter-productive.

STAY LOW WHILE YOU HIT

After you have turned your side to the net, crouch as though you are sitting on a stool or bench while you hit. Look the ball in the eye and stay down through the shot. As you swing forward, block the ball and try to make contact out in front of your position. Lift the racket head as you make contact to get the ball to rise over the net.

FOLLOW THROUGH COMPLETELY

Although the rest of the shot must be changed to compensate for the lack of time and unusual position of the ball, the follow through is relatively normal. Hit through the ball and continue your swing after contact. The follow through may be a little more upward than on other shots, but it should remain basically intact.

HALF VOLLEY PROBLEMS AND CORRECTIONS

1. **Standing straight up**—Since a half volley is by definition a shot hit immediately after the bounce, you have to get down there with it to see what is going on. If your eyes are at a level five or six feet higher than the ball and racket, you will have to be very lucky to return the ball.

2. **Pulling up with the shoulders too soon**—Once you get down with the shot, stay down there. If you lift your shoulders as you try to lift the ball, your shot is likely to sail out of the court.

3. **Hitting too hard**—Don't try to fight power with power. If the ball is coming fast at your feet (or anywhere else), use the power of your opponent by blocking or reflecting the ball back. If he or she hits hard and you panic by trying to hit just as hard, you will endanger the lives of spectators around the court. You will also lose the point.

REVIEW QUESTIONS

1. Describe the difference between the Eastern forehand, Eastern backhand, and Continental grips.

2. What are the comparative advantages and disadvantages of the Eastern backhand grip and the two handed backhand?

3. In what ways are the service and overhead smash techniques the same? How are they different?

4. What effects does the lack of time have on the technique of hitting volleys?

5. What differences are there in hitting a defensive and an offensive lob?

6. Describe the footwork necessary to prepare for groundstrokes.

7. List the fundamentals for hitting these shots:

- forehand
- backhand
- punch serve
- forehand volley
- backhand volley

- overhead smash
- lob
- drop shot
- half volley

Chapter 3

Strategy

BEFORE STRATEGY

Most tennis players go through several stages during their tennis play-ing lives. At first, they have no strokes and no game. Not only do they not know how to hold or swing the racket, they also don't know what to do with themselves or with the ball in most situations. As beginners start to master the strokes described in the previous chapter, they move into the second stage during which they look good hitting the ball, but have no game nor game plan. They are not sure whether they should push, hit hard, come to the net, stay back, or whatever. The most frequent complaint heard from players at the intermediate level is that they play people they should beat, but don't. Losses come to players with strange strokes, who wear funny clothes, who are frequently older, and who just do not appear to be good tennis players, but who somehow manage to win.

The purpose of this chapter is to help you, your students, or your team members move into the third part of their tennis lives in which strokes are intelligently blended into a complete tennis game. A mature player can de-velop a general plan to help himself defeat an opponent. That plan is called strategy. Wanting to comprehend and use tennis strategy is understandable, but there are some things you should know before getting too excited about the possibilities it will open for you or your players. Here they are.

In order to use strategy at all, you must be able to control and move the ball. That means you must have developed your strokes enough so that you are able to hit to specific areas of the court with a variety of pace and spin. If you are still struggling to keep the ball in play, you are not ready for strategy. You can learn where to position yourself for various shots, but keep working on ball control before worrying about strategy.

Strategy will help only if you have a reasonable degree of control over the match you are playing. Face it: if you are out there trying to survive the match without getting hurt rather than having a chance to win, there is no way you can utilize strategy. Very few players ever have the kind of com-plete control they would like, but there are times during a match when being able to control points or games is possible and productive.

One of the first steps toward using strategy is having some concept of what percentage tennis involves. You must know what the best shot is for a situation if you are going to use more than strokes to beat an opponent. If the shot is hit well, the hitter will win that point or be in a position to win the point a high percentage of the time. Most of this chapter will be spent on explaining percentage tennis.

In addition to knowing about percentage tennis, you also have to know what your personal percentage is. That means you may be able to hit shots in some situations even though normal percentage tennis would call for something else. For example, it is fairly common knowledge that you should not use drop shots very often in doubles. There are just too many people on the other side of the net who will be close enough to get to the ball for a winner. But some people are very effective with drop shots in singles and doubles. Their personal percentage on that particular shot is different from normal percentage tennis. Some players even hit drop shots from the baseline in singles, and it works for them. Try to learn which low percentage shots seem to work for you and for your opponent.

If you carry the personal percentage idea further, you will begin to realize that there are exceptions to every strategy rule. There is never an "always" situation. As soon as a player develops a pattern of hitting the same shot in certain situations, that player has become too predictable and may lose because the opponent knows where every shot is going. Some players may always hit the right shot and beat you, but they are probably better than you to begin with.

Assuming that you know the right shots to hit and how to use them to gain an advantage in a match, remember that a good shot or even a lucky shot may ruin the whole thing for you. You may hit the perfect down-the-line-approach shot—deep, low, close to line, and with backspin—only to have your opponent hit a crosscourt winner that could probably not be duplicated in ten attempts. That doesn't mean your strategy was wrong; just that on one point it didn't help you.

Strategy can change during a match. You may have a terrific game plan, only to realize that you have lost the first set and are down 3–1 in the second. In that case, take a quick, last look at your game plan and change it. Changing a losing game plan is not news and is not restricted to tennis. You will not be rewarded or remembered for out-thinking a player unless you also happen to win the match.

As you begin to think about strategy, take into consideration that there is strategy at the match, set, game, and point levels. You will have decreasingly less time to think about and execute each of those four plans as they are listed. It is not enough to have a vague idea of how a match should be played. That idea has to be put into the context of the stages of a match. If, for example, you are primarily a baseline player and are playing a hard hitting but out of condition opponent, how does that translate into a strategic game plan? At the match level, plan to be on the court a long time by pacing yourself and being in good physical condition. Don't panic if you get behind early in a set. Be patient, play conservatively, and don't be embarrassed if he or she blows you off the court occasionally when serving. Big hitters can do that, but they cannot do it forever. Fight to stay alive in every point and move the ball around the court as much and as long as possible. You may deviate from your strategy long enough to keep the other player confused, but stick to your plan if it is working.

Playing strategic tennis can be boring. Inside every player there is that desire to hit the spectacular shot even if the odds are against it. Using strategy effectively may require you to hold that urge inside for the sake of sound, rational tennis. Most percentage shots are not spectacular, but calculated shots designed to set up an opponent for the slow kill. It takes discipline to pass up a chance to hit a great shot in favor of hitting an everyday shot. Some people can never make that adjustment. They are destined to play a few spectacular points, games, or even matches, but to lose more than they win over a long period of time. The challenge for the percentage player is in winning, not in making the shot. If you cannot resist the temptation to hit the great shot for an entire match, at least wait until you are comfortably ahead in the game, set, or match before you go for broke.

Strategy requires practice. Chipping or slicing shots short and wide to the backhand sounds like good strategy against a two hander, but that shot is hard to hit in a match. Serving down the middle in the even court is good tennis, but that spot is difficult to hit unless you take time to work on it often. There are a hundred other examples, but the idea is that strategy without execution is useless.

No matter how well-designed your strategy is, the best player usually wins in tennis. Strategy can do three things for you: (1) it can close the gap between you and someone who is clearly better, (2) it can widen the gap between you and an inferior player, and (3) it can make the difference between winning and losing against someone your speed. Don't expect too much. Strategy will not enable you to defeat someone who consistently beats you, 6–0, 6–1, or 6–2.

Finally, feel free to disagree with some of the strategy you hear and read about. Some very prominent and reputable teachers and coaches disagree on relatively fundamental points such as where to hit a service return when the server stays back. Many books and articles on strategy are written with professionals or advanced players in mind. What works for them may not be practical for you. No one has all of the answers. But there are lots of answers to questions about strategy, and if you think you are ready to hear them, the following section is a presentation of the strategic options open to you on a stroke-by-stroke basis.

SINGLES STRATEGY

SERVE

1.   **Stand near the center of the baseline to serve.** From that point you are as close to every other part of the court as you can be while serving. That means you are in the best possible starting position to make your next shot after the service return. You can move away from the central position

as long as you think you can cover the whole court on your next shot. If you do decide to move out of the center, it is best to do it on the left side of the court. If the service return goes down the line to your right, you can probably cover the forehand side more easily than you could cover the backhand part of the court. Lefthanders may move to their right when serving to the even court and leave a little open space on the forehand side.

2.   Do not spend much of your energy or time trying to serve aces. You should let your opponent know you are capable of hitting an ace now and then, but save the shot for special occasions and to keep him off balance.[1] There are at least two times when the ace should be considered. One is when you are comfortably ahead in a set or game; the other is when you have run especially hard during the previous point and cannot afford to expend that much energy so soon. Other than in those situations, keep your serves deep, well placed to the corners, and hit with less than one hundred per cent velocity. When you try to hit as hard as you can, you increase the chance of missing the first serve, thus increasing the chance of having to serve twice on the same point. The serve probably takes more out of a player than any other shot. It is better to be smart than strong in this situation.

3.   Place the first serve to your opponent's weakest side or to an open area in the service court. The weakest side is the backhand for most players, but you will have to figure that out before or during the match. The open area will depend on where your opponent lines up to receive. Many players try to protect their backhands by moving a step or two in the direction of their backhands, leaving some daylight on the forehand side. There are obvious dangers to hitting to the forehand side even when it is left open, so be careful. If everything is equal, when playing righthanders serve from the right side deep and down the middle. From the left side serve deep and to the outside of the service court. Against lefthanders, from the right side go wide and from the left side hit down the middle. Figures 3-1 and 3-2 show target areas against righthanders and lefthanders, respectively.

4.   When you serve from the right side, be careful about serving to the righthander's forehand. Even though the other player may leave you some daylight, it is probably his strongest side and the side to which he can move easily. You might experiment with the wide-to-the-right serve to see how the points go. If he moves laterally to make the return, you may be able to exploit the open court and hit there to pull him out of position. If he moves diagonally and cuts your serve off early, you might be in trouble. If

---

[1] Masculine pronouns will occasionally be used to simplify descriptions. These pronouns are intended to designate both sexes.

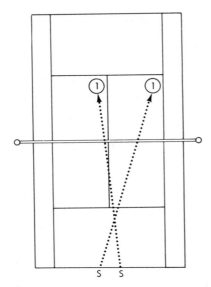

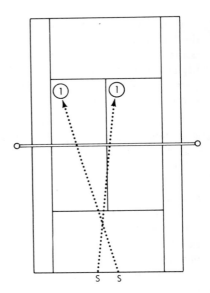

Figure 3-1 The circled "ones" indicate the primary targets for serves to a righthanded player.

Figure 3-2 The "ones" here show where to serve against lefthanders.

so, avoid the trouble by keeping most serves down the middle to his backhand. Be just as careful about serving to lefthanders' forehand on the left side of the court. When in doubt, serve down the middle.

5. **Use the righthanded slice serve to pull your opponent off the court to make a return.** If he has to go far enough, the return should be to your backhand and the opposite side of his court should be open for your crosscourt shot. A wide slice serve will be doubly effective against a lefthander in the right court. Not only will he have to move wide to make the return, he will also have to hit with his backhand. Figure 3-3 shows the probable sequence of shots when the wide slice serve is effectively hit.

6. **Serve wide to a righthander's forehand if he or she stands too close to the center of the court or well behind the baseline.** Either position opens up the corner of the service court for the wide serve. If the receiver stands behind the baseline, the short, wide slice serve is especially effective.

7. **Serve directly at the opponent who is good at hitting sharply angled returns.** If you serve wide to either side of this player, you give him a better chance to do what he does best—hit the angles. If you can serve right at him with a flatter and slightly faster than normal serve, he will not have

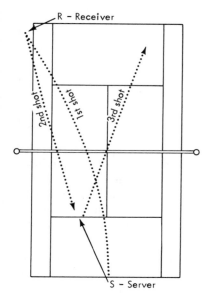

R – Receiver

2nd shot

1st shot

3rd shot

S – Server

Figure 3–3 The wide serve can set the server up for a crosscourt winner.

time to move to the side of the ball to execute his return. The angle of the return will be reduced, forcing him to return more shots toward the center of the court.

8. Serve directly at players who take big backswings on their groundstrokes. Again, the flatter, straight serve does not give your opponents time to wind up like they want to. Watch your opponent's racket head during the warmup. If you can see the racket come back behind his body as he prepares to hit a forehand or backhand or if the racket makes a loop near his head on the backswing, you know how to play the serve. This tactic of hitting directly at the stomach may also work on approach shots, and it is very effective on fast courts.

9. When you serve down the middle to the backhand, expect the return to come back down the middle. What else can the receiver do? If your serve has any pace at all, it will be very difficult for the player making the return to get out in front with the racket to hit an angled shot or a shot down the line. All that is left is the middle and the other line, and since you are standing to the side of the center mark, you should have both shots covered. Only a great angled shot could get the ball past you, and if the opponent is good enough to do that, you are probably going to lose, anyway.

The first serve is one of the most abused offensive weapons in tennis. Too many players try to knock their opponents off the court with the first serve, then follow it with a very weak second serve. Very few good players hit their first serve as hard as they can. Most use a combination of power and spin, with a little more power on the first serve and a little more spin on the second.

10. When you serve wide to the backhand of a player, let him have the crosscourt return until he proves he can beat you consistently with the shot. Following your serve, protect the middle and the sideline closest to where your serve hits. If you follow your serve to the net, follow the line of the ball a step or so toward the nearest sideline. If you keep getting passed with a crosscourt return, re-evaluate your strategy.

11. When playing in a crosswind, use the wide, slice serve to your advantage. The combination of your spin and the wind carrying the ball in the same direction makes it very difficult for the receiver to do much with his shot. It will probably take him farther off the court than usual, so fade to the same side the ball is going and expect it to come back down the line on that side. The opposite side of his court should be wide open for your next shot—either a crosscourt groundstroke or volley.

12. When playing someone who likes to come to the net behind his return, serve wide. There are two reasons for doing this: (1) he will have to leave more open court than if you serve at him or down the middle, and (2) he will have to travel farther to get to a volleying position where he can hurt you with the next shot. Since he is taking advantage of your serves, you can counteract at least part of that advantage by making him give you more room on the next shot and by making him work harder to get to the volley.

13. Do not follow your serve to the net unless your serve is very good and unless you can volley well. This sounds too simple, but many players watch tennis on television and see the pros serve, rush, and volley all the time. It is nice if you can do it, but very few players can. Your serve must be deep and to an open area or weakness, and your volley must be crisp enough to put your opponent in real trouble so you can finish the point with a second volley. If you get to the net and have to stay there for several shots, you will be in real trouble.

14. Serve the ball slower than usual if you need more time to get to the net. Remember that the harder you hit the ball, the less time that gives you to get to the volleying position. If you can take some of the speed off the serve but still hit deeply and with spin, you can establish a position on or in

84

front of the service line before hitting the volley. From that position, you should be able to volley crosscourt for a winner or for a shot that will lead to a winner. If you have to stop two or three steps short of the service line, your volleying position is much weaker.

15.   Use more spin and less pace on second serves. The idea is to avoid hitting two serves, but if you have to serve twice, keep your opponent off balance by hitting deep and using topspin to keep the ball in play and to make the ball bounce high. Try to develop a serving motion that is similar on both serves. Two seventy-five per cent velocity serves which look the same to an opponent are better than one bullet and one floater. A Continental or backhand grip is almost essential for the topspin serve.

16.   When serving, play aggressively when the score is 0-0, 15-0, 30-0, 40-0, and 40-15. The farther ahead you are in a game, set, or match, the more relaxed you should be and the more you can afford to take chances. While it can be argued that 0–0 and 15–0 are not really positions of strength, the 30–0, 40–0, and 40–15 scores do put you in command. Serve boldly and follow your serves to the net if you are a good volleyer.

17.   When serving, play more conservatively when the score is tied or when you are losing late in a game. If the score is close, you still have a chance to win because your serve gives you an advantage. Do not choke up and start punching your serves, but be patient and selective about when to hit forcing shots and when to move in to the net.

18.   Experiment with a variety of serves during a match. The object is to keep your opponent guessing about how hard you will hit, where you will hit the ball, and how much spin the ball will have. Keep him off balance by never letting him get into a groove with his return. If you play someone who just cannot handle a particular serve of yours, use it most of the time. Otherwise, move the ball around the service court.

RETURNING SERVES

1.   Position yourself so that you are in the middle of the two extreme sides to which the ball can be served. Every server is limited in how wide he or she can serve the ball by the service court boundaries, by his or her position on the baseline, by reach, by where you stand to return the serve, and by laws of physics. As you line up to return a serve, stand at a point where you can cover the widest possible angles of the serve. If the server stands near the middle of the baseline for a deuce court serve, you should be about a step to the left of the singles sideline.

If he moves to his right to get a better angle, you may have to move to your right to compensate for the change in his angle. From the left side, the normal position of return is slightly to the right of the singles sideline on the left side of the court.

2.　Stand as close to the service line as possible while still having time to make an effective return. If you move inside your baseline to return the serve, you cut down the angles the server has because you can get to the ball before it has time to reach the far corners of your playing area. The risk that you take by moving in closer is that you may not be able to effectively return a fast serve. Another advantage of standing close is that you improve your chances of returning the ball deeply, if that is what you want to do. Finally, standing closer to the service line reduces the time a server has to rush the net following the serve. If you can take two-tenths of a second away from the server, you will also be taking away some of the court position he is trying to establish.

3.　Stand closer to the service line than usual when you want to go to the net following your return. It is again simply a matter of time and distance on the court. The closer you are to the net when you return the serve, the closer you also are to a volleying position on the next show. Staying behind the baseline to return the serve would require more time and a greater distance to advance to the net.

4.　Leave part of your service court unprotected if you know your opponent cannot hit an ace to that area. If you want the serve to come to your forehand, move toward your backhand side. This will force the server to hit the ball where you want it to be hit—to your strongest side.

5.　Move toward the net a step or two after your opponent misses the first serve. This will give you a better position from which to attack the weaker second serve. Make your move at a time when the server can see you moving in. Do not do it to distract the server, but merely to let him know that you plan to take charge of the point.

6.　Learn to anticipate your opponent's second serve. It will have less pace and less variety because the server has to be more careful about getting the ball into the court. You can learn to anticipate by mentally recording where most second serves are hit and by watching the server's toss, swing, and racket face when contact is made.

7.　Run around your backhand occasionally on short, weak serves. You will be hitting a stronger shot and your opponent will have something else to worry about while serving. Do not try this tactic in crucial situations.

8.　When a righthanded server tosses the ball to his right, the serve will probably be a slice. The ball will bounce to your right side more than other serves. If the server tosses the ball straight ahead, watch for the flat, hard serve. If the ball is tossed to the server's left or slightly behind the head, watch for an American twist serve or a severe topspin serve. The

American twist should bounce to your left and the topspin serve will bounce higher than normal serves.

9.   **Return fast serves with a short backswing.** You do not have time to take a big backswing, and a short backswing should result in a shot hit at the feet of an opponent who is rushing the net. The idea is to use the power of your opponent. If the serve is hard, a block return will reflect the power of the serve. If the serve is softer, you may have to take a bigger backswing and supply some of the power yourself.

10.   **Return serves deep into the backcourt against players who stay near the baseline after the serve.** Keeping the ball deep is standard strategy for any groundstroke, including the service return in this situation. It makes the other player hit defensive shots and it gives you the chance to attack when a weak return comes back.

11.   **Avoid hitting service returns down the middle.** Practice returning the ball either down the line or crosscourt. More experts advocate the crosscourt return than the down the line shot, especially on shots hit deeply into the service court. Playing the return as a ground-stroke would dictate going crosscourt most of the time. Return down the line to exploit a weakness, open up the court for subsequent shots, or to keep your opponent guessing about what you will do.

12.   **Return short, weak serves down the line.** In this case, your return should be played as an approach shot if you go to the net behind your return. Since many approach shots should be hit parallel to the singles sideline, the return of weak serves should be, too. If you decide to hit crosscourt, it should be when the crosscourt shot will go to the backhand of the other player.

13.   **Hit the low, short return against players who serve and rush the net.** Pace is not as important as placement. It is very difficult for a player to hit a forcing shot if the ball has to be played at the feet. Chipping the ball straight ahead will reduce the angle of your opponent's next shot. Chipping wide to either side will not only force him to bend low to hit, it will also make him change directions to get to the ball. If you chip crosscourt, be sure to keep the ball low. Hitting higher or deeper may give the server time to reach your shot for a put-away volley.

14.   **Against high bouncing spin serves, stand closer to the service line and hit the ball before it has time to get away from you.** If that does not work, stand way back and wait for the ball to do its stuff before you hit. If that doesn't work, you are in trouble.

15.   **When you are having trouble returning a serve, stand slightly farther back than usual and try lobbing the return.** You will be hitting a

defensive shot, but at least you will be in the point one shot longer than if you missed a conventional service return.

16.   Experiment with different positions on the service returns. You may find that you are quicker than you thought or that you can take charge of the point even when returning. Do not automatically line up in the same spot against every type of server.

17.   When receiving serves, take chances at these times: at 40–0 because you have nothing to lose; at 0–15 because you have the double disadvantage of having to return the serve and of being one point down; at 0–30 and 0–40 for the same reasons; at 0–0 because you have a chance to offset the disadvantage of receiving the serve; and at 15–15 for the same reason. Do not take as many chances at 30–30 or deuce because you are close enough to winning the game without taking unnecessary risks.

GROUNDSTROKES

1.   Stand on or slightly behind the center of the baseline between groundstrokes. As soon as you hit one shot, start moving back to your base of operations. Do not wait to see where the next shot is going. As the point develops, you will have to shift from that central baseline position, but when in doubt go to that spot.

2.   Hit a majority of baseline shots crosscourt, deep into the backcourt, and high over the net. The crosscourt shot makes your opponent move, the deep shot keeps you on the attack, and the high bounce prevents a player from hitting with as much pace as on lower bouncing shots. Hitting crosscourt and high also gives you more distance with which to work and a lower net at the middle than on the side. There are obvious exceptions to the crosscourt pattern, such as when your opponent has a weak backhand or when part of the court is left unprotected.

3.   Protect the crosscourt side of your court when your opponent is hitting from the baseline. Assuming that your opponent knows as much about strategy as you do, he should be trying to hit crosscourt, also. Play a step in that direction to cut down the time and distance you have to travel to get those shots.

4.   When in doubt about where to direct shots hit from your backcourt, hit crosscourt. The reasons are the same as just given plus the fact that a crosscourt shot will stay in the air longer and give you more time to decide what to do next.

5.   Do not attempt to hit short, severely angled shots from your baseline. You leave too much open space down the line for your opponent's next shot. Besides, there are too many other things you can do with the ball rather than trying risky shots.

6.   Play shots at a safe height across the top of the net. Most mistakes are made into the net—not behind the baseline or wide. Shots that clear the net by three or four feet are not only safer, they are also more likely to bounce well back in your opponent's court.

7.   If you are weaker to one side than the other, tempt the other player to hit to your strong side. That can be done by playing a step or two to the right or left. Do not move over so far that you leave space for a winning shot; just far enough to get the shot you want to hit.

8.   Do not try to pass a player at the net cleanly on the first try. Hit the ball with good pace, and go for the winner on the shot after the first passing shot.

9.   Keep the ball low on passing shots. If your opponent gets to the shot, at least he will have to hit up on the ball with his volley. If you hang the ball high, he will probably put it away with a stronger volley.

10.   Consider hitting directly at the volleyer who has good reach and who is good at hitting angled volleys. Jamming the ball right at this player takes away one of his strengths and may reduce the angle of the volley.

11.   Against players who rush the net, chip the ball to their feet. Do not give them the privilege of using your pace for their volleys. Take a short backswing and chip the ball wide if their lateral movement is not good or directly at their feet to reduce the angle of the next shot. Making these players volley the ball up takes the offense away from them.

12.   Use your best stroke on all set-ups, even if you have to run around the ball to hit it. One of the differences between good players and great players is that great players have one "killer shot" in their arsenal. Find out what yours is and maneuver yourself into a position to use it for the last shot in a point.

13.   During a rally, develop a pattern, then break it. If you have some control over the match, you should be able to place the ball to various spots on the court. Three crosscourt shots followed by a down-the-line screamer might win the point. Try picking on someone's backhand so often that he moves over to protect it. Then break the pattern by going to his forehand. The combination of shots is almost endless, but the point is to lull your opponent into predictable series of exchanges, then change the pattern when it is least expected.

APPROACH SHOTS

1. **Use approach shots on balls that bounce near or inside your service courts.** The exceptions to this rule are when the shots have been hit with a sharp angle or with more than normal pace. If you can move or have to move forward several steps to get to the ball, an approach shot is probably in order. If you have to hit the ball from your baseline area, stay back after your shot regardless of where it bounced. Those shots do not give you enough time to hit and get to a position for a volley.

2. **Take a shorter than normal backswing on approach shots.** Since you are moving into the ball, the weight of your body moving forward will provide enough force to hit a strong shot. The forward movement and weight transfer plus a big backswing may cause you to hit the ball beyond the baseline.

3. **On most approach shots use backspin.** The backspin will keep the ball low after the bounce, and your opponent will have to hit up on the ball. Higher bounces also give a player more time to get to the ball. There are times when your opponent will give you a "sitter," a ball that bounces softly and higher than usual. On those occasions you might be able to use topspin on the approach, especially on the forehand side.

4. **Hit most approach shots down the singles sideline you are closest to.** There are many exceptions to this rule and they will be mentioned shortly. When you approach down the line, you will have less distance to cover to get to the net and your opponent will be forced to hit down the same line, down the middle, or to lob. If he hits a crosscourt passing shot, let him have it as long as it does not happen often. Be careful about approaching down the line to your opponent's forehand. Although it may work against some opponents, others may have good lateral movement and be able to pass you on the following shot.

5. **Occasionally hit approach shots down the middle or crosscourt.** Hitting down the middle can cause some players to change their strokes and it can negate the speed of others. There are also players who can hit better on the run than they can on balls directed right at them. Hitting crosscourt approaches often scores you points when the previous shot is very shallow and when the crosscourt corner is open. It also keeps your opponent from anticipating where your next approach shot will go. These crosscourt approach shots are especially effective when a righthander hits crosscourt to a lefthander's backhand or when a lefthander hits crosscourt to a righthander's backhand.

6. **Take a split step on the way to the net.** A split step involves momentarily squaring your feet to the net just before or as the other player hits

the ball. By taking the split step you can change directions, if necessary, to get into position to hit the next shot.

7.   Occasionally try a drop shot on an easy approach to the net. You may catch your opponent off balance if he or she is expecting a shot deep to the backcourt area. Do not try the drop shot in critical situations.

8.   When you go to the net after an approach shot, get there as quickly as you can without losing your balance before or as you hit. Try to get a step or two inside the service line before your first volley. Do not trot to the net. Run!

9.   Do not try to win the point with an approach shot. This shot should be hit so that you force the other player to hit a weak return. Then you can win the point with a good volley or smash.

10.   Stay away from the net if your opponent keeps passing you after your approach shot. You may be doing everything right, but a good baseline player can hit an even better passing shot than you can an approach shot. Find out what you can do and what the other person can do, then develop a pattern of attacking or defending.

11.   Be patient. Wait for the right shot before you hit an approach shot. If you are in doubt about whether or not to go, don't go. Hit your would-be approach shot to an open area of the court and then scramble back to the baseline to wait for a better opportunity.

Some players use a suicide strategy in charging the net. For apparently self-sacrificial reasons, they rush forward during a point courageously, but futilely. Others try to sneak up to the net as if to surprise their opponents (following a weak second serve, for example). Don't rush the net at all unless you can handle yourself once you get there.

VOLLEYS

1.   Play volleys from a position about eight to ten feet from the net near the center of the court. This position will change as the angle of your opponent's return changes. If he or she is pulled off to the side of the court to make a return, you will have to move in that direction to cover the angle from the new position. There will be times when you will have to play closer to the net or farther from it than eight to ten feet. If you are really attacking and get an easy shot to volley, you may be practically on top of the net before you hit. On weak approach shots, you may be forced to play a volley from on or behind the service line.

2.   **Place most volleys deep into the open part of the court.** If you can keep the ball deep, there will be less chance of being passed when your volley does not win the point outright. Look for daylight when you are preparing to hit and block the ball in that direction.

3.   **Volley shots that are hit down the line crosscourt.** A down the line attempt by your opponent gives you a good crosscourt angle for the next shot.

4.   **After a crosscourt volley, move in the direction of the open court in anticipation of the next shot.** If you don't win the point on the volley, you can expect the return to be an attempted passing shot down the other side of the court. If you get a head start, you can cut off the attempt with another volley.

5.   **Volley shots that are hit crosscourt down the line.** The reverse of the previous situation is also true. If you are at the net and the ball goes crosscourt, a down-the-line volley should win the point because that is where the open space is.

6.   **If you have to reach out to one side for a volley, try to move slightly forward as you go to the ball.** Since you are taking a short back-swing on the shot, the only way to get power is to move diagonally towards the ball. The forty-five degree angle into the shot allows you to use your body weight transfer to compensate for the lack of a bigger backswing.

7.   **Take at least one step in toward the net after every well-hit vol-ley.** By "closing" after a good shot, you improve your court position and maintain your role as the attacker. If you volley and stay in the same place, you may be passed or have to hit up on the next shot.

8.   **Use your first volley to set yourself up for a winning second vol-ley.** The first volley does not have to be a winner. If you can place the ball deeply or at a good angle, you can go for the put-away on the second shot. Never attempt a difficult shot when a less difficult one will accomplish just as much. If you hit a good enough approach shot, a simple tap on the volley will probably set you up to win the point.

9.   **Play volleys while the ball is rising whenever you can.** It gives the other player less time to prepare for your return and it lets you hit an offensive shot rather than a defensive one.

10.   **If you have to hit a volley from below the level of the net, go for depth instead of trying a winner.** It will take a great angle shot to win from the low volleying position. Most players cannot execute that shot well. Hit

deeply, keep yourself in the point by playing it safe, and wait for a better time to put the ball away.

11. **If your opponent has been pulled off the court or pushed behind the baseline, use the short crosscourt volley.** That's where the open court will be.

12. **When there is a doubt about where to volley, hit the ball deep to your opponent's weakest side.** That will at least give you more time to decide what to do with the next shot—if you get one.

13. **In rapid exchanges at the net, hit down the line or straight ahead until you are ready to attempt a winner.** If you try a crosscourt shot too soon, you will leave too much of your court open for your opponent to hit a winner. By going down the line you can make a mistake and still have a chance to win the point. If you make a mistake hitting crosscourt, you will be out of the point.

14. **Expect every shot to come back at you following a volley.** The pace of the point will be much quicker when you are at the net. You do not have time to admire your shots as you do sometimes from the baseline. Hit the volley, close toward the net, and immediately get the racket out in front of you for the next volley.

LOBS

1. **When you have to run wide to retrieve a deep shot, lob crosscourt.** That way your opponent will have less of an angle to hit the overhead smash. A down-the-line lob opens up too much of the court for his smash. With a crosscourt lob, you may get away with a mistake.

2. **If you are going to make a mistake on a defensive lob, make it deep rather than short or wide.** Direct your shots to the backcourt area by making the ball reach its peak near the opposite service line.

3. **Use the lob more often when your opponent has to look into the sun or into lights.** If the other players tries to take part of the court away from you by coming to the net, take some of his vision away by putting the ball between him and the sun.

4. **Follow good offensive lobs to the net.** This will put pressure on your opponent to hit a good return. An offensive lob is as good as an approach shot. Use it to take the net from your opponent.

5. **Lob at times just to make the other player aware that your lob is a threat.** If you don't lob now and then, he will play very close to the net without any fear of being lobbed over.

6.   Lob high if you are in a defensive position; lob low when you are trying to win the point with the shot. The offensive lob should barely clear your opponent's racket, and it is usually more effective to the backhand side.

7.   Use the offensive lob if the server is coming in to the net rapidly. If he is coming too fast, a lob may throw him off balance. This is a difficult shot, but at least see if it works against some players.

8.   Lob to the backhand if you can place the ball without risking an error. The high backhand shot is one of the most difficult in tennis. If the player at the net gets a racket on the ball, the return should not be very strong.

Overhead Smashes

1.   Let a lob bounce if you can do it without losing your offensive position. By letting the ball bounce, you will minimize factors such as spin and the effect of the wind on the ball. The exception to this suggestion is the short, low lob which can be put away when you are very close to the net.

2.   Do not let the ball bounce if by doing so you lose your offensive position. Most offensive lobs will have to be played in the air. If you let them bounce, you will have to retreat too far back for the next shot.

3.   Change the direction of two consecutive smashes. If you hit the first smash down the middle, hit the second at an angle. Open up the court by moving your opponent from side to side while he chases your smashes.

4.   Attempt severely angled smashes only when you are close to the net. Angled shots from the backcourt area are low percentage shots.

5.   Do not try to win the point with an overhead smash from your backcourt. There is too much distance for the ball to travel for it to be a winner. Hit the shot firmly and deeply, and wait for a shallow return for your put-away smash.

6.   If you are in good court and hitting position, hit away on the smash. Don't try more shot than you need to win the point, but hit the ball hard. Hold back a bit if your hitting position is poor.

Drop Shots

1.   Don't try drop shots from the baseline. It's too risky.

2.   Don't try drop shots when the wind is at your back. The ball may carry to your opponent's midcourt area for a set-up.

3. **Don't try drop shots against players who can run fast.** They can turn good looking shots into better looking shots for themselves.

4. **Be careful about using drop shots on hard courts.** The hard surface makes for a high bounce, giving the other player more time to get to the ball.

5. **Use the drop shot against slow moving opponents and against players who are not in good physical condition.** Make them pay for their weaknesses.

6. **Use the drop shot when your opponent expects you to hit a deep shot.** A drop shot when you are expected to hit a strong approach shot is not a bad idea. Keep people wondering what you will do next.

7. **Be ready to move forward after a drop shot.** One drop shot is often followed by another.

DOUBLES STRATEGY

SERVES

1. **Stand approximately halfway between the center mark and the doubles sideline to serve.** From this position you can cover the court from the middle to the alley when the return is made crosscourt. Your partner at the net can cover the other half of the court on everything but lobs (Figure 3-4).

2. **Serve at three-quarter speed deep to the backhand or to the open part of the service court.** The backhand is usually the weakest shot; putting the ball deep keeps the receiver from attacking your serve; and hitting at three-quarter speed is safe. It also allows you more time to get to the net following the serve.

3. **Serve wide to a righthander's backhand on the odd court.** The combination of the wide serve and your partner being stationed at the net reduces the possibility of a good return.

4. **Serve wide to a lefthander's backhand on the even court.** A lefthander shouldn't be playing that side, but take advantage of it if he does.

5. **Any time you serve wide to a receiver's backhand, cover the middle of the court on the return and let your partner cover the sideline area.** Leave the crosscourt area open until the receiver proves he can beat you consistently with the crosscourt return.

6. **Use more spin with your serves to give yourself time to get to the**

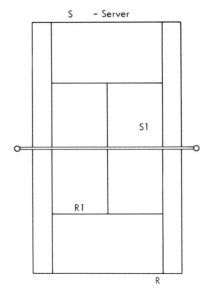

S   - Server

S1

R1

R

Figure 3—4   The server (S) should stand between the center mark and the doubles sideline. The server's partner is eight to ten feet from the net. The receiver is near the alley, and the receiver's partner is near the service line unless the server is very strong or the receiver is having trouble with the return.

net. A hard, flat serve may sound like a good idea, but if the ball comes back, it will come before you have time to reach a good volleying position.

7.   Let the strongest server begin serving each set. The order of serve may be changed each set, so use the rule to start out with a strong serve.

8.   Serve down the middle if your partner is good at poaching. A serve down the middle almost has to be returned down the middle and therefore can be anticipated.

9.   Use a variety of serves. Unless the receiver has particular trouble with one kind of serve, keep him off balance by mixing serves that are fast, slow, to the backhand, to the forehand, straight ahead, flat, and with spin. Never let the receiver get into a groove returning your serves.

RETURNING SERVES

1.   Receive the serve from a point approximately where the baseline meets the singles sideline. Since the server has probably moved to a position for a more angled shot, you will have to shift, also. Some players even stand behind the alley to return the doubles serve. Go back and look at Figure 3-4 to see where to stand.

2. Try to stand one step inside the baseline against players who do not have strong serves. That position will allow you to make a quicker return and it will also cut down the possible angles for a service ace. If the server is very strong, you will have to move back to the baseline or even behind it.

3. If the server remains on the baseline following the serve, return the ball deep and crosscourt, then get to the net. This applies only to intermediate and advanced players who have a good net game.

4. If the server's partner plays too close to the net, lob over him. Then go to the net following your lob. Your shot will have to be high enough to prevent a smash by the net player and low enough so that the server cannot run under it for a smash.

5. If the server comes to the net following the serve, return the ball crosscourt and to the feet of the server. This return forces the server to volley the ball up, frequently setting you and your partner up for a strong second shot. Returns to the center, to the net player, or down the line should be tried infrequently.

6. When you try to pass the server's partner at the net, direct your shot toward the singles sideline. If he or she is trying to poach, your shot will be placed well enough to pass and safely enough not to go wide.

Volleys

1. When your partner is receiving the serve, stand on or slightly in front of the service line two steps from the center service line. Face the server's partner. Be ready to advance closer to the net on a good return and to retreat on a weak shot. Again refer to Figure 3-4 to see the proper position.

2. If you are a beginner or an intermediate who is not comfortable at the net, line up on the baseline even with your partner. Some professional players begin the point from the baseline if the server is very strong.

3. When your partner is serving, stand about eight to ten feet from the net and two steps inside the singles sideline toward the center of the court. From this position you can cut off weak returns without giving up too much space for a return down the alley. You will also be in a good position to poach (Figure 3-4).

4. When your partner's serve goes wide, shift slightly toward the alley. You can cover the sideline and alley area and your partner can cover the middle of the court. Tempt the other team to try to pass your partner with a crosscourt shot.

5. **When your partner is serving, protect your side of the court, take weak shots down the middle, and smash any lobs hit to your side of the court.** Your responsibilities include much more than just protecting the alley. You actually have as much court to cover as your partner; only the starting position is different.

6. **When the receiver stays back after a service return, the server who has adanced to the net should volley down the center of the court.** The center-directed shot draws your opponents toward the middle and creates some confusion about who will play the shot.

7. **When the receiver follows his return to the net, the server should volley toward the receiver's feet.** He probably shouldn't be coming in so soon anyway, and if you hit to his feet, he will have trouble maintaining his balance and hitting at the same time.

8. **If the service return is high and back to the server, go for a winning volley by hitting at the receiver's feet or at his partner's hips.** Any high service return in doubles is a signal that your team is in charge of the point. Don't be reckless, but take advantage of the chance to volley down on the ball.

9. **In quick exchanges at the net, the last player to hit a shot should take the next shot if it comes down the middle.** Establishing this groundrule between partners can avoid confusion which sometimes leads to no one hitting the ball.

10. **If you get an easy volley at the net, hit at the opponent closest to you.** If you have to return a difficult shot with a volley, hit toward the opponent who is farther away from you. The first suggestion means that the other player has less time to react; the second gives you more time to prepare for subsequent shots.

11. **When you are at the net and your partner is serving, tempt the receiver to try a shot down your alley.** If he can do it once in a while, let him have it. If he does it often, move closer to the singles sideline.

12. **Go for a winner when you poach.** It is not a defensive shot. If you don't win the point with that shot, either get back to your original position or continue to the other side so your partner will know where to go. If your first volley doesn't win the point, part of the court will be left open until you and your partner recover.

13. **Poach occasionally, even if you lose the point.** Make the other team aware of the threat of the poach.

14. **Try poaching after your partner has returned the serve with a crosscourt shot.** This tactic, tried infrequently, can have the same effect as poaching on the service return.

15.   Poach more often when your partner is serving well. Avoid poaching if your partner is weak with the serve.

16.   When you poach, make your move just before the receiver makes contact with the ball. There is a moment when he must take his eye off of you and look directly at the ball. That is when you should go.

17.   Fake the poach at times. It gives the other team one more thing to worry about.

18.   Think about poaching on every point, but do it only when you are in control of the situation. If you are more worried about what the other team is going to do than you are about what you and your partner are up to, better not poach.

19.   Poach more often if your partner cannot cover the court well. The more space you cover at the net, the less he has to cover behind you.

20.   Poach on serves that hit deep in the service court or bounce high. Both kinds of serves make the return more defensive and more difficult.

21.   Be aggressive and cold blooded when you poach. Do not worry about hitting somebody with the ball. That is their problem, not yours.

22.   Move closer to the net with each volley when your team is on offense. Hold your position when you are on defense. Do not give up the attack by failing to close in on the net.

23.   Protect your alley when the ball is going to be hit from a point on your side of the center of the court. Shift with the ball and with the position of your opponents. Move slightly toward the middle of the court when the other team will hit from the side of the court away from you.

24.   During a rally, look at the racket faces of your opponents. Do not turn around and look to see what your partner is doing. You may get hit in the face and you will lose a split second in reaction time when you turn back to your opponents.

25.   Play a step or two farther from the net against opponents who use the lob frequently. You can take away some of their lobbing space.

26.   Play closer to the net against opponents who seldom use the lob. Take anything they want to give you.

27.   If you are farther from the net than your partner, be prepared to cover lobs on his side of the court. If you have to move over to return the lob, your partner should move across to your side and drop back to the service line to prepare for the next shot (Figure 3-5).

28.   Retreat quickly when your opponents are set up for a smash. Get back as far as you can before the shot, then dig in, stay low and put the

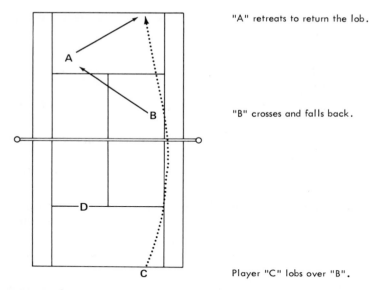

"A" retreats to return the lob.

"B" crosses and falls back.

Player "C" lobs over "B".

Figure 3–5 Cover the lob when it goes over your partner at the net. In turn, he or she should cross over and back to the service line to cover for you.

racket in front of your body. You may be able to deflect the ball back after the smash. Lucky shots are just as good as good shots.

29. Keep moving when you are at the net. Shift slightly with every shot to cover the open court or to make your opponents think about your position. If you stay in the same place, the other team can gang up against your partner without worrying about you.

30. If your partner's serve is weak, stand farther from the net than usual. You may need the extra time to react to the return of the serve.

31. Play farther from the net than usual if you are a stronger player than your partner. You may be able to take shots that he cannot handle. If you are weaker than your partner, play closer to the net. That way you give your partner more shots and more opportunities to set you up for winning volleys.

Lobs and Smashes

1. If you lob, lob over the player closest to the net. Then follow your lob to the net. The exception to this is when one opponent has a much stronger overhead smash than the other. Then lob over the weakest player.

2.   **Use the offensive lob if the net player poaches often.** His partner will get tired of chasing down balls on the other side of the court.

3.   **When in doubt, lob to the center of the court.** Almost every doubles shot hit toward the center is a good percentage shot.

4.   **Direct most smashes down the middle.** The smashes should be low if both opponents are at the net and high if they are in the backcourt. Once they move to the middle to protect against the smash, you may have an opening to the outside.

GENERAL STRATEGY

1.   **When your partner is forced to move out of his or her normal position, drift toward that side of the court until he or she has time to recover.**

2.   **Consider using the Australian doubles formation.** The net player lines up on the same side of the court as the server instead of at the net on the opposite side (Figure 3-6). This alignment takes the crosscourt return

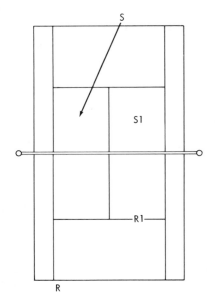

The server moves in to a volleying position in the right forecourt.

The server's partner lines up in the left forecourt to take away a crosscourt service return.

Figure 3—6   S (the server) and S1 are aligned in the Australian doubles formation before a serve to the left court.

away from the receiver and allows the server to move in and volley on the side where he is comfortable. The server has more court to cover, so there are disadvantages. The Australian formation requires a high skill level and partners who work well together, so be careful about when to use it.

3. **Play with someone you like and can get along with.** If you are compatible as friends, you should be good as partners. Don't fuss at your partner. He is trying to hit the ball well, and criticism will only lessen his concentration.

4. **Talk to your partner.** It can help you develop strategy and can keep you relaxed. Expressions such as, "Take it," "I've got it," "out," "no," "Get back," and "good shot," are common between doubles partners.

5. **Stay out of "no man's land" after you hit one shot from that area.** You may have to volley from a deeper position than in singles, but standing too far back will result in shots hit at your feet.

6. **Be more aggressive than normal if your partner is much weaker than you.** That does not mean to take shots that are not yours, but it does mean to assume the leadership role for your team. Somebody has to be the steady player and someone has to take a few chances. If you are the strongest player, take more chances.

7. **Unless you play regularly with the same partner, learn to play the left and right sides on the service return.** If a lefthander and righthander play together, most teams put the lefthander on the left side and the righthander on the right. Their backhands will be down the middle, but their service returns can be made with the crosscourt forehand much of the time.

8. **Protect the middle in doubles more than the alleys.** Give up passing shots near the sidelines until the other team begins to consistently hit winners.

9. **If your partner poaches, move in the opposite direction to cover the part of the court left open.**

10. **When you go for winners, hit to the extremities of the singles court.** Give yourself room to spare.

11. **When you and your partner are both playing in the backcourt, let the player with the forehand take shots down the middle.**

12. **When you and your partner are both in the backcourt and your opponents are at the net, hit low and down the middle.**

13. **If you are an advanced player, force the action.** Waiting for something good to happen is not good strategy. Make something happen.

SPECIAL SITUATIONS—SINGLES AND DOUBLES

PLAYING ON FAST COURTS

1.   **Get your racket back sooner and start your swing earlier than on slow courts.** The ball will bounce low and fast, and will tend to slide past you unless the racket is brought forward sooner. A shorter backswing may be necessary to meet the ball in time and in front of the body.

2.   **Play deeper than usual, especially on the service return.** The extra steps back will give you another fraction of a second to get ready and hit.

3.   **Attack on shots that would not be attacking shots on slower surfaces.** A better than average serve, volley, or approach shot becomes a great shot if the surface is fast enough.

4.   **Expect your opponent to be more aggressive on these courts than on slow courts.** You may have to defend against the serve and rush style of play against players who would not ordinarily play that way.

5.   **Play at a more intense pace than on slow courts.** Fast courts produce short exchanges on many points, so you may do less running. If you know you will be on the court a shorter period of time, you can pick up the pace during the match.

6.   **Be especially conscious of staying down low on groundstrokes.** Since the ball will slide more and bounce up less, you have to stay down there with the ball longer.

PLAYING ON SLOW COURTS

1.   **Be more deliberate than on fast courts.** You will have more time to prepare for shots, and you will be able to retrieve shots you would not normally reach.

2.   **Be patient.** It takes more time to beat somebody because the ball stays in play longer. The player who wants to get things over with in a hurry will become frustrated on these courts.

3.   **Don't wear yourself out trying to hit the big serve.** The ball will bite into the court and slow down considerably when it bounces. Pace yourself for a longer match and save your big serve for special occasions.

4.   **Use more spin on your serve.** The effect of the spin will be greater because of the increased friction between the ball and the court. The slice, topspin, and American twist serves will really do tricks on slow courts.

    5.   Be careful about advancing to the net. Even the pros are reluctant to follow a serve to the net on clay courts and slower synthetic surfaces. Approach shots have to be expertly placed before you follow the ball into the forecourt. Shallow serves and short approaches turn offensive tactics into positions of defense.

    6.   Use topspin groundstrokes more often. There is more time to set up and to bring the racket head up behind the ball than on fast courts. Be prepared to defend against the topspin shot in case your opponent has the same idea.

    7.   Don't underestimate the pusher or retriever on these courts. They are made for this player's game. Players who look slow, weak, and easy to beat on fast courts may be fast enough, strong enough, and tough enough to win on a slow court.

    8.   Be conscientious about your physical condition if you play most of your tournaments or matches on slow courts. You are going to be out there a long time—win or lose.

PLAYING IN THE WIND

    1.   Toss the ball lower than usual on the serve. Lowering the toss reduces the margin of error because the ball moves with the wind on a high toss. That could affect your service motion.

    2.   Do not attempt drop shots when the wind is at your back. The ball will sail instead of dropping.

    3.   Keep lobbing to a minimum. It is too risky, especially if the wind is gusting. If you have to lob, use the shot more when the wind is with you than when it is against you.

    4.   When the wind is with you, play a step or two closer to the net. When you are against the wind, play deeper than usual. If your serve keeps going deep, try standing a step behind the baseline. The added distance might compensate for the extra push the wind gives your serve.

    5.   Take more chances when you are playing against the wind. Shots that would normally be too high, too hard, or too deep often become well-hit shots against the wind. You may have to force the action or be blown off the court.

    6.   Play more conservatively with the wind. Shots that would usually be safe placements become winners when the extra pace is provided by the wind.

    7.   In doubles, let the partner with the strongest serve go against the wind. The weaker server can use the wind to make his or her serve stronger.

8. **Consider choosing to play against the wind the first game of the match.** Even if you lose the first game, you will change sides and have the wind at your back for the next two games.

PLAYING INTO THE SUN

1. **When you serve, toss the ball farther to either side of your head than usual, or toss it behind your head to avoid looking into the sun.** With either variation, the ball must be served with a lot of spin. Your opponent will have more time to prepare, but you will have more time to get to the net, if that is your plan.

2. **Remember that any lob your opponent hits will force you to look into the sun.** You may want to be selective about when to go to the net. If the other player comes to the net and is looking into the sun, don't feel bad about making him look up to hit a lob.

3. **In doubles, arrange a serving order that minimizes the problems of looking into the sun.** Right and lefthanded partners usually have an easier time avoiding the problem than two righthanders or two lefthanders.

PLAYING IN HOT WEATHER

1. **Don't waste energy on all-out serves during the first set.** While the big serve might win some early battles, it takes so much out of you that the war might be lost later. A big server who does not win in two sets will be in trouble in the third.

2. **Select some times during a game to serve and stay in the backcourt.** Points can be won without serving and rushing the net. It is very demanding to play that kind of game even in normal weather and more of a problem in hot weather.

3. **Try to make your opponent move around the court more than in cooler weather.** Now is not the time to blast him off the court, but rather to run him so much that he leaves voluntarily.

4. **Keep your racket handle dry.** Here are several ways that can be done: (1) Use commercial products that are sprayed or rubbed onto the grip. (2) Keep hand towels close to the court for quick dry offs during games. (3) Alternate rackets throughout the match. (4) Change wrist bands frequently. (5) Use sawdust as a drying agent. (6) Wrap adhesive gauze around the grip. (7) Carry your racket in the nonracket hand between points.

5. **Dress comfortably and coolly.** Loosely fitting clothes give your skin a chance to breathe. Lighter colored clothes reflect the sun's rays while

darker colors absorb the heat. Bring extra clothes if necessary for changes during the match.

6.   Stay in the shade as much as possible between points and games. A few seconds out of direct sunlight can give you a boost.

7.   Take water to the courts and drink it often. The fluid you lose during a match needs to be replaced quickly, not after the match has been completed.

8.   Wear a hat. It will keep hair out of your eyes and perspiration from running down your face. It will also provide a little shade and prevent you from being overexposed to the sun.

PLAYING AGAINST THE BIG HITTER

The big hitter probably has a heavy, flat serve, hard groundstrokes, put-away volleys, and a big overhead smash. He likes to serve and rush the net. His asset is power. His weaknesses may be lack of patience, mobility, and consistency. It is difficult to hit consistently big shots for an entire match. Watch for these weaknesses and be ready to take advantage of them. Most of all, don't be intimidated. These people can be beaten, even if they look better than you do while they are losing.

1.   Play a step or two deeper on the service return. The extra distance will give you a fraction of a second longer to read and react to the fast serve.

2.   Chip or block the serve and return it low and at your opponent's feet. Big hitters are frequently big people, and it is harder for them to get down on the low volley. When you chip or block, hold your racket tightly, take a short backswing, and use the pace provided by the server. The harder the serve is hit, the more you can act as a backboard to bounce back the power shots.

3.   Do not try to slug it out. Use the pace of the big hitter on groundstrokes. Place the ball so that he has to run, hit on the run, bend, stretch, and work hard. All of this should have a cumulative effect of weakening his power shots. He wants to hit a few hard shots and go home. You want to keep him on the court and moving as long as possible. The longer the match, the less consistent big shots become.

4. **Make the big hitter reach for volleys.** Keep the ball low on passing shots. If the volleyer has to reach wide or bend low, some of his power will be lost.

5. **Make the other player prove his overhead smash.** He will make you look bad on some points, but if that stroke is not fundamentally sound, it will fall apart later in the match.

6. **Take your time.** Do not let the player with a big game hurry through a match. If he has momentum, slow things down. You cannot delay the match, but you can take your one minute break on odd games, make sure you are completely set before the serve, and walk (not run) to pick up balls between points.

7. **Keep the ball deep.** This has been said before, but it is a must to prevent the big hitter from moving into every shot and following it to the net. The deep shot forces him to retreat and to give up some of the forward motion necessary to hit hard shots.

PLAYING AGAINST THE RETRIEVER

1. **Move the retriever up and back.** Make him run from the baseline to the net and back again. The pusher is not usually a strong net player, so get him to the net. Challenge his ability to hit a strong approach shot with a moderately short groundstroke. If he does not put the approach shot away or back you into a corner, he is probably stuck at the net or in mid-court. Then try a passing shot or a lob. If he gets out of that jam, do it to him again.

One way to beat the retriever is to change the rules. For informal matches, get him or her to play with the no-ad scoring system. If you know that games will not last more than seven points, you can pace yourself and at the same time take away the advantages of conditioning and patience that most pushers have. You may not win, but at least you won't kill yourself losing.

---

2. **Occasionally overpower the pusher.** It is important not to become impatient, so expect some put-aways to come back. Power mixed with short shots, deep groundstrokes, and lobs can be very effective. Anything that will keep him off balance and out of his groove will diminish his chances of winning.

3.   **Avoid playing the retriever's game.** He is better at it, conditioned to be on the court for a long time, and patient enough to let you beat yourself.

4.   **Attack the second serve.** You can gain control of the point early by moving in and stroking the weak serve deep to the backcourt or at an angle that will pull him off to one side of the court. From then on you will determine who wins the point. If you execute your strokes well, you will win. If you take the advantage but fail to put the ball away, watch out.

5.   **Respect the pusher.** You may not like the style of play, but pushers can beat people. They will beat you if you take them slightly or treat them as though they are inferior players.

PLAYING AGAINST LEFTHANDERS

1.   **Regroove your strokes to avoid hitting to the forehand side.** Most players remember to hit to the weak side at the beginning of rallies and during low pressure points. But at a crucial moment, many players forget and hit into the lefthander's strength. Only intense concentration throughout the match can help you avert this problem.

2.   **If you are righthanded, use a wide, slice serve from the deuce court.** Your righthanded spin will pull the lefty off the court and he will have to return it with a backhand. That means he cannot reach as far with power as on the forehand side.

3.   **Serve down the middle from the ad court.** You will be playing to his backhand and reducing the angle of the service return.

4.   **Expect the lefthander's serve to spin to your left.** If the ball starts out slightly to your right, it may jam you. If it starts directly at you, it can slide off to your backhand. If it starts out going wide to your backhand, you better move to your left in a hurry or you won't get there in time. You might even play a step to the left of your normal receiving position in the ad court. That way you can get a head start if he uses the wide slice to your backhand.

5.   **Against a righthander and lefthander in doubles, keep the ball down the middle.** Most doubles teams will put the righthander in the deuce court and the lefthander in the ad court. With this alignment, serves, groundstrokes, and lobs toward the center of the court will go to both the players' backhands.

Lefthanders have a tremendous advantage in tennis. No one is used to playing them and few people enjoy playing against them. Every shot seems to end up going to the lefthander's forehand. It takes almost a set to get used to the lefthanded serve. The only group of players who dislikes them more than righthanders is other lefthanders. It fouls up their games, too. Lefthanders may be discriminated against in society, but on the tennis court they are an elite minority. The number of successful lefthanded players is disproportionately high to the number playing the game.

STRATEGY ACCORDING TO THE SCORE

As you develop the ability to utilize plans and strategies in your game, you may want to give some thought to playing each point or game according to the percentages. The idea that some points in a game, set, or match are more important than others is not new. But to plan strategy accordingly requires a relatively sophisticated game. For beginners, adjusting your game on a point-by-point basis is impossible. For intermediate players, it is something to consider, but should not be the determining factor in how you play a match. For advanced players, knowing how to play each point is essential.

Generally the closer the score, the greater your effort should be to avoid unnecessary errors. For example, when the score is 30–30, deuce, or either player's advantage, that is not the time to be taking chances on low percentage shots or to play on the outer edge of your ability. You are in the game, you have a good chance to win the game, and you do not want to take a chance on losing by trying very difficult shots. Don't just punch the ball across the net, but hit shots firmly while giving your opponent at least an equal opportunity to make an error. The same strategy applies when you are tied in games, especially late in a set. At such a point play percentage tennis to the letter.

The time to be a bit more aggressive or to try those big shots that you really want to get out of your system is when you are far ahead or far behind. If you are ahead 40–0 or 40–15 in a game, or ahead by several games in a set, you should be relaxed and confident enough to play up to your maximum ability. If you lose a point because you attempt a difficult shot, you are still in good shape to close out the game on the next point. The pressure is on your opponent because he knows one mistake will end the game. Do not try absolutely wild shots, but use your big advantage in the score to put more variety into your shots.

If you are behind at 30–0, 40–15, or 40–0, you might as well be bolder to get back into the game. Chances are that your opponent will be playing more loosely than usual, so it will probably take a good shot or at least an aggressive shot to pick up a point. If you lose the point, it may be some consolation to know that you probably would have lost the game anyway. If, by playing more aggressively, you win a point and get back into the game, tighten up your strokes on subsequent points. In the context of a set, if you are ahead by a substantial margin, keep the pressure on. If you are losing big, try something different to make the score closer.

If there is one point in a game that is more decisive than others, it is probably the fourth point when the score is 30–15 or 15–30. If you are ahead and win the next point, you will have the game well in control. If you are behind and win the fourth point, it is a new game. What can you do about playing this point? Give an extra effort, concentrate, avoid an unforced error on the serve or service return, and don't hit to your opponent's strength. Give him shots he does not want to hit and try to set yourself up for your best shot.

A tennis playing Cajun was asked which is the most important game in a set. "The last one," he answered with indisputable logic. If the last one is the most important, the second most important game is probably the seventh game when the score is 4–2 or 2–4. If you are leading and pick up the seventh game, the 5–2 gap is almost impossible to close. If you are behind 4–2, winning the seventh game puts you right back into a competitive position, especially if you will be serving the eighth game. If you are pacing yourself in the set, do not hold back in the seventh game. Play it at full speed. It will be worth the extra energy you expend.

There are two other possible turning points in tennis. The first is any service break. As an intermediate or advanced player, you should be holding your serve more often than losing it. The same thing applies to your opponent. The best time to break a serve is following a service break. If you lose your serve, be ready to get that game back by really attacking your opponent on the first few points of the next game. He or she may relax after having worked hard to beat you on your serve. If so, take advantage of the situation. Conversely, if you win the other player's serve, be aware that he may be thinking the same thing.

The second turning point is the beginning of the second or third set. If you lose a set, concentrate on winning the first two games of the next set. There is a tendency to relax after winning a set, especially the first, because players know they have a cushion to rest on for a while. If your opponent lets down, put the pressure on before he or she has time to recover.

POINT-BY-POINT SUMMARY

Score: 0–0

Server's Strategy   Get first serve in; play your game; take charge

Receiver's Strategy   Be aggressive; you have to do something to compensate for the server's advantage

Score: 15–0

Server's Strategy   Keep the pressure on; retain control; relax, you are in good shape

Receiver's Strategy   Concentrate on service return; don't panic; do anything to keep the ball in play; hit away on easy set-ups

Score: 0–15

Server   No reason to get upset; it happens all the time; get the first serve in; regain control of the game

Receiver   Pressure is off for at least one point; be aggressive again, but not reckless; wait for your best shot

Score 15–15

Server   Play as you did on first point; nothing to worry about—yet

Receiver   You are one point closer to winning than you expected to be; play tight tennis; hit firmly; be bold if you get a chance

Score: 30–15

Server   You are on the right track; keep getting the first serve in and placed to a weak or open spot; get to the net if that is your game

Receiver   You are still one point from an even chance; don't try anything foolish; concentrate on keeping the ball in play; attack shallow ground-strokes or weak serves

Score: 15–30

Server   Time to get serious; no silly mistakes; give him your good serve; be as aggressive as your game will allow

Receiver   The server is worried and under pressure; keep it that way; service return is still the key to the game

Score: 30–30

Server   No reason to worry; don't change what you are doing; just do it better

Receiver   Things are looking good; no unforced errors; you are doing too good to give anything away; return serve deep if he stays back

Score: 40–30

Server   Time to put him away; go with your best shots; be bold, but not irresponsible; make him beat you; don't wait for something nice to happen

Receiver   He's coming after you on this one, so hold your racket tight and fight him; you are one shot from losing, so play slightly on the conservative side; you are also one point from deuce, so stay loose enough not to choke

Score: 30–40

Server   Stay poised; when you serve, you should win the point; no loose strokes, but don't push unless that is your style

Receiver   One step from glory; go after him; get the serve back and you have better than an even chance because pressure is on him; play good, tight tennis; you may not be in this position often

Score: Deuce

Server   This is serious; play things by the book; you still have the advantage because of your serve; get it in

Receiver   You're doing better than you are supposed to; relax; play your game; be ready for the kill

Score: Ad in or Ad out

Server   Play this point the way you did or would at 40–30 or 30–40, respectively

Receiver   Ditto

Score: 30–0, 40–0, or 40–15

Server   Relax and have a good time; just play tennis; you ought to win in spite of yourself

Receiver   You are in trouble; hit the strongest shot you can without taking an unnecessary risk; play one point at a time; try not to think about the score; if you do go down, go with style, not with a concrete elbow

Score: 0–30, 0–40, or 15–40

Server   Panic if you like, but don't give up; a good first serve will win the point most of the time; don't start punching or aiming the ball

Receiver   Go for the throat; don't hold back; give him your best shot; he's on the ropes, so knock him out

SOME STRATEGIC PARTING SHOTS

1. Move into every shot you hit.
2. Plan your moves before you go to the net behind a serve.
3. Shoot for a general target area in the backcourt instead of going for lines or corners.
4. Change strategy when you are losing.
5. If you are having problems with the surface, get to the net sooner and more often.
6. Play the ball instead of your opponent, especially in pressure situations.
7. Don't try a risky shot on a point you cannot afford to lose.
8. Seldom look at your opponent's face or eyes during a point.
9. If you are tired late in a match, try to win the point but don't over-extend yourself when you are losing 30–0 or 40–0.
10. Stay low on shots hit with backspin.
11. Play topspin shots on the rise.
12. Concentrate on winning the first point of every game.
13. Make your opponent prove he can keep the ball in play early in a match.

14. Return a high, softly hit shot before it bounces on your side of the court.

15. Give an extra effort in the first game of the second or third set.

16. Do not fight power with power.

17. Experiment on unimportant points.

18. Keep the ball very low or very high against players who hit with topspin.

19. Get to the net against players who hit a slice backhand.

20. Hit some shots directly at the stomach of players who hold the racket with both hands.

21. Hit low, wide slices to two-handers.

22. Don't worry about losing points early in the match against players who are in poor condition.

23. Learn to half volley as you get older because you will be out of position more often.

24. Rely on your best shots in crucial points.

25. Anticipate your opponent's best shots in crucial points.

26. Hit the simplest shot that will win the point.

27. Use your opponent's power by meeting the ball in front of your body.

28. Do not relax until you see the ball go into the net or bounce twice.

29. Expect every shot to come back.

30. Don't think too much during a match. Hitting is enough of a problem for most players.

REVIEW QUESTIONS

1. Strategy in singles and doubles dictates a difference in emphasis on certain strokes. What are the strokes and how is the emphasis different?

2. Develop a game plan against a righthanded big hitter playing on fast courts.

3. Develop a game plan against a lefthanded pusher playing on slow courts.

4. What are the advantages and disadvantages of serving to the various target areas in singles and doubles?

5. What do you consider the most important points in a game? How would you play these points differently from less important points?

6. Give some guidelines for hitting approach shots in singles.

7. Give some guidelines for returning serves in singles and doubles.

8. How would you adjust your doubles strategy if you were playing with a partner much stronger than you?

9. What are the factors which should be considered to decide where the receiver's partner stands to begin a point?

10. How can you use a strong wind to your advantage in singles?

Chapter 4

Thinking

CONCENTRATION

Concentration means the direction of attention to a single task or object. In tennis the task is to play the game as well as possible and the object is the tennis ball. There are many natural and man-made obstacles which can prevent you from concentrating on either the game or the ball. Before you get too involved in trying to attain a higher level of concentration, be sure that you want to. If you are one of the thousands of players who just want to go out, hit the ball, and have a good time, do not worry about directing all of your attention all of the time to the game you are playing. There is a great deal of enjoyment in talking with friends, socializing, being out of doors, watching others play, and just generally relaxing. However, if you are one of those players who is set on becoming highly skilled, competitive, and very serious about tennis, there are some problems and solutions when it comes to concentration.

The key to concentration is to block out as much as you can from your mind, leaving only the game to think about. Obviously that is almost impossible when you consider that tennis matches usually last from one to three hours. Nobody has an attention span that long. So the goal becomes one of mentally eliminating as many distractions as possible while you are on the court. First, consider some of the obstacles to concentration that are around the court where you are playing.

People are a major block to concentration. There are people on the courts next to you—talking, playing, hitting balls onto your court, and occasionally getting in your way or in your line of vision. Ignore them as much as you can without being discourteous. Do not watch their matches, even if their matches are more interesting than yours. Do not try to keep up with their scores. Play your own match. If your curiosity gets the best of you, get it out of your system by asking what the score is at a time when their match will not be interrupted. There may also be people in the stands or near your court watching your match. Keep your eyes out of the stands. Some players find it difficult to keep from glancing around to see who saw that last shot. If you are counting the house, you are not concentrating on what is happening on your court.

Even people on your own court can hinder your concentration. Some players may deliberately try to distract you or interrupt your thinking with an assortment of gamesmanship maneuvers. Some of the more popular methods of distraction are stalling instead of playing continuously, talking to you or to spectators, being overly dramatic after a point has been completed, and giving you a bad call just to upset you. There are two ways to handle these situations without totally losing your concentration. The first is to decide that nothing your opponent can do will bother you. If you expect trouble from an opponent or even if you get it unexpectedly, you must

117

make a conscious decision that you will retain your poise and concentration regardless of what happens. That is a difficult enough task in itself and it becomes even more difficult if you are losing. Then, even minor irritations become magnified. It is a lot easier to concentrate when you are winning than when you are getting beat. If a nonaggressive policy does not work, then you might as well confront the person who is bothering you and try to solve the problem before the match continues. There is no use putting up with distractions if you are going to let worrying about them interfere with your game. If you are thinking about the problems, you are not thinking about tennis. Stop the match, call your opponent to the net, and state what is bothering you. If he or she refuses to cooperate, ask for an umpire or get a ruling from the tournament referee, if there is one. If the match is supposed to be merely a social one, do a better job of selecting opponents. It would be better to walk off the court than to become so incensed that an incident or loss of friendship might occur.

Once a match begins, try not to worry too much about how good your opponent is. Even if he or she is great, you are stuck with each other, and it is best to go ahead and play your kind of game. If you walk around on tip-toes or fear that everyone of your opponent's shots will be a winner, you will play below your capability. If you can relax a little and play each point rather than worrying about the outcome of the match, you may even play better than you usually do. Superior players frequently bring out the best in inferior opponents. On the other hand, do not let your mind wander if you are playing someone who you should easily beat. Be nice, but try just as hard on every point as you would against someone who is your equal on the court. If you can win 6–0, do it. Never throw points or games in a match because you feel sorry for the person on the other side of the net. If an opponent cannot challenge your tennis skills, make the match a challenge to your concentration. Save your compassion for social tennis.

Noise can be a distraction if you are not used to playing where the noise level is high. If people are making enough noise to warrant a legitimate complaint, either tolerate it or ask the people to be quieter. If the noise is coming from traffic, from work being done near the courts, or from passersby, learn to live with the noise or choose a quieter place to play. Actually, once you learn to play with a lot of noise, your concentration should improve. If you can concentrate when it is noisy, you can surely concentrate better in quiet surroundings. Players who learn to play on public courts probably have an advantage over club players in this respect.

Some players allow the weather, especially the wind, to interfere with concentration. The solution to this problem may be to make it a point to practice as much as possible when it is windy. If you can adapt your game to windy conditions instead of worrying about them, that will be one less obstacle to concentrating on your game.

In spite of all of these outside distractions, most of the problems of concentration come from within our own heads. We let our minds wander, we think about families, jobs, or studies, we worry about people seeing us make a bad shot, and we think about a thousand other things. Since it is impossible to cut out all non-tennis thoughts, you can at least try to eliminate the most obvious ones. First, play one point at a time. Try to remember that your opponent is not likely to hit any shot that you have not at least seen before this match. Have a plan on each point. Do not just wait to see what happens. You should know after a while where you want to place the ball, what your opponent does best, what he or she has trouble doing, and where you want to be on the court. If you are playing somebody better than you, you may not be able to carry out your plan, but at least start out with one, even if the plan is to keep the ball in play as long as possible.

Avoid unnecessary talking. Too many players conduct eulogies after every lost point. They moan, groan, curse, shout, reprimand themselves, coach themselves, and even appeal to the heavens for help. If you are talking about a point, you are probably talking about one that has already been completed and that you can do nothing about. Instead of dwelling on the last point, think about the next one. Where am I going to hit the serve? Where is my opponent going to serve? Am I fresh enough to get to the net? Should I take it easy on this point? Do I play conservatively or aggressively on the next shot?

Also avoid talking to your opponent. Do not be rude, but do not get carried away with compliments after good shots or chatting during side changes. If you really want to concentrate, 99 percent of your talking during a match should consist of giving the score and calling shots out when they hit beyond the line. Never call shots "good" or "in" during the point. Just hit the ball.

Do not give up after a bad shot. You are in the point until the ball goes into the net, goes out of bounds, or bounces twice. Some players stop thinking and trying when the opponent has a setup. Make your opponent put the ball away. Do not concede anything. Your opponent could blow an easy shot and you could retrieve a would-be winner. Tenacity is a good sign that you are concentrating, and it can be demoralizing to the other player. Do not give up after you have lost a point. Games, sets, and matches can take a long time to complete. Every player is going to lose points, miss setups, and occasionally be embarrassed by a good opponent. You have too many problems in front of you during a match to be worrying about how bad you looked on one or two shots. Your time for the super shot will come if you have the patience to wait for it. A few bad points are part of the game; do not let them get you down.

Your concentration should improve if you practice as seriously as you play matches. Try to follow the suggestions already discussed every time you walk onto the courts. If you can develop the ability to block out distractions during practice sessions, concentrating in matches should be easier because you will have fewer outside distractions, greater motivation to play well, and better rewards if you win. Characteristics such as steadiness, poise, tenacity, silence, and concentration can be learned just as strokes can be learned. We do not inherit tennis behavior; we *learn* to act and think they way we do on the court.

Now what *should* you think about during a match? Since people can only direct their attention to one thing at a time, a priority of thoughts has to be established. At the top of the list is the tennis ball. "Keep your eye on the ball" should be more than a frequently used platitude. If you are serving, watch the ball until it leaves your racket strings. If you are receiving the serve, focus on the ball while it is still in the tossing hand of the server. Follow it with your eyes from the toss to the point of contact, across the net, and into your racket. Do not worry about whether the serve is in or out until after you have swung at the ball. There is no penalty for calling a shot out after you hit it. Continue concentrating on the ball throughout the point. Watch it when you and your opponent are preparing to hit and when you are hitting.

The second item on the concentration priority list is your opponent. As the ball leaves your racket, you will have a second or two to watch where your opponent is on the court and how he or she is going to hit the next shot. The place to give special attention is the face of the other player's racket. If you watch anything else to the exclusion of the racket and the ball, you can be faked out of position. Immediately after the ball is hit for the return to you, you must at least be aware of where your opponent is going to position himself or herself on the court. In this situation, your mind will have to move rapidly back and forth between priority items. You have to be observant enough to know whether your opponent is going to come to the net, return to the center of the baseline, or move to one side of the backcourt. Within a split second your attention must again return to the ball.

The third priority item on your think list is the method of hitting the ball. You are much better off if you automatically move into the proper position rather than having to think about it. Since preparation for a stroke happens at the same time you are trying to concentrate on the ball, you cannot literally think about both things simultaneously. If your strokes are grooved to the point of thoughtless but effective preparation, you can devote full attention to the ball.

As if trying to direct attention to the ball, your opponent, and your own form were not enough, there are other factors worthy of your attention. The score in the game, the set score, the weather, your physical condition, your opponent's condition, and your game plan are all worth thinking about during a match. The time to do that thinking is between points and games, not while the ball is in play.

Become as totally absorbed in the match you are playing as possible. Try to isolate your playing from the rest of your life for the short period of time you are on the court. Forget for a while that there are many other things in your life more important than playing a game. If you can (and want to), create a temporary attitude in which the next point, game, or set is more important than family, friends, or society. It is doubtful that you can accomplish that, but if you set that standard as a goal, any progress toward that attitude should improve your game by improving your concentration.

ANTICIPATION

Anticipation in tennis means to know where your opponent's next shot is going. It is very difficult to teach anticipation; good players acquire a sense of what is about to happen during a point through years of experience. If you have been in a particular situation only a few times, you might not know what to expect. If you have been in that situation hundreds of times, you have a very good idea not only of the possibilities but also of the one thing most likely to happen.

Spectators are often amazed when they see a good player moving to a spot on the court before the opponent even hits the ball. It appears as though the good player has some supernatural quality that sets him apart from lesser players. Not true. It is a learned response combined with the ability to think quickly during an exchange. If you play long enough, you don't even have to think about where the next ball is going. You automatically move toward the anticipated shot without consciously going through a mental process. The anticipation phenomenon occurs in every area of life, including family relationships, work, school, and social activities. We all know what to expect because we can read cues and rely on our knowledge of past experiences to make an educated guess about the future. In tennis it happens to be much more visible because a few people interact on a relatively small court in a short period of time where very little can be hidden.

Once a player begins to learn how to anticipate, that knowledge is one of the most valuable assets he or she can have. Anticipation can close the gap between players with great strokes and those with mediocre strokes. It can help older players compete with younger and stronger players, especially in doubles. It can frustrate even good players if you always seem to be in the right spot. It can save energy because your court movement becomes more efficient. Anticipation can also add an element to the game that will make it more challenging and fun. People who can anticipate the next shot or series of shots are figuratively and literally one step ahead of the people they play.

Where can you start learning this process? If you read the chapter on strategy, you already know where certain shots should be hit. This does not mean they will always be hit to the "right" place by the other player or team, but if they know what they are doing, they will hit the percentage shot much of the time.

Here are some situations which call for percentage shots. See if you know where the other player or players should place the ball. Answer the questions according to whether you are right or lefthanded. The answers will be different on some shots.

1. You hit a weak shot that bounces inside the service court to your left as you face the net. Your opponent moves in to hit an approach shot. Where do you think it will go? ·

2. Where do you expect the first serve to be hit when you are playing the deuce court? The ad court?

3. You are at the net and your opponent tries an offensive lob. To which side should it be hit?

4. You are at the net and reach wide to your forehand to hit a volley. Where should your opponent direct the next shot?

5. You are engaged in a baseline duel in singles. Where should most of your opponent's groundstrokes be going?

6. When should you anticipate that the other player will let your lob bounce instead of playing it in the air?

7. What would a good player do with an overhead smash hit deep from his backcourt?

8. You pull your opponent off to one side of the court and deep beyond the baseline. Where should his lob go?

9. On which kind of shots should you expect another player to come to the net?

10. When should you anticipate drop shots?

11. When you and your partner are both playing at the baseline, where do you expect shots to be hit?

12. When you are both at the net, where should shots come?

13. Where do you expect first serves to be directed in doubles when you are playing the right court? The left court?

14. When should the server's partner be expected to poach?

15. If you rush the net behind your serve, where should the return come?

16. If you stay back after your doubles serve, where will the ball be returned?

17. If you are at the net and the other team moves in to hit an attacking shot, where should the shot be hit?

18. If you are looking into the sun and playing the net, how are you vulnerable?

19. Who do you expect to hit shots that go down the middle in doubles?

20. When your partner is receiving the serve and the net player poaches, where should his volley be hit?

21. Your serve goes wide to an opponent's backhand. What part of the court should you protect on the return?

22. Your doubles serve goes down the middle to the left court. Where is the probable return?

23. Your opponent has just lobbed over your head. As you return to run and retrieve the lob, where do you expect him to be when you hit?

24. How should an opponent play your weak second serve?

25. When should your opponents come to the net on very slow courts? On fast courts?

If you know the answers to all those questions, you have a head start in knowing what to expect from good players. If you do not know many of the answers, go back and read the previous chapter. Most of the information will apply only to better players. Poor players either cannot hit percentage shots or they don't know what they are, so expecting the right shots from them won't do you much good.

What will help you is to be realistic about your own strokes. If you know what your weaknesses are, the people with whom you play regularly probably know them too. If they know what you cannot do, expect them to try to exploit your weaknesses. The most common ones are a soft second serve, a poor backhand, a weak backhand volley, an erratic smash, and general inconsistency. There are only two things you can do about faulty strokes. One is to improve them by taking lessons or practicing more than you do now. The other is to avoid hitting shots you know will get you into trouble. Getting your first serve in more frequently makes a weak second serve an academic concern; running around a weak backhand will solve that problem, but create others; and staying away from the net will save you from being beaten by your faulty volleys and smashes. The only way to beat inconsistency is to play people more inconsistent than you.

Another way to anticipate shots is to know what your opponents do in certain situations. Most tennis players have habits and patterns of play, so if you can correctly observe what they are, you can begin to make pretty good guesses about what is going to happen during an exchange. Watch for strengths, weaknesses, favorite shots on important points, strong sides, attitudes, and shot combinations. Find out from other players what a future opponent can or cannot do. If you can't do that, try to use the first part of a match to learn what to expect in the second or third sets. If you are really serious about this, make notes on upcoming opponents.

Watch for signs that will give you tips on what to expect. Some players will give shots away with their eyes. They will look to the spot in the service court where they want to hit. They will glance at the alley in doubles before trying to pass the net player. If you see a player peeking at a spot before a point or before a shot, you can change grips to get ready sooner, you can move a step in the direction of the anticipated shot, or you can simply feel more confident because you have an idea of where the next ball will go.

Other players will let you know what they are going to do with their feet and their rackets. Some players will only hit down the line or down the middle when they are in a closed stance. Others will only hit crosscourt from an open stance—that is, facing the net more openly with their shoulders and feet. Watching racket faces instead of just watching the ball will give you a tremendous advantage in anticipating. A low backswing can mean a topspin shot is coming. A high backswing might indicate backspin because the racket will have to be brought down on the ball. Most of all, if you can see the racket face, you can move in the direction it points. The strings have to be lined up in a position to direct the ball somewhere. If your eyes are good enough, you can tell where they are pointing before the hit.

Know what your opponent can do for certain positions in his court. Every player is limited by the circumstances he is put in by a given shot. For example, if you lob over a player at the net and he is running at full speed toward the baseline to try and chase down the ball, what can he do? He can't hit an overhead smash. He can't hit a screaming ground-stroke. He can't think about topspin or angles. All he can do is lob the ball back to you and that lob will probably be shallow. What should you do? Follow your lob to the net and anticipate his weak return. The worse the court position of a player, the more limited he is in choosing what to do with his shot. If he can eliminate some of the possibilities of returns, then you can concentrate more fully on the few shots he could make.

The last and simplest piece of advice concerning anticipation is to cover the open court. During each point, players move around the court to return shots. With every move, a portion of the court is left open. When you have to move to one side for a shot, as soon as you hit, start moving back in the other direction to cover the court. If you are pulled wide on a serve, hustle back to the center for the next shot. If you are caught deep behind your line, watch for the drop shot. If you are too close to the net, look out for the lob. If your partner has to run for a ball, cover for him until he gets back into position. If you see daylight across the net, hit toward that daylight. If you leave daylight on your side, expect your opponent to go for it. Try to stay one shot ahead of everyone you play.

USING PSYCHOLOGICAL ADVANTAGES

Remember that the better player usually wins a tennis match. So although there are things you can do to improve the physical and mental aspects of your game, there is no one psychological tactic that is going to enable you to knock off that person who always beats you. Also remember that it is difficult to psych out people with whom you play frequently. After a while you get to know each other so well that nothing anybody does is a surprise. However, in matches or tournaments when you compete against players who are about your speed, you may be able to use some psychological moves to your advantage. It should be emphasized that you should not spend so much time or effort trying to psych out somebody that you neglect the two most important aspects of winning tennis: good shots and sound strategy. Within this context, here are some suggestions that may give you a psychological edge in certain situations.

Before a match begins, do not offer any information about your game or your ability that may hurt your chances when play begins. Weekend tennis players are almost neurotic when it comes to worrying that an unknown opponent may be a great tennis player. There are all sorts of little pre-match games played off the courts in which players try to find out how good the other person is. Questions are asked such as, "Are you ranked?" "Is she seeded?" "How did you do against Fred?" "Did you ever play college tennis?" "Has she ever played Arlene?" "How does he play on this kind of surface?" If a prospective opponent finds out that he or she frequently beats someone who has beaten you, that player's confidence may zoom. Do not volunteer that kind of information. On the other hand, if your opponent is nosy about how good you are and if you have something to say about your game that might be intimidating, do it. Do not force anything, just subtly and casually let it be known by your responses to the questions. The less your opponent knows about you, the better off you are. Reveal your game, style, and ability during the match, not before it.

Once you get onto the court for the warmup period, warm up seriously. Do not waste time chattering. Play shots on the first bounce as much as you can without wearing yourself out. Establish an attitude of serious tennis. Make sure that you get to practice all the shots that you expect to use when the match begins. When you practice serving, loosen up adequately, but do not necessarily hit your best serves. If you can save your match serves for the first game, you may pick up a few points on unreturned serves just because it takes a while for your opponent to get used to your style, velocity, or spin. If you use your good serves during the warmup, your opponent gets a chance to practice returning them. At the same time you are not showing your best serves, you should practice returning balls he or she serves during the warmup. You will get used to the other player's kind of serve, and you may also demonstrate that you can handle anything that player has for you.

Once the match starts, move in a step or two on your opponent's second serve, and do it at a time when he or she can see you moving in. The first reason for this move is that the second serve is likely to be hit with less velocity than the first and probably be hit shorter in the service court. By moving forward, you will be in a better position to make the return. If you stay back, you will have to run up and get into position before you hit. The psychological reasons for advancing at a time when your opponent can see you is that the move can intimidate the server. By stepping toward the other player as he or she serves, you are sending a nonverbal message which says: "Your second serve is weak enough for me to move up on you; I am going to do something special with my return; and I am taking charge of this point." One other comment about returning the second serve: occasionally run around the weak second serve hit to your backhand side and really tee off with a blistering forehand shot. Even if it does not win that point, it will give your opponent something to think about the next time he or she gets ready to hit that serve.

During a match, mix up your shots. Do not fall into a pattern of play that your opponent can predict and anticipate. If you are a power player, occasionally use some junk shots just to keep your opponent off balance. If you are a retriever, show that you are capable of hitting the strong passing shot. Mixing up shots may even mean hitting a low-percentage shot occasionally. Be judicious about when to attempt high-risk shots, but the person you are playing should always have to think, "What is that guy going to do next?" It would be even better if your opponent thinks he or she knows exactly what you are going to do, only to see you do something completely different. The more things the other player has to worry about, the better off you are. Do not force shots to prove you are unpredictable, just use the unpredictable shot occasionally—preferably when losing a point will not cost you a game or a set.

One of the best potential psychological weapons at your disposal is your temperament. One good weekend player tells this story: "I had a match against a guy who was good enough to beat me as often and as badly as he wanted to. He was ranked in the state, experienced, had all the shots, and was in good shape. When the match started, I played as well as I have ever played in my life. I hit shots consistently that I had never been able to control before. At the same time, my opponent was playing terribly. He was missing easy shots, double faulting, making mental errors, and generally playing poor tennis. Yet, even with the score 5–1 in my favor in the first set, he never said a word, never looked worried about losing, complimented my good shots, and did not blink an eye after his bad shots. You would have thought he was the player ahead, 5–1. His attitude got to me. Here I was playing tennis as well as I could ever hope to play; here he was looking like a hacker; and he did not appear the least bit distressed about his chances of coming back and winning. He won, 7–6, 6–1. Judging only by his court presence, the score could have been 6–0, 6–0."

The moral of that story is to maintain your poise regardless of what the score is. If you get behind and begin to talk to yourself, curse, make excuses, complain about bad luck, and act like you are beaten, your attitude has to give your opponent a psychological lift. Do not give that advantage. Try to present a calm, confident, determined front no matter how bad things are going. If you come back and win, you will have proven to yourself that you can do it, and you will let the other player know that regardless of the score, you are always in the match. Your opponent will never be completely confident of beating you until the match is over.

There are several things you can do in doubles to make the other team worry about things they should not have to worry about. One thing you can do is poach. Let the other team know that you are a threat to go at any time your partner is serving. Be sure not to risk the loss of a crucial point by poaching just to prove you can do it, but be selective and get out there to pick off a service return now and then. Even if you lose that point, you have given the opponents one other little problem to think about. If you find out that one of the players on the other team really has problems with the return of serve, poach frequently. Intimidate the player as much as you can. Also, fake the poach at times; once you have established the fact that you are a threat at the net, take a quick step toward the middle just before the service return, but get back to protect your side of the court. Do not jump around at the net; make your fake look as much like an actual poach as possible. Let your partner know that you may try a fake poach, so he or she will not pull up and be faked by your move instead of the opponent.

If you play doubles regularly with the same partner, consider using signals when your team is serving. For example, the partner at the net can show a closed fist behind the back to indicate he or she will not poach, one finger to show an intention to poach on the first serve, and two fingers to mean poaching on both serves. Signals also give the other team something to think about, and they can also help the serving team because the server will know exactly what part of the court must be covered after the serve. Signals work best when both players are used to watching for and responding to the signs. If a team is not accustomed to using signals, they can do more harm than good.

When you are returning the serve in doubles, there are at least two tactics you can use. First, glance at the alley being protected by the net player just before the serve. Just as a baseball pitcher looks a runner back to the bag, look your opponent back toward his alley. Make sure that players sees your glance. If your look keeps the person a little more honest about protecting his or her side of the court and not getting a good jump to poach, you will have more room to hit the crosscourt return. Second, hit down the line every once in a while and try to lob over the net player's head on some service returns. If you try either shot earlier in the match, you may force your opponent to play more conservatively than if there were no threat of shots directed to his or her side of the court. Regardless of when you hit down the line or try the lob, these shots keep you from falling into a predictable pattern of service returns. While percentage tennis says that the return should go crosscourt or down the middle, those shots will be easier to execute if your opponents think you might not always hit the percentage shot.

Finally, keep your eyes and ears open for conversations between your doubles opponents. Do not turn your back to them. You will be surprised to find out how much you can learn about what is going to happen if you watch and listen to what is being said. Players at the net will sometimes tell their partners (without a signal) that they are going to poach. Servers might tell their partners that they are going to serve to the forehand or backhand. They might mention a weakness they have spotted. If you are not paying attention to what is being said or indicated, you might miss a tip that could win a point or game for your team.

PERSONALIZING YOUR GAME

As you play more and more tennis, your game will begin to take shape. You will be known as a certain kind or style of player. Your strengths and weaknesses will become more obvious to you and to your opponents. Your strategic approach to tennis will also become somewhat predictable. Even though your game will be determined to a degree by factors over which you have no control, there are some things you can do to shape your own game. You can become the kind of player you want to be within the limits of your ability, experience, opposition, amount of time to practice, and competitive attitude. Players who do not believe this or who do not have the interest or time to mold their own games are destined to go out and play without a style of their own, erratically, and with very little control over what happens on the court.

Those of you who think you do have some control over your tennis destiny should first look very closely at the things you do best on the court. Most players have one or two shots which they can really execute well. For some it is the big serve, for others a powerful forehand, a consistent backhand, or a good net game. Whatever it is you do best, try to create situations during your matches so that you get to use your best shots. If consistency is your strength, forget about trying to make spectacular shots and make the other player beat himself. If you have a strong forehand, play a little to your backhand side so that more shots have to be hit to your forehand. If you are comfortable playing at the net, get up there as often as you can. If your backhand is good, play a bit toward the forehand side of the court.

At the same time you cash in on your good shots, you can do two things about your weak shots. You can avoid having to hit them during a match. In the same way that you run around certain shots in order to hit your strongest strokes, you can move on the court in such a way as to avoid hitting weaker strokes. If you are weak at the net, there is no rule that says you have to move up there to play the game. If you are inconsistent, you can hit forceful shots to end points quickly rather than letting your opponent wait for your mistakes. The second thing you can do about weak strokes is to use matches to work on improving problem areas. Play against people you know will try to exploit your weaknesses. Sometimes if your opponent hits enough shots to one weak stroke you have, that stroke begins to get stronger because of the practice you are getting.

In order to learn exactly what your strengths and weaknesses are, you may consider charting your matches. In some cases, what you perceive to be happening during a match and what is actually happening are not the same. In the heat of a match, a few good shots or bad shots may stand out in your mind even though more subtle facets of your game were the determining factors in winning and losing. If you can get someone to watch a couple of your matches, it is relatively simple to keep a record of how points and games are won and lost. Charting merely involves recording how a series of points were completed. There are elaborate systems used by college coaches and observers of professional tennis players, but the average beginner or intermediate could use something like Figure 4–1 (p. 130).

It is obvious that several games will have to be charted in order for a pattern to be established, but if someone has the time to watch you and to make notes, it could help you to find out without a doubt what the strong and weak points of your game are. The possibilities for abbreviating or coding your shots are unlimited. There is also much that could be added to the

Error Chart

Game	1	2	3	4	5	6	7	8	9
1st serve									
2nd serve									
Forehand serve return									
Backhand serve return									
Forehand groundstroke									
Backhand groundstroke									
Forehand volley									
Backhand volley									
Lob									
Smash									
Drop shot									

Winning Shot Chart

Game	1	2	3	4	5	6	7	8	9
1st serve									
2nd serve									
Forehand serve return									
Backhand serve return									
Forehand groundstroke									
Backhand groundstroke									
Forehand volley									
Backhand volley									
Lob									
Smash									
Drop shot									

Figure 4–1

information shown here. If you decide to keep a chart on your matches, begin with a simple system and add to it if the results warrant a more thorough record of how you are playing.

Once you know what you can and cannot do, develop a style of play with which you are comfortable. If you know what kind of player you are, you can set realistic goals and develop a style that you like. If you are always seeking something new or different with your game, you can never have the security of knowing who you are on the court. You will tend to second guess your shots and your strategy. This does not mean that you should stop trying to improve your game; just spend more time in developing what you already have than in trying to revamp your style of play. Do not worry about the books which teach only one way to play tennis. There is nothing wrong with pushing if pushing wins. A two-handed backhand may not be right for 99 percent of the players, but it may be best for you. Running around your backhand is not recommended by teaching professionals (and it should not be taught), but it may win points for you in some situations. Do what is best for *you*, as long as you are successful. If peculiarities in style begin to get you into trouble or prohibit you from developing your overall game, then consider making changes.

Play a game consistent with your physical capabilities. If you are middle-aged and get to exercise only a couple of times a week, be careful about playing the kind of tennis that overtaxes you. Either slow down your pace or play more doubles. Most people, as they get older, have to pace their game downward to compensate for the lack of time they can give to tennis. Toning the game down does not necessarily mean becoming less of a player. It just means that you have to rely more on technique, strategy, and consistency than on physical strength and speed. The situation is comparable to that of the baseball pitcher who begins his career as a fastballer and who develops into a finesse pitcher once the fast ball leaves him. He still gets good results; he simply changes the means of getting those results.

At most levels, points, games, and matches are lost rather than won. Most players who rely on big shots to win, will not. Keep the ball in play. Give your opponent the opportunity to make mistakes. If that doesn't work, then try a few forcing shots when you get the right balls to hit.

Play a game consistent with the amount of time you have to practice. Tennis is a difficult sport in which to maintain skill levels. If you cannot play several times a week, forget about trying to play a game that requires you consistently to make extremely difficult shots such as hard serves, forcing volleys, and strong overhead smashes. You cannot play shots close to the lines as a normal part of your game unless you practice those shots frequently. Drop shots and lobs require a delicate touch that is not easy to maintain without regular play. That leaves the weekend player with challenging, but limited groundstrokes, volleys, and well-placed serves in his repertoire.

Play against people who can challenge your skills. If you play only against people you can easily defeat, you will probably win without having to think about and execute demanding shots. You will get the satisfaction of winning a match, but it is doubtful that you will benefit from playing. If you play people of your caliber, you can practice your good shots and improve on your weak ones at the same time. If you play against someone who is out of your class, consider it a free lesson and learn as much as you can while you are being drubbed.

As much as possible, force your opponents to play your style of game. If you do not have a game, you are going to have to change your style of play every time you walk onto the court. If you know what your game plan is, you can at least begin the match by sticking to your shots. If you try to blast with the big hitter or push against the retriever, you will never develop the consistency to play your own game. If your opponent is a lot better than you are, you will not be able to control the match. However, against lesser players, you will be more successful if you play it your way, not theirs.

Finally, be honest with yourself about your commitment to the game. If you are not interested in playing serious tennis, try not to get upset about the quality of your playing. Occasional players and recreational players do not have the right to expect their shots and games to go well. The players who get out there several times a week and work hard to develop their strokes have the luxury of being frustrated when things go badly. Tennis is not an easy game to play well. Everyone who plays deserves to have a good time. Only those who put a lot into tennis deserve to have a good time and to play consistently winning tennis.[1]

REVIEW QUESTIONS

1.   What are some obstacles to concentration? How can they be overcome?

2.   Give ten examples of how the use of percentage tennis by your opponent can help you anticipate his or her shots.

3.   How would you exploit the weaknesses in your own game?

4.   Give some examples of how players tip off or telegraph shots?

5.   Think of a specific player. How does he or she tip off shots?

[1] Jim Brown, *Tennis Without Lessons* (Englewood Cliffs, N.J.: Prentice-Hall, Inc., 1978, 112.

6. How are players limited in their shot selection by their body positions or their positions on the court?

7. How can you gain psychological advantages over an opponent without being unethical or unsportsmanlike?

8. What are your best shots? How can you play so that you get the maximum use of those shots?

9. How can you reduce the frequency of having to hit your weakest shots?

10. How can physical capabilities and limitations affect a person's style of play?

11. Predict how your error chart would look after a match. Then play a match and have someone chart your errors. Compare your predictions with the actual results.

12. Compare your predictions with actual results on the winning shot chart.

Chapter 5

Teaching

CHILDREN

It is exciting and gratifying to see so many smooth-stroking, court-wise tennis players under the age of twelve. But it is also misleading. Whenever we see a ten-year-old serving, stroking, and volleying like an adult, we probably assume he or she is also thinking like one.

With due respect to the intellect and judgment of the twelve and under age group, it is important to remember that their approach to the game and their technical problems are different from those of older groups. These differences must be recognized in order to ensure the proper psychological approach during the formative years.

All of us have psychological needs. Perhaps the four most basic needs are (1) the need to belong, (2) the need for security, (3) the need for recognition, and (4) the need for love. Each of these needs must be satisfied, and they can be partially satisfied by participating in a well-conducted program of tennis instruction.

Young players usually need to belong—to be part of a group. Initially, the group may consist of only two people: the instructor and the student. If you are the instructor, you may have to sell yourself to the student before you can begin selling the game. You must have the kind of personality attractive to children, and by now you know whether you do or not.

Learning to play tennis can be difficult and frustrating, especially to children who have not matured physically or emotionally. The typical under-twelve-year-old beginner has little chance of immediate success in mastering the skills of the game. He or she must be attracted to the peripheral aspects of the sport such as the instructor, the other players, the lead-up games, and the total tennis program (lessons, competition, work, recreation, fellowship, and related social activities).

Once an interest in the game has been instilled in the young player, you must wean him away from you and encourage participation with a peer group of players. The mother who brings her boy or girl to the courts and waits while he or she takes a lesson cannot expect that child to become much of a tennis player. Children in the seven to eleven age group have a strong need for group associations. Since tennis is primarily an individual activity, the group need must be satisfied in some other manner. It is an excellent idea for a group of friends to go to the courts together, play together, and go home together. The most valuable contribution that the instructor can make with respect to the need to belong is to push the reluctant beginner forward and to develop his skills so that the other young players will want him to be part of their group.

Although all of us are insecure in one way or another, no one is more insecure than the eight year old who is hanging on to a racket almost as big as he is, while attempting to defend himself against balls which are attacking him and trying to master a game that 99 percent of the people in the world has failed to master. With the young player facing such overwhelming odds, the instructor has an obligation to provide a little security and stability for his student. The child's relationship to adults is very important in satisfying this need, and the tennis instructor is one of those adults who can play a definite role.

The instructor should know every pupil by his or her first name, he should know something about the child's interest other than tennis, and he should know about the child's family. The instructor should maintain a regular schedule of lessons so that a child knows that he or his group will get special attention at least during that time period. The instructor should be there for scheduled lessons, not delegate the teaching to someone else. The teacher's actual approach to learning is important. Educational research shows that youngsters prefer teachers who are fair, firm, consistent, and friendly. All of these qualities will make the beginning tennis player more secure as he learns the game.

You can criticize Little League Baseball for many things, but you must admit that much of its success stems from the recognition given to the players. They have uniforms, coaches, sponsors, leagues, publicity, awards, ballparks, and other fringe benefits that attract kids to the game. Since tennis is an individual sport, not as well organized at the junior level, and more difficult to publicize than baseball, the instructor is again called upon to help satisfy a basic need—recognition. There are both subtle and direct means of providing recognition for those who need it.

Children have a powerful desire to be first, to be noticed, and to be singled out for attention. A simple statement such as, "Amanda hit that forehand better than I could have hit it," made in front of a group may be the equivalent to the Wimbledon trophy for many beginners. Other forms of recognition such as applauding a good shot, paying attention to a student's match, and giving students bulletin board publicity also serve as valuable psychological tools. Giving expensive trophies as a method of recognition is overdone, but awards such as certificates, ribbons, medals, and prizes can be used effectively to reward and recognize students' achievements in practice as well as in tournaments and matches.

Finally, everyone—adults, adolescents, and especially those in the seven to eleven group—needs love. In the instructor-student relationship, it is a very simple kind of love which means, "I trust you," "I know you can do it," or "Let's figure out how we can solve this problem together." It is the kind of love that develops out of mutual interest and the mutual challenge to achieve a goal.

A good tennis instructor should be just as interested in teaching tennis as the pupil is in learning to play. If not, his lack of interest in and understanding of his pupil will be evident. The beginner will either lose interest in the game or he will find another instructor. It is difficult for some people to recognize that when a tennis instructor goes to the courts, he is going to work, not to play. But even though the teacher's work is somebody else's play, the instructor has to enjoy or perhaps even love that work. If he does, some of that love will rub off on those he teaches. Here are other psychological approaches to teaching tennis to the elementary age group:

1. **Develop standards of achievement based on an individual rather than a group rate of improvement.** Consider the readiness factors (physical, mental, and emotional) in each student.
2. **Provide an opportunity for success regardless of the child's ability.** Hitting five forehands over the net in a row could represent enough success to keep a seven year old coming back for more instruction and play. Eve Kraft's *Tennis Workbook* offers excellent ways of setting reasonable goals and measuring a player's success.
3. **See that young players enjoy the activity that tennis provides.** Playing tennis beats standing in right field for two hours, butting heads at left tackle, and running a mile. Kids enjoy hitting a ball over a net, and the instructor should see that they get to do that frequently and with a minimum of standing around waiting. Two other suggestions:
    a. Make sure that your students achieve a degree of skill at a technique before going on to something new.
    b. Stop the practice of an activity while the interest is still high. This will guarantee some enthusiasm the next time the activity is presented.
4. **Tell students why you are asking them to do whatever they are doing.** Many teachers never explain, probably because they do not know the reasons for tennis mechanics themselves. For the elementary group, a detailed explanation is not necessary. A simple, direct statement or answer is enough. Too much explaining will provide more information than most children care to have.

The better tennis instructors have learned these psychological principles through training and experience. Unfortunately, there are many young instructors with good tennis skills but little or no background in psychology or physical education. In order to be effective with any age group, the teacher must have a combination of technical ability and an understanding of people. If mistakes are made with children trying to learn the game, they may quit and never return.[1]

If you teach or coach an extremely talented junior player, be very careful about making predictions regarding that player's future. Almost every teaching professional has one player who has the potential to become great. The chance of that happening is not very good. Many things can happen during the adolescent years to prevent him or her from becoming great. Girl friends, boy friends, studies, lack of practice time, inadequate teaching, economic factors, parent pressure, getting tired of tennis, and poor competition are just a few of the things that can get in the way of tennis greatness. By publicly stating that a player should be or will be a great player, you will add more pressure to an already stressful situation. If you predict greatness and it doesn't happen, both you and the player suffer. If you avoid those kinds of predictions and the player makes it big, you both benefit.

ADOLESCENTS

No other age group has been written about more than the adolescent. Articles and books are seldom seen about people in their twenties, forties, or sixties, but everybody seems to have opinions about the attitudes and behavior of adolescents, especially the specific group in that range known as teenagers. Parents have trouble communicating with them. Colleges offer courses in adolescent psychology to study them. Children idolize them. Are adolescents different from any other segment of the population? Most psychologists agree that they are different.

For example, there are three stages of adolescence: preadolescence, which begins to appear in nine and ten year olds; adolescence, which begins at about twelve years and continues to emerge until the late teens, when the late adolescence period starts. The lines dividing these phases are vague. They may not be consistent from person to person, or the same person may develop different characteristics at various times during the entire age span.

Adolescents are different because our society expects and even forces them to be different. As a result, they have social, emotional, and physical

[1] Jim Brown, "Psychological Factors in Teaching Tennis to Pre-Teens," *Scholastic Coach*, 41, no. 8 (April, 1972) 104.

problems not characteristic of other groups. The tennis teacher or coach has to take these differences into account in order to be effective in working with this age group. This part of the book will point out some of the special problems teaching adolescents presents and suggest ways to solve these problems.

GROUPING

Whether you are teaching a physical education class, coaching a team, or working in some other instructional capacity, you are going to have to make some decisions about grouping players for instruction, practices, or recreational tennis. There are several factors to consider when you start grouping adolescents. One factor is grouping by sex. The early adolescent, roughly those in the ten to thirteen age group, will probably feel more comfortable working in a group of his or her own sex. Since girls tend to mature physically and emotionally a little sooner than boys, the girls might be more at ease in a mixed group. They will probably be more skilled in tennis, also. But the boys generally want to be with other boys, to compete against other boys, and not to be compared to girls in any way. As both groups move into the middle adolescent years, it will be easier for you to mix them in various tennis activities. During late adolescence, you may even have to segregate them by sex again to get anything done as far as serious tennis is concerned.

Grouping by ability is important for several reasons. The emphasis on individualized instruction in the schools necessitates designing instruction for each student. You cannot accomplish much if there are beginners, intermediates, and advanced players in the same group. You will be underteaching some and teaching over the heads of others. The advanced players will be bored, the beginners will be intimidated and possibly discouraged from coming back, and the intermediates will be looking over their shoulders to see what is going on with the other two groups. As much as possible, keep the three levels in separate units with activities designed for their skill levels. If students of varying abilities must be mixed because of time or space limitations, use practice drills in which one group can be used to set up shots for another. Advanced players may also be used to help you teach basic skills to beginners.

Grouping by age and particularly by grade in school is a factor to consider, especially in urban areas. Our system of education emphasizes highly graded schools. One of the results is that many students prefer to study, work, socialize, and play tennis with other students their age or in their grade. Since adolescents will develop their tennis skills at varying rates, some mixing of age groups is inevitable. But if there are problems of motivation, communication, or students getting along with each other, at least consider the possibility that age grouping might be the cause.

The last problem with grouping is to separate those who want to play the game seriously from those who want to play "giggle tennis." There is a place for those who just want to play for the fun of participating without being overly competitive or very serious about the game. They should be provided with a program that will meet their needs, and the first essential of that kind of program is to find others who are looking for the same thing. Those who want to play tennis for the sake of competition, rapid improvement, and recognition must have a more rigorous regimen of practicing, playing, and conditioning. The two groups are vastly different and should be separated on the courts.

MAKING TENNIS FUN

Adolescents are frequently looking for experiences that will help them to learn about themselves. They are rehearsing for roles they may have to play later in life. In our society, boys have traditonally tried to compete in sports requiring skill, strength, and sometimes courage. In the past, girls have been more interested in developing social skills, but that concept is changing. The continuing emergence of women as participants in all areas of endeavor has been a tremendous boost to the increased interest in tennis. It is no longer unfeminine to run, jump, work hard, and perspire. The change in values means that women are a vast natural resource for participation in all athletics, and especially in tennis.

With these concepts in mind, it is the responsibility of the tennis instructor to attract people to the game. It is time for tennis to stop losing the best athletes to football, basketball, baseball, drill squads, and social clubs. The best way to attract players is to make the sport attractive and fun. Here is a quick review of some tennis selling points:

1.   **It is good for health and fitness,** as evidenced by the fact that you can build strength and burn as many as six hundred calories an hour simultaneously.

2.   **Tennis can be used for social purposes by introducing the player to a new group of friends.**

3.   **Compared to other sports, tennis is a timesaving way to get a workout.** Playing an hour of tennis is equal to several hours of playing golf, bowling, or playing most positions in baseball.

4.   **Tennis is economical when compared to other activities.** A person can get started with an investment of ten to twelve dollars. Compare

that with the cost of golf clubs, hunting and fishing equipment, or football gear.

5. Tennis is a lifetime sport. When the last high school or college football game is over, some athletic careers end. Those who have been playing tennis are just getting started.

6. Tennis can be a tough, challenging, competitive sport for those who want it to be. In a list of all the physical and mental qualities necessary to play the various sports popular in this country, tennis will be near the top. For the high school athlete trying to withstand the pressure of friends, parents, and coaches who want him to play another sport, try showing him the list of skills and appeal to his athletic spirit. The list could include speed, strength, endurance, power, flexibility, reflexes, ability to stop and start quickly, ability to make split second decisions, ability to track and hit a moving object, ability to perform alone in singles and with a partner in doubles, etc. Again, tennis will compare favorably with any other sport.

7. Tennis is fun. It beats most of the other sports for pure enjoyment, and it really beats them in that it can be just as much fun to practice as it is to play. This is where the good instructors are separated from the bad ones.

It is your job to make sure the adolescent enjoys playing tennis. If he does not, there are many alternative activities competing for his attention. Classes, lessons, or practice sessions for the teenager should involve activities in which he can enjoy himself and at the same time improve his skills. This does not mean that practicing and playing is not hard work. It just means that anybody can enjoy working hard. The work-enjoyment combination requires a teacher who is capable of planning and directing activities to fill both needs.

KEEPING THEM BUSY

If there is one almost universally recognized characteristic of the adolescent, it is his restlessness. It is almost torture to make a teenager stand in line, sit and listen to a lecture, or to be part of anything passive. The message for the tennis instructor is to keep them busy. Have something for them to do every minute they are under your supervision. If they are not hitting, they can be throwing to someone else. If they are not thowing, they can pick up balls. If there are no balls to pick up, they can be running or doing weight work. If nothing else, they can keep charts on players. Work them to death. If you allow them to sit around doing nothing (except during required recovery periods after intense work), you are not only wasting their time, you are probably giving them a chance to get into or give you trouble.

RECOGNIZING PHYSICAL CHANGES

Remember that the adolescent is undergoing a period of rapid and sometimes difficult physical changes. His tennis thinking may be ahead of his physical capabilities. He will want to try shots that his body will not let him make consistently. It is your job to be patient with the awkward teenager, to be understanding with the adolescent who does not experience the rapid growth changes, and to challenge the physically gifted students. To do the job effectively, you will again face problems of individualizing instruction to meet everyone's needs.

PROVIDING A ROLE MODEL

The typical adolescent is uncertain of his status. He is making the trip from childhood to adulthood, and he is not sure how he is supposed to behave in between. He will complain that his parents do not understand him and that they treat him like a child, but he is not yet ready to assume all the responsibilities of living as an adult. He certainly needs adults to look up to in addition to his parents, and the teacher or coach fulfills that need. Be professional in your behavior around students without being aloof. Be friendly without being their buddy. Most important of all, give them opportunities to work, play, compete, socialize, and enjoy themselves in a way that will help them grow into maturity.

ACKNOWLEDGING INTELLECTUAL ABILITY

In spite of all his seemingly strange behavior, do not overlook the fact that the adolescent is quite capable of handling himself intellectually. In fact, intellectual capacity peaks during adolescence. Applied to tennis, this means the average teenager can understand tennis tactics and strategy and their relationship to his game. Unfortunately, the intellectual ability to recognize the importance and logic of strategic tennis is offset by the lack of playing experience. Dumb players who play the game long enough eventually develop some sort of game plan. Bright young tennis players will develop a thoughtful approach sooner. The teacher should be able to talk with the adolescent student about game strategy and mechanics of strokes. Eventually, the body will catch up with the mind.

Now that you have read about all of these adolescent characteristics, forget them for a minute. Keep in mind that each person, regardless of age, is unique. There are teenagers who exhibit every trait just discussed; there are others who do not fit into any category. Some will by physical adults and emotional children. Others will be just the opposite. Know your students well and you can design your teaching to fit their personalities and capabilities.[2]

ADULTS

Teaching adults presents some challenges, problems, and experiences that are different from teaching children or teenagers. The challenges are there because this group has usually passed its prime athletically, and only a good teacher can take what is left of that ability and develop the person into a good player. The problems center mostly around your ability to deal with the diverse personalities of the students. The pleasant part of the job is the fact that you can help some people who really want help and who are not there just because their friends are there or their parents want them to take lessons.

Every adult player is going to come to you at a different level in terms of their previous tennis experience, their athletic ability, and their commitment to learning how to play. Take each player where he or she is. Do not try to re-make everyone into a factory produced player whose strokes look like yours. If you get a good athlete who has not played or who is capable of changing strokes, you may be able to help that person develop a technically sound set of strokes. If you teach men and women who are either less athletically gifted, weaker, older, or unable to change old habits, set realistic goals about what they can do with their games. People do not have to have perfect strokes to enjoy playing tennis. It is very possible that you will have to get as much mileage as you can out of limited capabilities in many students. That is not bad. You may be doing a better job of teaching by turning a mediocre prospect into a respectable player than if you teach a gifted athlete how to become an outstanding player. Anyone can teach the good ones; only good teachers can teach the bad ones.

Almost all players are able to learn one shot on which to build their games. Part of your job is to find that stroke in each person you teach. The easiest shot for most players is the forehand. It is a relatively natural stroke

[2] Jim Brown, *Tennis: Teaching, Coaching, and Directing Programs* (Englewood Cliffs, N.J.: Prentice-Hall, Inc., 1976), p. 58.

that even the weakest of players can develop to some degree. Most players can also learn to have a consistent serve. Some of those may also be able to serve with power, but many beginning adults will never have a strong serve. They will just have to accept that fact unless they want to start lifting weights, and there is no guarantee that will help. The backhand is going to be the biggest problem for most adult learners. You may be able to teach them how not to lose with the backhand, but very few will be able to use a backhand as an offensive weapon. The forehand volley is reasonably easy for anyone to handle, but the backhand volley is as much of a problem as the backhand groundstroke. Some adults will never learn to hold the Continental grip at the net. They are destined to hit the ball pretty well on the forehand side and to lose points on the backhand side. They end up either trying to hit a backhand volley with a forehand grip or they get caught trying to make the change in grips when they don't have time. The overhead smash can be taught to this group. It may not be great, but it can be adequate for most and a strong shot for others.

At some point toward the beginning of a series of lessons, you are going to have to make a diagnosis of each student's strokes. At that time, you and the person being taught will have to decide whether to start from scratch and learn (or re-learn) a stroke completely or to do the best you can with a faulty grip, stroke, or swing. Be honest with the student. It's their game and their money, so they should have some control over what goes on. Take into consideration how much time these people will have to work out problems with their strokes. If they can only play once a week, there is no way they can make drastic changes in the way they play the game. Give them your best advice, tell them the benefits and risk involved, let them make the decision, then go to work.

Handling personalities can be the most difficult part of teaching tennis. Coaches in any sport will tell you that the easiest part is the "X's and O's"—the technical part. The hard part is keeping people happy, boosting egos, avoiding conflicts, and generally seeing that things move along without disruptive incidents. If you teach at a country club or tennis club, you are going to be dealing with people who are used to being waited on, accommodated, or obeyed. Keep in mind that you are being employed by the club, but that does not mean you have to compromise your professionalism by catering to any one group. Get your ground rules straight before you start to work about what your responsibilities are. In a diplomatic way, the message must be understood that you are a professional who is providing a professional service. You are not a message person, a delivery boy or girl, or a bartender. Your job is to teach people how to play tennis. As long as everybody pays the same amount of money for your instruction, everybody is treated equally.

It may be best for the club pro to maintain a social life somewhat apart from the club itself. The pro who gets mixed up in club life also becomes involved in a thousand little games that are played among members. Rather than being accused of siding with one group or another, stay out of those situations. You will hear enough about complaints, jealousies, relationships, and problems as part of your working day. You are asking for punishment if you decide to become more involved in those things after work.

The kinds of personality problems are predictable. First of all, there are going to be some people who don't like you or your teaching. It doesn't matter if you are the best teaching professional in the world; you are not going to please everyone. That is an occupational hazard you must live with. You don't have to like it, but try not to worry about it too much. There are only two good ways to handle those people: ignore them or be even nicer to them than you are to other people. Both strategies are effective because they do not give the other person anything to fight against.

A second problem is that someone in the group you are teaching will not like someone else. The reasons do not matter; they just don't get along. The solution is simple: keep them apart. Put them in separate groups or schedule them at times so they don't even see each other. If you do happen to get them on the same court, keep them so busy hitting they will not have time to demonstrate their dislike for each other.

There will always be those who think they are better than the other players in their group or on their court. They will approach you privately and tell you how good they are or that they are too good for everyone else. Either explain your reasons for the group's makeup, stall for time, or arrange a match with someone they see as not so good. A well-planned loss for that person can put things into perspective very nicely.

Some people will complain that they are not getting enough work during a private or group lesson. If they are right, give them more work. If they are wrong, give them more work. Give them so much that they will want to go back to the previous level of activity. Keep an eye on them, however. Some adults have difficulty in pacing themselves during a workout. You may have to set the pace.

Watch out for the talkers. They want long explanations on everything and they want to give you equally long explanations about their games. Do not let them slow up the rest of the group or cheat themselves out of valuable lesson time. Save the conversations for breaks.

Male-female conflicts can also surface on the tennis court. Men seem a lot less likely to want to take lessons than women. Women seem to be very secure about asking for help and taking advice. Men may not be so secure out of their working or family environment. Husband and wife teams taking lessons can be grim. Men frequently try to coach or teach their wives instead of letting you do it. Women call you over to the side to get you to make a correction in their husbands' games. If you are not careful you can become a pawn in a family argument.

In spite of all these problems, teaching tennis to adults can be rewarding, productive, and fun. Most adults have a very good perspective of where tennis fits into their lives. They want to learn, are receptive to your ideas, and appreciate your knowledge of the game. Seeing someone who took up the game in their twenties, thirties, or forties do very well or simply enjoy playing a game makes teaching tennis worthwhile. You can encourage them in a variety of ways. Give them positive reinforcement, both privately and in public. Figure out a way to say good things about their games rather than always finding something wrong with the way they play. Phrases such as "You can improve that stroke by . . ." or "You might be more effective if . . ." sound a lot better than, "That's wrong; do it this way." Be patient with these people. Don't expect them to learn something as quickly as you did or as a better player did. The money is the same whether you are patient or impatient, so why not be nice to the customers? Help them arrange matches and hitting sessions with players of similar ability. Many adult learners are hesitant to ask someone else to play with them. Finally, give them a maximum effort. They deserve as much attention and work as your best junior prospect. If you do your job right with adults, you will be a better teacher and tennis will have gained more followers.

PRIVATE LESSONS

The expression "Private Lessons" in this chapter means teaching individuals and being paid for the lessons. The fact that you will be paid directly by the students or their parents imposes a kind of quality control on instruction. You must either have a monopoly on the tennis teaching market in your area or you must give your clients their money's worth. If not, you will be out of business just like any other businessperson. Here are some ideas on how to operate your tennis teaching business effectively and profitably.

Attracting customers is the first priority. If you have established a reputation as a player or teacher, people will come to you. If not, newspaper advertisements, radio-television spots, and bulletin board posters at clubs, city parks, recreation centers, and sporting goods stores can be effective ways to promote business. People seeking tennis instruction frequently call high school and college physical education and athletic departments for information. Having contacts in those places can result in referrals.

The only equipment you need is a court, your racket, a basket of reasonably firm and fuzzy tennis balls, and enough tennis clothes to dress professionally. This does not mean that you must dress in whites only, but that you should be dressed neatly and comfortably. If you are going to teach professionally, you should dress accordingly. In addition to the equipment and clothes just mentioned, many clubs and city programs provide ball throwing machines for their instructors. These machines can be an effective teaching aid and should be used as an aid, not as as a substitute teacher.

Once you are set up with people to teach, a place to teach, and equipment with which to teach, the next step is to plan what to teach. This obviously depends on factors such as who is to be taught, playing level, age, time available, and what the students want to learn. But there are some general principles which apply to almost any individual or group enrolled for instruction. Every lesson should be planned before you arrive at the courts. The planning should include what your goals for the day are, the teaching activities to be implemented, and a minute-by-minute timetable. Merely arriving at the courts ready to hit with your students is not enough. Try to get input from those being taught to help you decide about lesson content, but take the responsibility of planning what to do yourself. If you have several individuals taking instruction separately but during the same time frame (weekly, for instance), it might be a good idea to keep a file card on each one. The card should contain information such as the name, address, and telephone number of the student, the lesson schedule, money paid or due, and a record of what has been done in previous lessons. Trying to keep track of two or three groups and several individuals without records is difficult.

Progression of learning is vital. Most teachers begin with a series of lessons emphasizing baseline fundamentals such as the ready position, moving to the ball, and hitting the forehand, backhand, and serve. As the students' skills improve, the teacher moves into halfcourt and forecourt skills, including approach shots, volleys, and overhead smashes. Below is a more detailed progression for beginning players. If you are working with a player twelve years old or less, the shots hit from the forecourt might not be included until the child begins to play matches. Full explanations for drills are given in the last chapter.

FOREHAND

1. Demonstrate the grip and stroke
2. Downs (dribbling the ball with the racket)
3. Ups (air dribbling)
4. Up-Bounce-Up-Bounce (alternate air dribbling with letting the ball bounce on the court)
5. Hit-Bounce-Hit-Bounce (instructor and student alternate hitting the ball up, then letting it bounce)
6. Hit-Bounce Over the Net (same as #5, but ball is hit across the net; a few fundamentals are introduced during the hitting, such as getting the racket back early, turning the side to the net, etc.)
7. Ready-Pivot-Step-Swing (instructor and student go through the swinging-hitting motion facing each other; fundamentals are reviewed or introduced, as necessary)
8. Toss to Forehand (instructor tosses balls to forehand at close range)
9. Running Forehands (instructor tosses balls where student has to run a few steps to hit with the forehand)
10. Hit to Forehand From Forecourt (instructor hits easy shots to student; instructor at net; student in backcourt)
11. Hit to Forehand From Backcourt (same as above, but instructor puts ball into play from backcourt)
12. Counting Forehands (instructor and student count number of balls kept in play without missing)
13. Placement Forehands (instructor feeds balls; student hits to specified areas of the court)

BACKHAND

1. Demonstrate Grip and Shot
2. Ready-Pivot-Step-Swing
3. Toss to Backhand
4. Running Backhands
5. Hit to Backhand from Forecourt
6. Hit to Backhand from Backcourt
7. Counting Backhands
8. Placement Backhands
9. Alternate Hitting Backhands and Forehands

SERVE

1. Demonstrate Punch Serve (racket starts behind back)
2. Demonstrate and Teach Grip
3. Demonstrate and Teach Position of Feet
4. Demonstrate and Teach Toss
5. Demonstrate and Teach Starting Position of Racket
6. Toss and Hit From Net
7. Toss and Hit From Service Line
8. Toss and Hit From Baseline
9. Demonstrate Full Swing Serve
10. Demonstrate and Teach Downswing
11. Demonstrate and Teach Downswing to Backscratch Position
12. Demonstrate and Teach Downswing, Backscratch, and Reach for Ball
13. Down Together—Up Together (coordinate the racket hand with the tossing hand)
14. Down Together—Up Together—Toss—Hit
15. Down—Up—Toss—Hit—Follow Through

VOLLEY

1. Demonstrate Grip and Forehand Volley
2. Volley From Fence (student stands with back to fence or wall; instructor tosses to forehand volley)
3. Volley From Net (student at net; instructor at mid-court)
4. Hit to Forehand From Forecourt
5. Hit to Forehand From Backcourt
6. Demonstrate Backhand Volley
7. Volley From Fence (instructor tosses to backhand)
8. Volley From Net (instructor tosses to backhand)
9. Hit to Backhand From Forecourt
10. Hit to Backhand From Backcourt
11. Toss to Forehand or Backhand (instructor mixes up tosses)
12. Hit to Forehand or Backhand From Forecourt
13. Hit to Forehand or Backhand From Backcourt
14. Placement Volleys

OVERHEAD SMASH

1. Demonstrate Shot
2. Demonstrate and Teach Grip and Preparation
3. Demonstrate and Teach Swinging Motion
4. Lob to Student (instructor in backcourt; student very close to net; gradually move student away from net)

There is a temptation to tell a beginner or intermediate everything you know about the strokes. While the intent may be good, the student simply cannot assimilate that much information in a short period of time. If you and your students can concentrate on one component of a stroke at a time, all of the components will fall into place later. Overteaching tends to confuse and discourage many inexperienced players. If they are not very successful at first, they might conclude that there is just too much about tennis to learn and drop the sport. Teaching one concept at a time presents a problem. Repetition is essential, but it can be boring. It is your job to disguise the repetitive nature of learning strokes by designing enjoyable, variable, and constructive learning activities. Examples of drills are presented in the last section of this book.

Most people taking lessons want to learn something new every lesson and they want to feel that they have worked hard physically. Unless specific requests are made prior to a lesson by the students, the teaching sessions should be a combination of technical advice and stroke polishing and appropriate physical activity. Adults especially like to feel that they have gotten a workout when you are through with them. Give the people what they want. It is probably better to get to the technical part of a lesson first and to follow it with demanding drills and play. If the order is reversed, your students may be too tired to listen or learn.

If it is possible, try to arrange for some type of follow up to your lessons. Encourage your students to practice what they have learned by playing with others, hitting against a wall or a ball machine, or by going through serving drills alone. Be a match maker for students taking separate, private lessons. A group that takes lessons together is a natural for a weekly doubles match to complement the formal instruction.

Private (individual) lessons may be taught for one hour or half-hour periods. The pro who teaches half-hour lessons is either very well organized and knowledgeable about the game or very business minded. A teacher who works with a student for only thirty minutes must be very good to keep his customers. There is no set number of individual lessons a beginner should take, but one or two sessions a week should bring results. There should be some time for students to work on what has been covered in the last lesson. Private lessons may last weeks, months, or for indefinite periods of time, but after so many lessons the instructor is probably repeating himself or correcting old mistakes rather than introducing new information or techniques.

Suggesting what you should charge for private lessons is risky because of inflation, supply of teachers, and demand for lessons. College players and semi-professionals charge from seven to fifteen dollars for an hour lesson, and they are more likely to teach for an hour than a half hour. Club pros get anywhere from fifteen to fifty dollars an hour. Conscientious teaching pros can work out some kind of sliding pay scale for younger players or those who cannot afford the high prices of instruction. Many instructors allow students to work for their lessons by shagging balls, stringing rackets, or clerking in the pro shop. Payment for lessons should be made by check for record keeping and tax purposes, and should be made before a series of lessons. If people pay you at the beginning of the lesson series, they feel a commitment to continue. It is best if they sign a ticket for the amount of the lesson. Then the club collects money owed rather than the pro. Students should let you know in advance if they cannot be present for a lesson so you can arrange your schedule accordingly. If they don't show up, bill them anyway.

There are several abilities that the tennis teacher should possess. First, he must be willing to do hard, physical work. Standing and moving on the courts in all sorts of weather while constantly talking to students is not an easy way to make a living. Most people do not understand that even though tennis is recreation for them, it is an occupation for the teaching pro. While that occupation can be rewarding in many ways, it is not quite as glamorous as most people think. Second, the teacher should be good at names—good enough to know every student by his or her first name during the first lesson and to remember it the next lesson. Believe it or not, there are professional tennis instructors who still address some of their students as, "Hey, you!" during the fifth or sixth week of instruction. That kind of behavior is not only rude, it is also bad business. The instructor should also be a good tosser and hitter. A good tosser can place the ball exactly where it should be placed and at the right speed for each student. For young beginners, tossing underhand may be appropriate for technical and psychological reasons. A good hitting teacher can keep the ball in play, hit it to the desired spot, and watch the student's movements rather than watching the ball. He must also be capable of carrying a hand full of balls while running about the court and hitting. This technique is terrible for the instructor's game because it requires a short backswing, little follow through, no opposite hand support, and no pace. Few top notch instructors can maintain their playing level while teaching heavy loads.

There is a question in the minds of some inexperienced teachers and coaches that if the gifted player executes the fundamentals of the game correctly, what is there left to teach? There are several options. First, very few junior players hit every shot well. Look for or ask about the shots that give the player problems. Look beyond the routine groundstrokes, volleys, and serves. Half volleys, approach shots, high backhand volleys, and second serves are examples of shots which even good players need to improve. A second option is to see that the above average player makes efficient use of practice time rather than wasting it. Good, bad, and average players can benefit from demanding, structured practices. A third alternative is to arrange matches for the good player against better players. You can then observe the matches and look for areas that need improvement.

GROUP LESSONS

Group lessons can last any length of time, but most groups practice or play an hour or an hour and a half. The number of lessons also varies—once or twice a week for four to eight weeks. Groups should have a minimum of three students and a maximum of eight per teacher. One of the most common ratios is one teacher for every four students. With this format, there is usually one pro in charge with assistants helping on each court. Four, five, or six people can be taught on one court if the instructor is well organized. Teaching huge groups is possible, but not as effective. See the section in this chapter on teaching physical education classes. Prices for group lessons range from one-third to one-half the cost of private lessons. Here are some suggestions on how to make small group instruction worthwhile for the students and profitable for the instructor.

Plan the content and order of teaching activities before you go to the court. Each student should be hitting, throwing, or picking up balls most of the time. There should be a minimum of waiting in lines to hit. Many people take lessons not only to learn how to play but also to get exercise. You can help them achieve that goal by having something for them to do every minute they are with you.

Make brief explanationns. You can explain things while your students are hitting as well as you can while they are standing still. If you have to have their complete attention to get a point across, make your explanation in less than a minute. Say what you want to say, then let them start hitting again. During your explanations, make only one or two points. They won't remember more than that, anyway.

Group players according to ability. When people sign up, see that they are placed in the right kind of group. If you don't know them, ask questions about their tennis background to find out how long they have played, if they have taken lessons, or who they can beat. When possible, group them by age. Even though the tennis ability of a twelve year old and an adult might be the same, the lessons will go better if people are compatible socially as well as athletically.

Make sure that everyone is successful with at least one activity. Adults have needs just as children do, and one of them is achievement. If they are completely unsuccessful at everything you give them, you will lose them. Hitting individually with each player in the group at some time during the lesson helps. That way you get to know each person better and can give every student some special attention. You can also find at least one thing that player can do and reinforce the skill by letting him practice it with you.

To increase interest, vary your drills slightly with each lesson. Do not use all of your best drills during the first couple of times the class meets. Keep the drills short. It is hard to concentrate on anything that lasts more than ten or fifteen minutes. Introduce an idea, set up the drill based on that idea, then move on to something else. Instead of bouncing from one activity to the next, move in a logical sequence of learning exercises. Alternate rigorous drills with less demanding ones or with a time out to pick up balls. Make everybody pick up balls. There are people who think that picking up balls should be done by somebody else. Change their minds.

Use combination drills to make effective use of limited time. If one group is serving, another can practice returning their serves. While some practice lobs, their partners can hit smashes. Half of the players can work on volleys while hitting to others working on groundstrokes.

Finish the lesson with a demanding drill. Give them something to remember. A lot of players will go away completely satisfied if they are fatigued at the end of the lesson. Don't disappoint them.

THREE AND ME

The Three and Me format for group lessons is popular and workable. It consists of three students and the teacher or pro utilizing one court and at least one hundred balls. Any number of lessons can be scheduled, but one hour a week for four weeks is about right. The advantages of Three and Me for the students are:

1.   splitting the cost of instruction three ways,
2.   having a group small enough so that everyone gets personal attention, and
3.   having the pro involved in most of the drills.

Three and Me can be used for beginners, intermediates, or advanced players. The hour of instruction should be divided into five to ten minute segments, and all of the strokes should be practiced each lesson. The emphasis is on hitting as many balls as possible during the hour. Every drill should either involve all three students hitting or one or two hitting with a third person picking up balls. Spend as little time as is necessary with detailed explanations, but go slower with beginners than you do with intermediates and advanced players. Organization is crucial, so plan ahead.

When people call about group instruction, suggest the Three and Me arrangement as an alternative. You can match people who call separately, but it is best if they form their own groups. That cuts down time you would have to spend organizing groups and it helps in forming groups in which the players are friendly and matched by ability.

The price for Three and Me sessions can be the same as you charge for private lessons. Just split the total three ways. The amount of time and effort you must give is the same—private or group. If you do your job well, the participants will get enough instruction and exercise for their money.

Here are sample schedules for beginners, intermediate, and advanced groups. See the chapter on drills for details.

Beginners

Time	Activities
10 mins.	Ups, Downs, Halfcourt Hitting
10	Ready-Pivot-Step-Swing (Forehand; 1 on 3)°
	Running Forehands (1 on 3)
10	Ready-Pivot-Step-Swing (Backhand; 1 on 3)
	Running Backhands
10	Halfcourt Serve (3 serving simultaneously)
	Full Court Serve
10	Volley From Fence (2 on 2)
10	Running Groundstrokes (1 on 1)

Intermediates

10	2 on 2 Groundstroke Warmup
10	2 on 1 Volleys
10	3 on 1 Monster

Intermediates

10	1 on 2 Overhead Smashes
10	3 Serving or 2 on 2 Serving
10	1 on 1 Get Everything or 1 on 1 Approach Shots or 1 on 2 Hitting From Backcourt

Advanced Players

10	2 on 2 Down-The-Line and Crosscourt Groundstroke Warmup
10	3 on 1 Monster
10	2 on 1 Volleys
10	2 on 2 Lobs and Smashes
10	2 on 1 Serve-Rush-Volley
10	1 on 1 Get Everything

* 1 on 3 means one instructor facing 3 students; 2 on 2 means teacher and one student against two students

Six on Six

Six on Six is a group lesson format providing near individual instruction at group rates. In order to use this idea you must have six (an arbitrary number) hitters or assistant instructors. They should be advanced high school or college level players. Teaching experience is helpful, but not essential.

In Six on Six, the six assistants you hire are matched with six students who want group instruction. Each student has his or her own private hitter or assistant instructor for the entire lesson, but players and hitters can be rotated throughout the lesson. Two students and two hitters share one court. Lessons can last from an hour to an hour and a half. Shorter periods are not worth the effort or money; longer periods are too rigorous for most players. Your job is to oversee all three courts.

What you do with the group depends on the abilities of the people taking lessons. It can be a drill session, a series of introductory lessons, or a time for intermediate players to compete against someone better. The best part of Six on Six is that you do not have to do the same thing at the same time with every student. Two players may want to practice serving on one court; two others can be developing groundstrokes on the second court; and the last two can alternate playing singles or combine to play doubles on the third court. Players don't even have to be grouped by ability since every student is working independently of the others. More than three courts could be used, but it creates problems of supervision, getting qualified hitters, and having enough tennis balls for that many people.

You will have to decide on pricing, but there is a guideline for charges

155

and paying helpers. That guideline is whatever amount is paid to you by the student, you take half and the hitter gets half. For example, if you charge each student ten dollars for a one hour Six on Six session, your total intake would be sixty dollars. You take half that amount and make thirty dollars. Each of your hitters is paid half of the ten dollars—five dollars for an hour's hitting. You can run as many as three groups during a morning, afternoon, or night series. Once a week is enough for most people, and they may sign up for as many sessions as they want to. Remember that part of the money you take in will be spent in organizing the lessons, publicizing them, hiring workers, and buying tennis balls.

NINE PLAYER GROUPS

If you use three courts, three instructors, and nine students, the Nine Player Group becomes a Three and Me format run simultaneously on three courts. The teaching methods and drills are the same, the pricing is approximately the same, and the organization is comparable. The problems are finding enough students who fit your teaching schedule, finding three competent assistants, and organizing the series of lessons effectively. The benefits are increased profits for you and the capacity to teach larger numbers of people without occupying too many courts.

LARGER GROUPS

Teaching tennis in situations where there are more than four players to a court is difficult, but not impossible. The organizational ability of the head instructor will be severely tested. The main problem will be to keep everyone active instead of waiting in line to hit. Many of the drills in the last chapter of this book show how to arrange lots of students on the courts for effective instruction. Here are some additional suggestions.

Use all of the space on and around the tennis courts. There is room on the court for at least three separate groups of players. One group can use the middle area and the other two can use the sideline areas, including alleys (Figure 5-1). There is room between courts or between a court and the fence or wall for another group to work on certain shots. Where there is a practice cage or building wall, some of the players can be assigned to those areas. In some throwing drills, the students can line up facing each other from sideline to sideline rather than baseline to baseline (See the Toss to Forehand drill in Chapter 8).

Use as many tennis balls as you can get your hands on. If the flow of activity has to be stopped too often to pick up balls, interest will diminish.

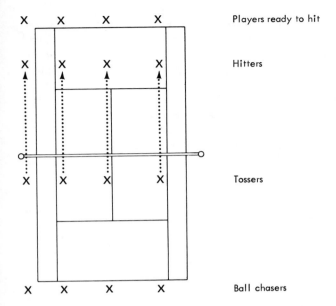

X   X   X   X   Players ready to hit

X   X   X   X   Hitters

X   X   X   X   Tossers

X   X   X   X   Ball chasers

Figure 5–1 By using all of the space inside the court and some outside, as many as sixteen or more players can be accommodated in limited space.

Use tennis balls provided by the sponsoring agency (school, city, club); use some of your personal supply of balls; ask for old tennis balls from adults in the program or area; and request that the participants bring at least a can of balls to contribute to the program.

Try to have something for everyone to do on the court at all times. For example, on a single court and surrounding area, five people could toss balls; five others could be across the net hitting groundstrokes; five more on deck ready to hit; five behind those five simulating forehand swings; five counting the number of shots hit; and five picking up balls. That takes care of thirty students on one court. They may not all be practicing a specific tennis skill, but they are engaged in a tennis related activity and not looking for ways to get into trouble.

Establish some basic goals of instruction like teaching everyone how to keep score and at least presenting the serve and groundstrokes to all players. There will be many who can do much more, but there will also be some who cannot do that much.

Watch for talented players. In spite of all the disadvantages of mass instruction, the real hungry tennis players usually come out of the public court, free lesson environment. It is part of your job to recognize them, teach them, and give them an opportunity to develop their talents.

Develop some system of rewards or awards for large groups of students. Since there will not be enough time or space to play individual matches, you can devise contests to evaluate progress and stimulate interest. Teams can compete against each other for the number of forehands, backhands, or serves hit into the proper court in a given time period. Individuals can get recognition for the number of times a ball is kept in play. Slower learners can be rewarded by prizes for showing the greatest improvement or being the best helper. Talented players can be chosen to represent your group against other groups in the area. Awards can consist of certificates, ribbons, patches, or just privileges like not having to pick up balls or moving to a more advanced group.

PHYSICAL EDUCATION CLASSES

There is a wide range of competencies among the people now teaching tennis. The demand for instruction is so great, almost anyone who can play at the intermediate or advanced level will eventually be asked to teach some individual or group how to play the game. Although the demand for tennis teachers is encouraging, the quality of instruction is rather low. People who can play the game well cannot necessarily teach others how to play. While clubs, municipalities, and individuals are free to employ anyone they choose and can afford, schools should be as selective as possible in providing teachers who are not only tennis oriented, but educationally oriented.

The person reading this chapter has either already been selected or is interested in teaching tennis in a physical education program. If that decision has already been made, it would be useless to tell you what competencies you should possess to be qualified to teach tennis in schools. However, there are skills, teaching techniques, and information the tennis instructor should possess. If you do not have these competencies, it would be professionally advantageous to work toward certain goals in order to improve while you teach.

There are some great tennis teachers who have never had any formal training program to prepare them as instructors. Through experience and by using common sense they have reached high levels of competency. But for most people, there should be at least some tentative standards of preparation, and the following general guidelines are offered as suggestions to establish these standards:

1. The tennis instructor should have several years playing experience.
2. The tennis instructor should have competed in city, state, regional, or national tournaments.

3. The tennis instructor should have completed some formal program of tennis instruction (series of lessons, a tennis course, a clinic, etc.)

4. The instructor should have completed some formal educational program of methods in teaching tennis or physical education.

5. The instructor should have completed a course in human growth and development or psychology.

6. The instructor should have some experience in organizing various forms of competition.

7. The instructor should be a member of some professional organization related to tennis, physical education, or recreation.

8. The instructor should subscribe to at least one professional publication related to tennis or physical education.

PREPARING TO TEACH A COURSE

If you know you are going to teach a course, there are many areas of preparation to consider before the series of classes begins. The nature of your students—physical education majors, nonmajors, students required to take the course, students taking an elective course—has a lot to do with how you will prepare. Some of the decisions that have to be made may have already been determined by school or departmental policy, tradition, or unwritten guidelines of other teachers. If this is the case, all you have to do is check with your supervisor to learn what the policies are. If not, you should decide on the items below before you meet the first class. The intent here is not to suggest policies, but to alert you as to what must be planned.

1. **Who will furnish tennis balls and rackets, how many will be needed, how should they be marked, and where will they be stored?** Some schools provide all equipment for their students and others require the students to bring their own rackets and two or three marked balls. If the students bring their own balls, time will be needed at the end of each class to retrieve and sort out everyone's balls. Storage can be provided by the school or made the responsibility of the students.

2. **Have the courts been cleared for use by your class?** Check to see that there is no schedule conflict with other teachers, other departments, private groups, or varsity teams. Also check to see if the courts are in good playing condition.

3.   How will students dress and what provisions are there for storage and cleaning of clothes and towels? The alternatives for dress are no special requirements, gym shorts and T-shirts, and school PE uniforms. As with equipment, storage can be the responsibility of the school or the students.

4.   What are the objectives of the course? If not already established, they will vary with the nature of the students taking the course. If you are asked to write objectives, they will probably have to be written in behavioral terms (meaning in terms of student behavior, observable, and measurable). For example, "The learner will demonstrate proficiency in the serve by successfully serving seven of ten balls using the proper grip and a full swing motion."

5.   Is there a course outline to follow? If not, an outline should be developed with a scope (content) and sequence (progression of learning activities) format. Suggestions for an outline are presented in this chapter.

6.   What will students be assigned in addition to class activities? Written reports, magazine articles, participation in extraclass competition, attendance at tennis matches, unit plans, lesson plans, and field trips are possibilities, depending on the group taking the course.

7.   How will the students be graded? Factors which may be considered are skill tests, written tests, written work assignments, attendance, improvement, and attitude. Examples of skill tests, written tests, and outside assignments are given in this chapter.

8.   What is the policy on injuries? If a student is injured and cannot participate in the activities, there must be some policy established. Some schools give incompletes, others require the student to drop the course, others allow grading based on written work only, and some set a maximum grade which can be attained without full participation.

9.   What is the policy on absences? Some programs build in an automatic penalty for missing classes. In others, as long as work is successfully completed, attendance is not a factor in grading. A plan for making up work missed must also be devised.

10.   How will the class be organized? A class routine will be necessary for checking attendance, arranging for lectures or demonstrations, and learning activities. Many instructors assign students to permanent groups for drills. Groups of four or less per court is ideal; six in a group is crowded, but manageable; and more than six is undesirable.

11.   How will the class be taught on bad weather days? Make sure there is some place for your class to meet, and prepare some classroom presentations in advance.

Lengths of tennis courses vary with the schools. Some meet daily for an entire semester. Others meet two or three times a week. Class periods range from forty minutes to two hours. Required physical education tennis courses frequently consist of on the court work only. Classes for future teachers usually combine playing time and classroom instruction. Regardless of the length of the class period or course, the most important factors are the content and the sequence of progression of learning activities. Here is an outline for a tennis class of nonmajors which will meet thirty times (five days a week for six weeks). Each class period will last sixty minutes with approximately forty to forty-five minutes of actual court time.

1st Day	Introduction to course
	Format and instructions on procedures
	Assign students a tennis article to read
2nd Day	Explain and demonstrate ready position, forehand grip and stroke
	Large group drills followed by partner or small group drills
3rd Day	Review fundamentals of forehand
	Demonstrate how to drop ball and put it into play
	Repeat forehand drills
4th Day	Explain and demonstrate backhand grip and stroke
	Class and small group drills
5th Day	Review fundamentals of backhand
	Repeat drills
6th Day	Classroom lesson on rules, equipment, and terms
	Discussion of articles; assign second article
	Questions and answers
7th Day	Explain and demonstrate punch and/or full swing serve
	Class and group drills
8th Day	Review fundamentals of serve
	Repeat serving drills
9th Day	Explain and demonstrate forehand and backhand volley
	Partner or small group drills
10th Day	Review fundamentals of volley
	Drills for the volley

11th Day	Explain and demonstrate overhead smash
	Drills for the smash
	Repeat drills for other strokes or free play
12th Day	Classroom lesson on singles and doubles strategy
	Questions and answers
13th Day	Singles or doubles play
14th Day	Singles or doubles play
15th Day	Explain and demonstrate lob and drop shot
	Drills
16th Day	Drills for groundstrokes
	Singles or doubles play
17th Day	Drills for the serve
	Combination drills
18th Day	Drills for the net game
	Singles or doubles play
19th Day	Singles or doubles competition (Tournament)
20th Day	Singles or doubles competiton
21st Day	Singles or doubles competition
22nd Day	Singles or doubles competition
23rd Day	Classroom lesson; discussion of second reading assignment
	Review for written test
24th Day	Practice for skill tests
25th Day	Practice for skill tests
26th Day	Skill tests; play for those not taking tests today
27th Day	Skill tests; play
28th Day	Skill tests; play
29th Day	Skill tests; play
30th Day	Written final exam

GIVING SKILL TESTS

The teacher who designs or administers skill tests for physical education activity courses will always be faced with the problem of whether to consider improvement as a factor in the final grade. Pretests and posttests should be considered as a measurement technique, but both have negative aspects. The student who comes into your class never having played tennis is more likely to show progress than the person who has some playing experience. It makes sense to reward the beginner for improvement, but the intermediate or advanced player should not be penalized for something over which he has little control.

A second problem is whether to grade on accuracy, form, or a combination of the two. Some of the standardized tennis tests award grades on accuracy. For example, a student can punch the ball on the serve using a Western grip and probably score high on accuracy. A second student may attempt the full swing serve using good form, but hit fewer shots into the target area. A combination of form and accuracy seems to be the most equitable alternative, but it leaves part of the grading to a subjective evaluation by the teacher. If you are not ready to assume that responsibility, it might be better to grade objectively and solely on the placement of shots.

The third problem to be solved in giving skill tests involves which skills to test. The level of competence among the students should be the determining factor in your selection. For beginning players, the following aspects of the game should be sufficient to establish a fair skill grade:

1. Demonstration of the ready position
2. Demonstration of proper grips
3. Put ball into play by dropping and hitting
4. Return hit or thrown balls with forehand stroke
5. Return hit or thrown balls with backhand stroke
6. Serve—punch or full swing
7. Return hit or thrown balls with forehand volley
8. Return hit or thrown balls with backhand volley
9. Return hit or thrown balls with overhead smash
10. Overall playing ability

Intermediate or advanced players should be able to perform the same skills at a higher level of competence as well as these:

11. Demonstration of proper footwork for each stroke
12. Demonstration of variety of serves
13. Demonstration of the lob
14. Demonstration of the drop shot
15. Demonstration of the half volley

Often there is not sufficient time to test each student on all skills. In that case, certain skills should be selected as indicators of overall ability. The number of attempts allowed each student per stroke should not be less than five and not more than ten (because of time considerations). Each student should be allowed to practice a few shots before beginning a skill test.

In addition to individual stroke skills, some provision should be made for the students to hit against another player who can keep the ball in play or against the instructor. The overall hitting ability should be taken into account as part of that player's skill grade. A student may do poorly on individual shots attempted out of a game context, but do quite well by keeping the ball in play and using a variety of shots while moving. The overall hitting score should carry more weight than the scores achieved on separate strokes. That score is not only more important, but it also gives the instructor the opportunity to use his judgment in determining the final skill grade.

A skill test form is shown on the next page. The students have been tested on eight variables valued from one to five points. One was the lowest a student could score; five was the highest. Grading was based on a combination of form and accuracy. The overall hitting grade was scored from one to ten. The final skill grade may be decided by a predetermined number of points necessary to achieve an "A," "B," "C," "D," or "F," or the scores may be curved to allow for the group's skill level. In this example, the scores were curved.

GIVING WRITTEN TESTS

The most commonly used items on written tests are true-false, multiple choice, identification, discussion, matching, fill-in-the-blank, and listing. Matching items are not very demanding and allow for guessing by the process of elimination. Fill-in-the-blank questions are too structured and give no opportunity for original responses. Listing items requires memorization, which is a rather superficial way to learn. The other types of written tests should be more reliable and valid, but they also have advantages and disadvantages. True-false tests can be an effective method of evaluation, but care must be taken to use words familiar to the student and to structure statements so that they will not appear vague or ambiguous to the students. Properly constructed true-false tests should have a majority of true statements. People tend to remember as fact what they read, whether it is true or not. Multiple choice tests should have at least three items from which to choose and not more than five. Identification of terms may constitute part of a test, but an entire test of identification items again requires too much memory work. Discussion items are the best way to ascertain what a student knows, but the time required for grading this type of test may be prohibitive. A written test should include a maximum of three different kinds of questions. Anything beyond this becomes more of an obstacle course exercise than a measure of what has been learned. On the following pages are sample true-false, multiple choice, identification, and discussion items.

Skill Test Form

NAME	Serve	Forehand	Backhand	Forehand Volley	Backhand Volley	Overhead Smash	General Play	Total Score	Skill Grade
Viccellio	3	3	2	4	1	3	6	22	C
Moore	4	5	4	4	3	5	8	33	A
Salinas	3	3	4	3	4	3	6	26	B-
Buck	2	3	2	4	4	2	5	22	C
Quarles	3	4	3	4	3	3	7	27	B
Milburn	5	5	4	3	4	5	8	34	A
Frazee	3	3	3	2	3	4	5	23	C
Hebert	4	4	5	3	3	5	9	33	A-
Lundy	4	4	3	3	4	2	8	28	B
LeBato	2	2	3	1	1	2	3	14	D
Soulier	3	3	3	3	2	4	5	23	C
Farst	2	3	2	3	3	2	6	21	C
Garbo	1	3	3	4	3	3	7	24	C+
Gamblin	5	5	5	5	4	4	9	37	A
Hogan	2	1	1	2	2	3	4	15	D
Yu	4	4	3	2	3	2	6	24	C+
Kesava	4	4	4	4	2	3	7	28	B
Chavanne	5	4	5	4	3	3	5	29	B
Davidson	5	4	3	2	3	2	5	24	C+
McElveen	3	3	2	2	4	1	5	20	C
Butler	4	5	2	4	3	3	6	27	B

Figure 5–2

These questions are not presented as a test but as possible questions from which a teacher may choose.

True or False

T   1. When the score is 30–15, the server is winning the game.

T   2. Balls that land on lines are in play.

F   3. It is illegal to serve with an underhand motion.

T   4. A let serve is repeated.

T   5. A player may not reach over the net to strike a ball.

F   6. The backswing used to hit a volley is the same used to hit a groundstroke.

F   7. Clay courts are faster than concrete courts.

T   8. A doubles team may change the order of serve at the beginning of a new set.

T   9. Davis Cup play involves international competition for men.

T   10. The governing body for amateur tennis in the U.S. is the United States Tennis Association.

F   11. The player about to receive a serve may purposely attempt to distract the server.

T   12. A player must win at least eight games and be ahead by at least two games to win a pro set.

F   13. The server must have at least one foot in contact with the ground when the ball is served.

T   14. The grips for the backhand and advanced serve are similar.

T   15. The arm should be fully extended at the point of contact on the serve.

F   16. The lob should only be used as a defensive tactic.

T   17. A shot with backspin is called a chop.

F   18. A short stroke with a wrist snap is recommended for groundstrokes.

T   19. A maximum of 90 seconds is allowed for players to change ends of the court after an odd number of games.

T   20. In some instances, the player who wins the toss or racket spin should choose a side rather than first serve.

T   21. A foot fault should be called when a player walks or runs as part of the service delivery.

T   22. A shot is good if it is returned outside the net post and lands in the proper court.

T   23. In a nine point tie-breaker, the player due to serve the next game with the score 6–6 serves the first two points.

T   24. Playing an Australian doubles formation, the server and his partner line up on the same side of the court.

T   25. If other variables are equal, a flat serve will have more velocity than a twist serve.

F   26. Passing shots should be hit as high over the net as possible.

F   27. Professionals and amateurs are not allowed to compete in the same tournaments in this country.

T   28. A service toss may be repeated if the ball is not swung at or hit.

F   29. In hitting a backhand, the ball should be struck at a point even with the center of the body.

T   30. When both opponents are at the net in doubles, the best place to hit is low and down the middle.

T 31. In doubles play, lefthanders are usually more effective returning a serve from the left side of the court.

F 32. The net is the same height in the middle as at the sideline.

T 33. A player attempting a topspin shot can hit the ball higher over the net than with other shots.

T 34. Put-away overhead smashes should not be attempted from a position behind the baseline.

T 35. Drop shots should not be attempted when the wind is at a player's back.

T 36. In tournament competition, players should be allowed at least fifteen minutes between matches.

T 37. Most points are decided by errors rather than by winners.

F 38. The height of the player is not a factor in executing a serve.

T 39. Most approach shots should be hit down the line.

T 40. The Wightman Cup is awarded to the winner of a dual match between women of the United States and England.

F 41. Gut strings are water resistant.

T 42. Metal rackets generally allow a player to hit with more force than wooden rackets do.

T 43. Hard court surfaces are easier to maintain than soft surfaces.

F 44. The server's partner in doubles should stand in the alley.

T 45. The server's motion in tennis is similar to the throwing motion in baseball.

T 46. In singles, keeping the ball deep is more important than hitting shots that barely clear the net.

T 47. Most groundstrokes should be hit crosscourt.

T 48. Backhand shots are more likely to be hit with backspin than forehand shots.

T 49. Lobs should be directed to an opponent's backhand.

F 50. The racket should be brought back on the backswing just as the ball bounces in front of the hitter.

Multiple Choice

1. Which of the following tournaments is considered to be the most prestigious in the world?
   (1) U.S. Open, (2) French Open, (3) **Wimbledon,** (4) Australian Open.

2. You are serving and the score is 30–40. Your opponent wins the next point. The score is now
   (1) **game,** (2) 30–45, (3) deuce, (4) ad out.

3. What is the minimum number of points possible in a game?
   (1) 3, (2) **4,** (3) 5, (4) 6.

4. What is the maximum number of sets played in women's competition?
   (1) one set, (2) one pro set, (3) **two out of three sets,** (4) three out of five sets.

5. Where is the best place to wait for the ball during singles play?
   (1) center of the court, (2) **middle of the baseline,** (3) on the service line, (4) anywhere in the backcourt.

6. Which of these scores would be called deuce?
   (1) each player has two points, (2) each player has the same number of points, (3) **each player has three points,** (4) 30–30.

7. In doubles, shots hit down the middle should be taken
   (1) **by the player with the forehand shot,** (2) by the player closest to the net, (3) by the player with the backhand shot, (4) by the last player to hit the ball on the previous shot.

8. Players must change ends of the court after every
   (1) point, (2) game, (3) set, (4) **odd game.**

9. The height of the net at the center of the court is
   (1) 2½ feet, (2) **3 feet,** (3) 3½ feet, (4) none of these.

10. The serve should be hit with the ball
    (1) **in front of the body,** (2) directly over the server's head, (3) slightly behind the head, (4) to the left of the server's head.

11. A shot hit with topspin will
    (1) **bounce higher than usual,** (2) bounce lower than usual, (3) have the same bounce as any other shot, (4) bounce to the left of the opponent.

12. A closed stance may indicate that the hitter is going to hit
    (1) **straight ahead,** (2) crosscourt, (3) a lob, (4) a slice.

13. Which is the least effective grip for hitting a backhand shot?
    (1) Eastern, (2) **Western,** (3) Continental, (4) handshake.

14. In doubles, the receiver's partner should stand
    (1) just in front of the baseline, (2) two steps from the net, (3) **on the service line,** (4) in the alley.

15. In doubles, when the ball is lobbed over the net player's head, he should

(1) stay where he is, (2) **cross to the other side of the court,** (3) try to beat his partner to the ball, (4) move to the center of the court.

16. Which shot would be the best to use against a short lob?
    (1) drop shot, (2) **smash,** (3) lob, (4) topspin backhand.

17. If a ball rolls onto the court during a rally, the point
    (1) should be continued, (2) is given to the player on whose side the ball is rolling, (3) **should be replayed,** (4) is awarded to the player on the other side of the court.

18. The United States Open Tennis Championships are played in
    (1) Los Angeles, (2) **New York,** (3) Dallas, (4) Miami.

19. The receiving formation of a doubles team
    (1) **may be changed at the end of a set,** (2) may not be changed after the match has begun, (3) may be changed at any time during the match, (4) is not restricted by any rule.

20. The most popular type of tennis tournament is the
    (1) double elimination, (2) **single elimination,** (3) round robin, (4) ladder.

21. The best grip to use in hitting the volley is the
    (1) **Continental,** (2) Western, (3) Eastern, (4) modified Eastern.

22. If a ball is touched by a player who is standing behind the baseline before it bounces,
    (1) **he loses the point,** (2) he wins the point, (3) the point is replayed, (4) the umpire may rule for either player.

23. In the last point of a nine point tie-breaker,
    (1) the players flip to determine the court to be served from, (2) the server decides on which court to serve from, (3) **the receiver decides on which court he prefers to receive,** (4) the umpire decides on which court to be served from.

24. A player who has been drawn off to one side of the court behind the baseline should attempt which shot?
    (1) **a lob,** (2) a drop shot, (3) a smash, (4) a crosscourt groundstroke.

25. Which of the following strokes will involve movement of the wrist?
    (1) forehand, (2) backhand, (3) volley, (4) **smash.**

Definition or Identification of Terms

U.S.T.A.	baseline	flat
slice	service line	Australian doubles
chop	alley	tie breaker
pace	advantage	straight sets
push	foot fault	round robin
seed	pivot	ladder tournament
gut	racket head	pyramid tournament
deuce	racket throat	love
American twist	topspin	rally
Continental	approach shot	volley
half volley	passing shot	poach
bye	ace	rush
VASSS	stop volley	double elimination
chip	closed stance	open stance
default	semi-finals	quarter-finals
Wimbledon	W.C.T.	Davis Cup
Bill Tilden	Billie Jean King	Rod Laver
Pancho Gonzales	Walter Wingfield	Althea Gibson

Discussion Questions

1. Explain the scoring system in tennis.
2. Explain the nine point tie-breaker system.
3. Diagram and discuss the positions for advanced doubles.
4. Name and explain the three basic tennis grips.
5. Discuss the advantages and disadvantages of metal and wooden rackets.
6. Name and discuss the advantages and disadvantages of the various kinds of racket strings.
7. Name and discuss the advantages and disadvantages of the various kinds of court surfaces.
8. Trace the history of tennis from the 1800s to the present.
9. Give some examples of basic singles strategy.
10. Give some examples of basic doubles strategy.
11. Discuss the possibilities for positioning the different combinations of righthanded and lefthanded players in doubles.
12. Explain how a round robin tournament is drawn up and conducted.

13. Explain the procedure for seeding players in a tournament.
14. Compare tennis to golf, bowling, swimming, and handball in terms of endurance, strength, balance, speed, flexibility, and quickness.
15. Outline and discuss the organizational structure of the United States Tennis Association.

ASSIGNING WORK FOR FUTURE TEACHERS

Physical education majors, minors, and others who will eventually teach tennis to groups of people should develop their own resource units for future use. Although books such as this one are a type of teaching unit, students will be more likely to use something they have worked out for themselves. They certainly will be more familiar with the material they decide to include in a unit than with the information in a book. Some college teachers require their students to develop a unit plan and others ask their students to prepare a series of daily lesson plans. Below are content suggestions for unit and lesson plans.

Unit Plan Outline

I. Introduction
   A. History
   B. Values
II. Unit Objectives
   A. General objectives or goals
   B. Specific objectives
      1. Written in terms of the learner
      2. Related to general objectives
      3. What is to be accomplished by each individual
III. Development of the Activity
   A. Skills or techniques to be taught
   B. Key teaching points
   C. Lead-up games or special activities
   D. Tennis-related information (principles, rules, strategy, etiquette, etc.)
IV. Class Organization
   A. Division of students into groups
   B. Assignment to teaching stations
V. Equipment
VI. Health and Safety Precautions
   A. Safety rules
   B. Physical examinations

   VII. Motivational Devices
- **A.** Audio-visual aids
- **B.** Tournaments
- **C.** Field trips
- **D.** Special events

  VIII. Evaluation and Measurement
- **A.** Skill tests
- **B.** Written tests
- **C.** Assignments

   IX. Block Plan
- **A.** Time table of lesson plans
- **B.** Progression of learning activities

    X. References
- **A.** Books
- **B.** Periodicals
- **C.** Miscellaneous material

Daily Lesson Plan Outline

    I. Objectives (written in behavioral terms)
   II. Equipment (items necessary to conduct the class)
  III. Time Allotment (how many minutes for each class segment)
  IV. New Material (outline of lecture notes, if any)
   V. Activities (explanation and diagram of learning activities)
  VI. Evaluation (self-evaluation or notes on lesson taught)
 VII. References (sources of information used in this lesson)

PUBLIC SUMMER PROGRAMS

Many summer programs begin with free group lessons for junior age players. These programs frequently begin the first Monday after the last day of school in May or June. If there is a time gap between the end of school and the beginning of tennis lessons, the children may become too involved in other activities to be interested in tennis. The lessons are usually given in the morning because the people in this age group are free at that time, and because there is not a big demand for use of the courts by adults.

Lessons may be given at a central tennis center or they may be given at various locations throughout the city or county. Both systems have advantages and disadvantages. Tennis centers have many courts, and a large number of players can be supervised by a few instructors. It is also easy to keep tennis traffic moving at a large complex of courts. The disadvantage is that school age children may not be able to get transportation to take lessons or to play at a tennis center far from their homes. If the lessons are taught at neighborhood courts or schools, more children have access to program activities. However, either more instructors must be hired to teach and supervise at the various sites or the same few instructors have to move from place to place throughout the city during the day.

Group lessons last about an hour a day, two to five days a week, for a period of about four weeks. The hour long session is about as long as the younger players can concentrate on learning, as long as the instructors can teach one group effectively, and as long as the schedule of court use permits in many cities. The five-days-a-week schedule is preferable, but may not be possible if there are many groups to be taught. Four weeks of daily lessons is about the maximum length advisable. Many programs run for shorter periods. In the city recreation type of program, however, the children are going to be in and out because of vacations, ball games, and other summer activities. Very few participants will be there every day for a month. If there is a demand for more instruction, a new cycle of lessons can be started every three or four weeks.

Any experienced summer program director will testify that a lot of baby sitting goes on during free tennis lessons. Some of the kids want to be there and are enthusiastic about what is happening; others would just as soon be doing something else; and a third group is there because their parents dropped them off at the courts and told them to take lessons. It is difficult to plan a program of instruction for such a wide range of participants. As much as possible, separate the players by age groups and ability. Eight, nine, and ten year olds seem to get along with each other, eleven and twelve year olds stick together, and the thirteen to fifteen group should be separate from the younger players.

Municipal programs ought to provide group lessons for older adolescents and adults during the summer months. These lessons attract more people if they are taught late in the afternoon or at night when adults get off work. The exception to that suggestion may be lessons for housewives taught during the morning. The lessons should last for several weeks, but adults will not be able to attend daily as the juniors can. Two or three one hour sessions a week are enough, provided the participants get to practice on their own in addition to the classes.

JUNIOR DEVELOPMENT PROGRAMS

Junior Development Progams are conducted at many tennis and racket clubs and at some municipal facilities. Their primary function is to further develop the tennis skills of junior players who have already had some tennis experience.

Groups may come twice or three times a week for four to eight weeks. Those who want to continue after one series of lessons may sign up for another one. The group lessons or practice sessions last from one to two hours, depending on the age of the players and the amount of time the program director can give the groups.

Players should be divided by age and ability. The twelve and under group might come on Monday and Wednesday, and the high school players on Tuesday and Thursday. Within each group the juniors can be divided by ability on separate courts.

Arrange the price of being in a development program so that it is inexpensive enough to encourage participation and lucrative enough to help you earn a living.

Assistants should be used on every court with the twelve and under group. The helpers can be advanced high school students, but you must be on the courts to supervise them at all times. Restrict the number of twelve and under players to four per court. You may have to arrange additional sessions, but at this level, they need someone out there to help keep the ball in play.

You may be able to handle as many as twelve to sixteen high school players alone or with one assistant. More advanced players need your attention and advice more than they need you to hit with them.

What you do on the court with each group is very similar to a team practice. It is a structured setting in which players get their practice time in under supervised conditions. Most juniors will not practice enough on their own. They prefer to play. Under your direction, they should hit a specified number of forehands, backhands, serves, volleys, smashes, and drop shots. You may have time for some competition if court space allows.

J. D. programs seem to work best in the spring and fall seasons. Good players are busy playing tournaments in the summer, and during the winter it is either too cold or there is not enough indoor court space in northern areas of the country. In the spring and fall the program fits nicely around school schedules. The only possible conflict is a high school spring tennis schedule. Some of your players will have to be given extra sessions to make up time missed to play dual matches or tournaments.

To summarize, your responsibilities include overseeing the entire program, organizing and supervising each session, hiring and supervising assistants, and trying to make constructive changes in your players' games. A good program can be the foundation both for good tennis among those who participate and for your tennis future at a club or public facility.

CLINICS

Tennis clinics are usually held when a nationally or regionally known player or teacher is present to attract participants. However, any knowledgeable high school or college coach can direct a clinic for beginning, intermediate, and advanced players. A one day, do-it-yourself clinic can be an interest stimulator in the off-season, an event to begin a season, or a promotional idea any time of the year.

Many courts, instructors, and balls would be ideal for such a clinic, but an effective session can be conducted to accommodate up to one hundred participants with three courts, three coaches, instructors or advanced players, and three balls provided by each player who attends. Each of the three teachers should have at least one helper—preferably, but not necessarily, an experienced player.

Assuming that the clinic will be directed toward more than one age group, the natural divisions are adults, college age students, high school students, junior high school students, and a group for those in grades one through six. None of the groups should work more than an hour and a half, and if more than one age group is to be involved the same day, a time gap between sessions should be provided for in the schedule.

Regardless of the age or ability level of a group, a few major skills should be introduced, demonstrated, and practiced rather than attempting to cover every phase of the game in a short period of time. For beginners, the clinic will be successful if participants can learn a little about the forehand, backhand, punch serve, and how to keep score. For intermediate players, work on groundstrokes, the volley, and the serve is enough for one ninety minute period. Tournament level players can be put through a brisk practice session for the same amount of time.

For the same reasons that relatively few skills should be practiced, relatively few teaching points should be emphasized. The objective of a one-shot clinic is to drive home a few ideas well, rather than to use the shotgun approach, hoping that a little bit of everything will hit everyone. Following are some suggestions regarding organization, drills, and teaching points to be emphasized for beginning, intermediate, and advanced groups:

Beginning Group

10 Minutes Explain and demonstrate the ready position, forehand grip, and footwork for the forehand stroke. Have the players line up in rows facing the instructor. The players follow the instructor's lead in a "ready-

Pivot-Step-Swing" drill. In the same formation, players can practice dribbling a ball against the court or in the air, using the correct forehand grip. This drill helps to develop ball control and also aids the beginner in establishing the hand to racket head distance relationship.

Points to Emphasize

1. Keep the racket well up and in front of the body (pointing toward the net) in the ready position.
2. Pivot forward on every shot.
3. Make sure that the forehand grip allows the face to be perpendicular to the court as striking the ball is simulated.

20 Minutes   Players line up on the opposite side of the net from the instructor's aides, who throw easy, waist high forehand shots. The instructor stands with those players doing the hitting. If aides are not available, players may be used as throwers. Those waiting to hit are used to retrieve balls.

Points to Emphasize

1. Get the racket back on the backswing as the ball is thrown, not as it bounces.
2. Step into the ball.
3. Watch the ball leave the hitter's strings.

10 Minutes   Explain and demonstrate the backhand grip and stroke. Repeat the "Ready-Pivot-Step-Swing" and dribbling drills, using backhand techniques.

Points to Emphasize

1. Use the nonracket hand to guide the racket back on the backswing.
2. Pivot forward.
3. Follow through as if trying to slap the net with the back of the hand.

20 Minutes   Have the aides throw backhand shots, employing the same procedure used in practicing the forehand.

1. Get the racket back early.
2. Use the opposite hand to aid in changing grips and to push the racket foward.
3. Strike the ball in front of the right foot (for righthanders).

10 Minutes Rest period. After the players get a drink of water, explain the fundamentals of scoring as they rest.

5 Minutes Explain and demonstrate the punch serve.

Points to Emphasize

1. Grip the racket with a forehand grip.
2. Toss the ball in front of the body.
3. Toss the ball as high as the server can reach with the arm and racket extended.

15 Minutes Serving drill. Half of the group takes turns practicing the punch serve while the other half retrieves balls. Care should be taken to avoid having more than one person hitting at a time, and to see that balls are returned along the sides of the court so that the servers will not be interrupted.

Points to Emphasize

1. Toss the ball without spin.
2. Contact with the ball is made with the arm fully extended.
3. Transfer the weight of the body forward as the serve is delivered.

Intermediate Group

30 Minutes Allow this much time to look at the group's groundstrokes. The throwing drill may have to be utilized, but having four players on one court at all times is preferable. If necessary, six players can fit onto one court for forehand and backhand practice. The players should be rotated frequently so that everyone gets plenty of action. Players not hitting should retrieve balls.

1. Be consistent in form and types of shots attempted. (Players at this stage frequently want to try everything, usually at the expense of further developing solid, consistent, basic strokes.)
2. Take an efficient, relatively short backswing. Big wind-ups are impractical.
3. Concentrate on keeping the ball in play.

30 Minutes   Two-on-one volley drill. Two players alternately hit two balls each to a third player at the net. Use both sides of the court if enough balls are available. Other players and aides pick up balls.

Points to Emphasize

1. Bend at the knees and stay low.
2. Hit the ball before it gets even with you. The ball should be hit while it is still rising, not as it drops.
3. Use a Continental grip and take a short backswing.

30 Minutes   Serving drill. Two players serve, two play the net, and two return serves. The instructor concentrates on the servers. Players rotate among all six positions.

Points to Emphasize

1. Be consistent in tossing the ball prior to the serve.
2. Use a rhythmic, continuous motion in hitting the serve.
3. Place the ball at designated spots in the receiving court.

Advanced Group

30 Minutes   Use a three shot, serve-rush-volley drill. The players serve alternately from the right and left sides. Servers follow the serve to the net. The player on the opposite side practices the service return by trying to pass his opponent. The server then attempts to volley that return. Play stops after three shots. Players rotate positions every five minutes. The instructor roams from a position behind the servers down the side of the court to the net.

Points to Emphasize

1. Get set for the volley as the opponent strikes the ball, then make a secondary move for the volley. Rush behind the serve to establish a position in front of the service line before making the volley.
2. Hold the racket tightly on the volley and place the volley crosscourt to set up the opponent for the put-away shot.
3. Watch the opponent's racket head in order to anticipate where his return will be placed.

30 Minutes   Two-on-one volley drill. Use the same procedure and points of emphasis as with the intermediate group.

15 Minutes   "Quickie" drop shot games (doubles, if necessary). Score as usual. Only drops and angles are allowed. Everything beyond the service line is out.

Points to Emphasize

1. Take the drill seriously.
2. Hit to open spots
3. Disguise your shots.

15 Minutes   Two-on-one overhead smash drill. The procedure is the same as in the volley drill, except that those players at the baseline hit lobs.

Points to Emphasize

1. Get the racket back quickly.
2. Take many short steps in preparing to hit.
3. Point to the ball with the nonracket hand for balance and position.[4]

OTHER CLINIC FORMATS

There are many other ways to organize clinics. They can be divided into those in which people participate on the court and those in which they watch or listen to a few speakers.

[4] Jim Brown, "Do-It-Yourself Tennis Clinic," *The Coaching Clinic*, 11, no. 1 (January, 1973), 9.

For participation type clinics, any of the methods described for group instruction can be adapted for clinic situations. The "Three and Me," "Six on Six," and "Nine Player Groups" are excellent ways to organize clinics where multiple courts are available. Any combination of teachers and participants is acceptable as long as the players can actively participate in the instruction. If they spend more time listening and waiting to hit than they do hitting, it would be better to conduct a lecture-demonstration type clinic without group participation.

There are also many ways to present the lecture demonstration clinic. If there is adequate seating at courtside and a good public address system, a clinic or workshop can be conducted at a school, club, or convention center complex. If the court idea is not feasible, a large room with seating and sound facilities can be used.

With this format, a wide range of subjects can be presented by one or more speakers. Here are some topics typically covered at clinics:

- Strokes
- Singles Strategy
- Doubles Strategy
- Equipment
- Group Instruction
- Coaching Techniques
- Advanced Coaching Techniques

- Innovative Teaching Ideas
- Club Programming
- Model Lessons
- Public Relations
- Treatment of Injuries
- Umpiring
- Pro Shop Management

There are some ways to make the one man or one woman show more attractive to participants:

1. Divide the sessions into time periods that do not exceed an hour and a half. Remember that no matter how good you are as a speaker, demonstrator, or player, people can concentrate for only so long.

2. Begin with something to get attention. A hypothetical situation, a controversial statement, an interesting statistic, or a well-designed visual aid can get you off to a good start.

3. Try to cover material that the majority of the audience is interested in. To do that, find out as much as you can about the group before you begin preparing for the presentation. Tell them the major points to be covered near the beginning of the session. Don't be intimidated by those in the audience who know more than you, and don't let novices slow you down if most of the listeners are more knowledgable.

4. If there is more than one session, try to have a variety of speakers. Again, no matter how good you are, a new face and approach will help to keep interest levels high.

5. Provide handouts outlining the subjects being discussed. People want to go away from workshops and clinics with something in their hands they can use in their jobs or with their games. Give the handouts at the end of each session. If they are given out at the beginning, people will read them instead of listening to what is being said.

6. Check out audio-visual equipment well before time to start. If there is any doubt about the availability or working status of projectors, screens, or microphones, make arrangements to bring your own.

7. When people ask questions, repeat the questions so the entire audience knows what you are talking about with the answer. Sometimes questions cannot be heard by everyone.

8. Stick to your subject and your schedule. Rambling and going over the time allotted causes confusion among the listeners and shortchanging of other topics or speakers.

9. Summarize important points at the end of the presentation. The summary will reinforce learning and serve as a checklist for you.

10. Make yourself available during breaks to those attending the clinic. Do not allow yourself to be hustled off by a sponsor or monopolized by one or two talkers.

REVIEW QUESTIONS

1. What are some psychological factors to be considered in teaching children? Adolescents?

2. What should be considered when grouping adolescents for instruction?

3. What kind of role model should the instructor provide for children and adolescents?

4. What can the teacher do for an adult learner with limited athletic ability?

5. Describe some personality problems most instructors can expect in teaching adults?

6. Design a ten lesson series for a middle aged beginner.

7. What is a "Three and Me," a "Six on Six," and a "Nine Player Group?"

8. Name some ways to reward students in large group teaching situations.

9. What are some competencies tennis instructors should possess?

10. What policies must be decided upon before teaching a physical education class?

11. What methods of evluation can be used for physical education classes?

12. Suggest guidelines for a summer tennis instruction program in your community.

13. How might a junior development program differ from other forms of instruction?

CHAPTER 6

Coaching

INTRODUCTION

Many high school and college coaches do not have a strong background in tennis. Some faculty members are assigned the job whether they want it or not. The tennis coach may be an assistant football coach, a science teacher, anybody who has mentioned that he or she likes tennis, or someone else just as unqualified. If you are an experienced high school or college coach, you may already be familiar with the material in this chapter. If you can identify with some of the people just described, this chapter should be helpful.

Although it is almost impossible for an inexperienced coach actually to teach someone to play tennis, that person can become a good coach. Coaching and teaching are different. Coaches spend a lot of their time recruiting players, making schedules, holding practices, baby sitting, and promoting the tennis program. Teachers show players how to hold the racket, how to swing it, how to move on the court, and later, how to win matches. Although a coach without a tennis background may learn enough about the game to do some teaching, it is too much to expect him or her to be both a coach and a teacher at the beginning.

An inexperienced coach can do some homework to get ready for the job. Tennis organizations, sporting goods companies, colleges, and teaching pros promote interest in the game by conducting clinics for players and coaches. Watch the papers and tennis magazines for information about clinics in your area. You can also increase your knowledge of tennis by reading tennis literature. There are several good magazines and hundreds of books which have instructional material for players, teachers, and coaches. For those of you who really want to become more involved in all aspects of the game, read the section in this chapter entitled "Developing Professionally."

RECRUITING

The high school coach should start looking for players when school begins in the fall. Set up a team meeting during September or October, and publicize it on the public address system, in the school paper, and on bulletin boards around the school. Invite anyone interested in playing varsity tennis to attend the meeting. The majority of your team will consist of those who played the previous year. You will also pick up a few former junior varsity players, transfers, some students up from junior high or middle school, and a few strays. Ask those who attend if they know others who might be interested in playing. There will always be a few students who don't attend the first meeting because of absences, other commitments, or not knowing about the meeting. Be on the lookout for athletes who have proved themselves in other sports and show an interest in tennis. A good athlete can improve enough during a school year to give your team depth at the lower positions.

From a coaching point of view, try to avoid the nonathlete who is not good enough to participate in any other sport. There are enough good tennis players around today in most communities so you don't have to take in rejects from football, basketball, and baseball. From an educational outlook, let as many students participate as you can while considering the time, courts, and supplies available for your program. Remember that the more players you have, the more tennis balls you must supply for practice. If you have to cut the squad, direct those who don't make it to intramurals or public programs until they are ready for a varsity team.

At the high school team meeting in the fall, get as much information about the squad members as you can. Get the players to write names, ages, addresses, class standing, class schedules, home rooms, and anything else that will help you keep in touch with them or give you information about their tennis backgrounds. You could distribute an information sheet like the one shown here (Figure 6-1).

TENNIS TEAM INFORMATION SUMMARY

Name _____

Address _____ _____

Age _____ Height _____ Weight _____

Home Telephone Number _____ Home Room Teacher _____

Class _____Tennis Ranking (if any) _____

Tennis Experience _____

_____

_____

_____

Class Schedule

8:00 _____   12:00 _____

9:00 _____   1:00 _____

10:00 _____   2:00 _____

11:00 _____   3:00 _____

Figure 6—1

The team meeting can also be used to explain the fall tennis program, if there is one. Sometimes so many people show up for the first meeting, the obvious problem becomes how to sort out the good players from the ones who cannot help the team. It will not be unusual for a few beginners to attend these meetings. Unless you are prepared to teach people how to play the game in addition to coaching a team, you need a system of determining who can play and who can't. One way is to group your players and have them play round robins within each group of four or five players. There will not be time for a complete round robin tournament unless you have access to many courts and require your players to attend daily fall practice sessions. Play small round robins (which are explained in the next chapter), but compute the results on a total point basis. For example, if twenty-one point games are played instead of sets, have the participants report the exact scores to you. If a player wins, he or she gets twenty-one points. The loser gets the number of points won in losing the match. Both players carry their totals into the next match. The player who totals the most points during the round robin wins. With this system, every point counts, even when you lose. As a coach, you can get a better idea of how the players match up than if you just record wins and losses. The top finishers in each group can compete in a final round of competition for further evaluation. By that time, you should have a very good idea of who will be playing for you in the spring.

College recruiting is complicated, time consuming, costly, and the most important factor in the success or failure of teams and coaches. You do not have the luxury of making mistakes in evaluating prospective players as football coaches do who carry fifty to one hundred recruits for a game that can be played with eleven people. Most colleges in the United States are limited to five tennis scholarships and many schools give less than five. You are going to win or lose with the five or six players you recruit, so recruit them carefully.

The first place to look for players is in area high schools. Get in touch with high school coaches and let them know you will be interested in their best players. Ask them to send you a schedule of matches and tournaments. Read the papers to learn about tournaments where you can scout players. Attend as many junior events as you can. Become well enough known at tournaments that parents, coaches, and players identify you with your college or university. Then they will start coming to you instead of you always having to take the initiative.

If there is not enough local talent, look to other parts of the state, region, or even the country. Attend U.S.T.A. sanctioned events for junior players. Join the organization and you will receive a book with all the players ranked in your section. Get their names and start writing letters.

Get to know as many high school players as possible, but decide which ones can help your program and give them the most attention. If you want to improve the quality of a team, always try to recruit a player who can beat at least some of the players you already have. If you recruit for the bottom of your lineup, it will be difficult to catch up to other teams. Look for good strokes, good attitude, and a good record. If a player has good strokes, his game can continue to improve more than one with unorthodox strokes. If he has a good attitude toward school, competition, discipline, and work, he will adjust to a college program easily. A high school or junior tournament record should be impressive to merit a scholarship. The tournament record is more important than interscholastic competition, so make sure it looks promising. You may find a few sleepers out there, but not many. Most players will have established themselves as number one types or number five types by the time they reach college. Shoot for the number ones.

A second source of college players is junior colleges. The advantages of junior college players are:

1. You can get a better idea of how good they are because they have had more time to compete than high schoolers.

2. They are more mature because they are two years older.

3. They have a better idea of how to fit into a college environment.

One disadvantage is that you only have them for two years, meaning you have to recruit twice as often as with high school students. These transfer students are also often academically weak, which is why they may have started at a junior college in the first place. These players will usually have developed their games about as far as they are going to, so you must be doubly careful about judging their ability.

There was a time when a few foreign players could turn a program around in one year. Those days are gone. One reason they are gone is because of the huge number of good American players being produced by various teachers and programs throughout the country. Another reason is because so many colleges have gotten into the foreign player market. It is no longer enough just to have a foreign player; you have to have an outstanding player. There are colleges and universities in the United States who have had almost all foreign players on their squads, only to have losing seasons.

There are still good prospects to be found in countries outside of the United States, so don't give up on the idea. The amount of work involved in finding them is discouraging, but worth the trouble. Write foreign embassies and tennis associations to get started. If you can afford it, advertise in *World Tennis* and *Tennis* magazines. Give yourself and the recruit plenty of time when you decide to go for foreign athletes. Communications problems are difficult to overcome, and those problems are complicated because of special entrance requirements for foreign students at many schools. Send every piece of correspondence by air mail; regular delivery may take months. Your best selling point is an American education, so emphasize it as well as the tennis program.

When you decide on which players you want, keep in touch with them. Send them all of the literature about your school you can find. Don't send it all at once; it is better to develop a continuing relationship with players. They should be looking for something in the mail box almost every day. Get them placed on the athletic department mailing list, if there is one. Send them clippings about your team from school and local newspapers.

Find out what each prospect wants in terms of an education and a tennis program. Talk tennis with the prospect if he wants to, but talk academic standards, job opportunities on graduation, personal attention, and the conditions of the scholarship with the parents. A major university will sell itself to some students, but if you coach at a smaller school, emphasize the friendly atmosphere, low teacher-student ratios, and the idea that a player can move right in as a freshman and help the team. Sell yourself to the player and his or her parents. They have to believe in you as much as the school you represent.

Use the players on your team to help find and recruit others. If you have a good team, the word will spread. Just give the prospective player a chance to spend some time away from you and with your team members. Be careful about friends recruiting friends. Sometimes that kind of recruiting can get you two good players; other times it will just get two good friends. Listen to what your players have to say about players they think will be interested in scholarships, but get an objective opinion from someone else before you sign anyone.

Split your scholarships if you can. With the abundance of talent out there, you may be able to get two players for the price of one. It is a coach's market as long as schools are restricted to five scholarships. If you normally play six singles and three doubles in dual matches, you need eight or nine players. Injuries, attrition, school problems, and other unforeseen factors make it necessary to have backup players. Having a few more than six also keeps those six awake. If no one is going to be pushed from a position on the team, motivation will be difficult.

SCHEDULING

Start working on a spring schedule during September or October. Before you begin, try to get an idea of how good or bad you expect your team to be. Then make a schedule consistent with your team's talent. Whatever you do, don't deliberately schedule yourself into a losing season. While it helps to have good competition, it hurts to play so many teams out of your class that your players lose confidence in themselves. If you are loaded with talent, schedule anybody. If you are not so strong, arrange to play a variety of teams with whom you will be competitive. Schedule tough teams in the middle or latter part of the season. Getting off to a good start will help your players get their bodies and games in shape and to establish a winning reputation. You are going to be judged on your win-loss record, not on the names of schools you play.

Once you have decided who to play, the next problem will be deciding how frequently to play and how many total matches and tournaments should be scheduled. The solution to the first problem is relatively easy. Play often enough to make the season interesting, but not so often that they miss too many classes or get tired of tennis. One or two matches a week when the spring weather breaks is common for most teams. At the college level, fifteen to twenty dual matches and two or three tournaments is a full schedule. The toal number of matches will be affected by your budget, the weather, available competition, and district or conference rules. If you have home and away matches against every school in your league, that may not leave much time for outside competition.

If you have a choice, the dual match format for high school and college competition gives more players the opportunity to contribute to your team's success than single elimination tournaments. Tournaments reward one or two outstanding players that many teams have, but it reduces the importance of having a well-balanced team. If a dual match consists of six singles and three doubles, the players at number four, five, and six are just as important as those at the top of the lineup. If you do not have a choice about competitive formats and the single elimination tournament is popular in your area, try to provide alternate forms of competition for the less talented players. Intrasquad matches, ladders, and junior varsity programs can help keep interest up and provide a training ground for future varsity players.

Confusion about the details of dual matches can be avoided by an exchange of letters between coaches spelling out the conditions. Simply agreeing on the dates is not enough. Complaints are frequent about things such as the number of matches to be played, which courts will be used, what kind of tennis balls, and what happens in case of rain or darkness. Here is a form that could be exchanged between coaches which would eliminate potential problems (Figure 6-2).

```
┌─────────────────────────────────────────────────────────────┐
│                  DUAL MATCH AGREEMENT                        │
│  Teams Competing _____ vs. _____    │
│                                                             │
│  Date _____ Time _____    │
│                                                             │
│  Location _____  │
│                                                             │
│  Number of Boys Singles Matches _____   │
│                                                             │
│  Number of Girls Singles Matches _____   │
│                                                             │
│  Number of Boys Double Matches _____   │
│                                                             │
│  Number of Girls Doubles Matches _____   │
│                                                             │
│  Number of Mixed Doubles Matches _____   │
│                                                             │
│  Total Number of Matches _____   │
│                                                             │
│  Number of Completed Matches to Determine Winner _____   │
│                                                             │
│  Method of Scoring _____   │
│                                                             │
│  Type of Tennis Balls _____   │
│                                                             │
│  In Case of Delay or Interruption _____   │
│                                                             │
│  Agreement Regarding Coaching During Matches _____    │
│                                                             │
│  _____       │
└─────────────────────────────────────────────────────────────┘
```

Figure 6-2

SUPPLIES AND EQUIPMENT

Before you can do anything about buying supplies and equipment for your team, you have to check with the principal or athletic director to find out how much money is available and where the money will come from. Expect the worst when you go in to get this information. Tennis budgets are traditionally small. Do not be surprised if you are told that your money must come from self-generated funds earned in programs sales, car washes, concessions, or other rather unglamorous projects. It might be appropriate to complain about the amount of money allotted to tennis and to inquire about the sources of funds for other interscholastic athletics. Since you are a relatively new coach, your complaints probably will not get any immediate results, but you can start wearing down the establishment early. Once you have become known as a responsible coach and the program has earned some respectability, you will be in a better position to ask for a bigger tennis budget.

With the money available for tennis, you must then decide on a priority list of items in terms of what you need and what you can afford. The first item on most lists will be tennis balls. It is difficult to advise you on how many balls you will need because that will depend on how many players you have, how many matches at home your team will play, and how many months your fall and/or spring practices will run. It may be best to schedule your matches first, then determine the number of balls needed for home matches. With that number as a base figure and counting on match balls for practice sessions for two or three days following a match, you can begin to get an idea of how many balls to order. If you are still not sure, order a few dozen to get started, and place a second order when a pattern of use has developed. Solicit bids or at least compare prices before making a decision on which balls to purchase.

In addition to providing tennis balls, you will also have to consider racket restringing jobs, clothes and tennis shoes, and money for out-of-town matches and tournaments. Having rackets restrung can deplete a budget rapidly. A few high schools have enough money to pay for all restringing jobs, some schools allow one or two per varsity player, and others make their players pay for their own work. Here are four suggestions that may help you save money on racket strings:

1. Learn to string rackets or at least how to patch strings yourself. Not all breaks require a completely new set of strings.

2. Encourage your school to purchase a stringing machine so that players can string their own rackets. The initial investment for a machine could range from seventy-five to several hundred dollars, but the long range savings would be even more substantial.

3. Use racket string that is worthy of competition, but less expensive than gut. There are several kinds of nylon string that are relatively inexpensive and more than adequate for the average high school player.

4. Buy racket string in large quantities directly from the manufacturer instead of having to buy thirty-three feet of material in separate quantities for each stringing job done at a pro shop or sporting goods store.

The tennis clothes and shoes problem can also be sticky, but most schools provide shirts or blouses with the school emblem and perhaps one pair of shoes for each team member. The players have to buy everything else. Items such as socks and supporters may be available from supplies purchased for other school teams.

Finally, you will have to allocate some money for travel expenses such as gasoline, meals, and housing. It is not uncommon for tennis players in high school to be transported by parents, to buy meals with their own money, and to spend the night in homes of friends or host team players. This is not the way the football team travels, but you were told to expect the worst when it comes to tennis budgets. If you have the money available, take your team first class. You need no advice on how to do that.[1]

College coaches should order supplies and equipment during the summer semester or early in the fall semester. It is difficult to say how much money is needed to field a team, but you need enough money to purchase forty to eighty dozen tennis balls, new nets, and an average of five to ten restringing jobs per player. Some schools save money by buying stringing machines and letting the players restring their own rackets. Some companies provide free sets of strings to schools that qualify. Enough money should be allotted for shoes, socks, shirts, supporters, and tennis shorts in men's programs. Women's teams should be outfitted with shoes, socks, and either tennis dresses or skirts and shirts. A few colleges give their players free rackets. Travel budgets depend on the college or state policy, but mileage, meals, and housing have to be taken care of. Eating in school cafeterias and staying in guest dorms saves money.

PRACTICES

If there is a key to successful tennis programs in high schools and colleges other than having quality players, that key is the organization of the program. That part of the program which requires the organizational skills of the coach most is the planning and directing of productive practice sessions. Effectively organized practices are important at the high school level because the coach usually has a large number of players and a limited amount of space and time to work with them. If the coach cannot carefully plan how to use that space and time, the players are deprived of the opportunity to develop their games and the coach reduces the chances of winning tennis matches. The college coach has fewer athletes with which to deal and usually has better facilities in which to work, so he can be more flexible in organizing practices. However, the practice sessions are no less important than in high school. The college coach may be under more pressure to win, and purposeful practices can help a team achieve the goal of winning. College players may have developed their fundamental skills to a high degree. Planned practices help to maintain and reinforce their playing skills and also give the players a sense of discipline and team unity not always found in individual sports.

[1] Jim Brown, "Coaching Without a Background," *Scholastic Coach*, 40, no. 6 (February, 1971), 42.

If there is one ability of a tennis teacher or coach that will help you earn the respect of your students or players, it is probably the ability to observe what a player is doing wrong and to make a correction that solves the problem. A player will have confidence in someone who can suggest a change that brings immediate, observable results.

There are many activities from which to choose when planning practices. Some of these activities include warmup exercises, drills, singles competition, doubles competition, playing for position, free play, strategy sessions, weight training, and running. Which activities you choose to make up an individual practice period depend on the number of players on the team, the abilities of your players, their physical condition, the amount of time and space available, the time of year, and the purposes of a practice. Before considering all the activities mentioned above, here are some general suggestions for practicing team tennis.

If possible, conduct practices as a team with all members arriving and leaving at predetermined times. This is easier to do in high school because most students finish classes at about the same time. At the college level it may be harder to accomplish because students have classes at various times during the afternoon. However, if everyone knows that practice will begin at a certain time and that everyone is expected to be there, the feeling of discipline and team togetherness begins to develop. Some coaches impose penalties on team members who do not arrive at practice on time.

Make the practices enjoyable. As mentioned earlier in the book, tennis has the advantage over most sports of being a game that is fun to practice as well as to play. It is part of your responsibility to see that tennis does not lose that advantage. This philosophy does not rule out hard work such as drills and conditioning exercises. Your players will understand that their hard work is productive and will contribute toward improving their tennis playing ability. Enjoyment will come from the progress made as well as from the joy of playing. Practices can be made more enjoyable by using a variety of drills, by maintaining a balance of time spent working on fundamentals and time spent playing sets or matches, and by allowing players to practice with a variety of team members. Do not overwork your players. Plan practices that last long enough to achieve your goals for the day, but not so long that your players are too tired to eat or to study. Sessions should probably last from an hour and a half to two hours. Tournament circuit players have to put in more time than this, but tennis is their top priority. Your players should be concerned about their academic work as much as their tennis game. Give them an occasional day off. Tennis players can get stale, and a break away from the courts may help their game more than practicing.

Maintain a role as coach, observer, and director of the entire program rather than a role as player. There are times such as when emulating a certain style of play or filling in as a doubles fourth that you can play with or against your team members. But do not compete with your players on a regular basis or try to impress them with your playing ability. If you are a good player, your students will already know it and it will do nothing for their confidence if you beat them. If you are not a good player, you may lose their respect and you will do little to improve their skills by playing against them. Also, if you spend too much time playing during the practice sessions, you will not give enough time to the players who need your help as a teacher and coach. You cannot concentrate on your game and your players' games at the same time.

Treat all the players on the team equally. School tennis is a team matter and every player has something to contribute to the team. There is a temptation to give more time and attention to the number one and two players than to those lower in the lineup who probably need help the most. Try to promote a feeling of respect and loyalty among the players. The number one player should be just as willing to go get water for the number six player as the sixth player is for those who are better. Now look at some of the things that can happen in practice.

WARMING UP

When players begin arriving at the courts, there are several ways for them to loosen up before beginning strenuous work. Some coaches have the players jog around the tennis complex or jog a quarter-mile. Others prefer calisthenics or stretching for a few minutes. Stretching will be given special consideration next. The most traditional and probably least effective way to warm up is by hitting. It is the easiest way to get started, but there is a tendency not to exercise all of the muscles until actual play or difficult drills begin. When that happens, there is a greater chance of injuries. A warmup period should prepare a player for strenuous activity without tiring him in the process.

STRETCHING

Teams in many sports begin their warmup period with stretching exercises. Stretching is a more systematic form of warming up which athletes have engaged in for centuries. Joints in the body have normal ranges of motion through which they move. Muscles control these ranges, and tightness in the muscles will decrease the amount of movement in a joint. With increased flexibility, the range of motion will be increased while the probability of injury to the joint and surrounding muscles will be decreased. That is the bottom line on stretching—more flexibility and less chance of strains and sprains. Tennis players should do the exercises daily or at least on days they play. Flexibility is not a fixed factor. It can be improved or reduced. Jogging prior to stretching stimulates circulation. If you use the exercises illustrated here, follow the order as presented. Hold each stretch ten seconds unless otherwise indicated. Set a goal of at least five sets of each exercise if you have that much time. If not, consider doing some of the exercises before you go to the courts or taking a longer than usual warmup hitting the ball.[2]

Figure 6–3   The player on the left is holding her neck and head upright and stretching her neck alternately to the right and the left. The player on the right is rotating his body to the right and left, trying not to rotate his hips in the process.

[2] The information on stretching was provided by Jim Murphy, athletic trainer at McNeese State University.

Figure 6–4 Camille (left) is leaning forward and down with both feet pointing straight to stretch the Achilles tendon. Alan (right) is leaning forward and down, but the front foot is pointing forward and the back one is sideways to stretch the groin.

Figure 6–5 Camille (left) is standing with her legs straight and feet together, reaching to grasp her legs as low as possible. Alan is reaching to touch his ankles and should be trying to touch his knees with his chin.

Figure 6–6 Camille alternately tries to touch each knee to the ground, then tries with both legs at the same time. Alan slides his hips toward his feet without moving his hands. This stretches the shoulder girdle.

Figure 6–7 Camille goes through the serving motion several times with the racket cover on the racket. Alan holds his racket at the ends and reaches back as far as he can.

Drills are an effective way to master the various mechanical components of any sport, and some time should be given to drills in almost every practice. The problem many coaches have is in determining how much time should be given to drills and how much time should be programmed for competitive play. Some people feel that teams should spend more time drilling during the fall season or early during the spring semester before matches begin. When the schedule starts, they prefer to prepare their players for matches by spending more time in intrasquad competition. Other coaches do not share that opinion. They feel that preseason practice should consist of competition and that drills should be used during the season to prepare for specific situations or to correct problems which have developed during competition. If you are undecided about how much time to allot to drills, experiment with both methods. What works for one team or coach may not work for another. A compromise balance between drilling and playing will probably develop in each team's case.

Regardless of when drills are used and how much time is spent on drills, there are principles which apply to this segment of the practice routine. First, drills should have a purpose, and that purpose should be explained to the players. Drills should simulate game situations as much as possible. Any potential game situation or probable sequence of shots can be made into a drill. Within reason, drills should be fun. If the players dread going through some drills, it may be because the coach is not utilizing a variety of activities. Players will respond better to a variety of drills, and the response may also be better if a drill is completed while interest in it is at a peak. Players will look forward to practicing that drill the next day rather than hoping the coach will not include it in the practice schedule. Use tennis drills that are simple to explain and simple to understand. Too many x's and o's are confusing. Finally, remember to plan drills so that a progression of learning or practicing is possible. Difficult drills for beginning or intermediate players may do more to discourage them than to improve their skills.

SINGLES COMPETITION

It is important that the coach plan who will play against each other in singles and doubles during practices. If the players are always allowed to make these decisions, there is the possibility that the same players will always want to play each other, that grudge matches will take up too much practice time, or that cliques will develop among the squad members. If the coach arranges the matches, he can ensure that everyone gets to practice against a variety of styles and that there is a balance of competition within the team. He can also do a better job of planning other practice segments if he knows in advance who will be available.

DOUBLES COMPETITION

Practicing doubles is one of the most neglected phases of team tennis. The young players are usually more interested in the activity and challenge provided in head-to-head singles play, and the coach knows that most of the team's dual matches will involve more singles play than doubles. Consequently, practicing doubles frequently becomes something the team does after all other work is completed. The emphasis on singles is understandable, but regrettable. Doubles can be as enjoyable as singles, as rewarding, as demanding, and as important to team success. All close dual matches will be decided by what happens in doubles competition. Teams of equal strength usually split the singles matches, and the team with the best doubles combinations is in a position to win.

The point of all this information is to encourage you to spend time during practices on doubles. Try to arrange your combinations early in the preseason workouts so that teammates have time to get used to each other and to develop a successful partnership. In planning practices, allocate time for doubles work just as you do for singles, drills, and other parts of the daily routine.

PLAYING FOR POSITION

While doubles competition is neglected in practices, playing for positions in the lineup is overemphasized. What happens may be seen in the team that begins serious workouts for the spring season immediately after the Christmas holidays. The first few weeks are spent in conditioning and trying to regain some of the preholiday form. After that period, everyone really begins to get into a groove by working hard on strokes. All of a sudden, the first match or tournament of the season is about two or three weeks away, and the coach realizes that the lineup is not set. A round robin is hastily arranged, and everybody plays everybody else every day for two weeks. There are several problems that this approach creates. First, you probably do not have time to finish the round robin. With poor weather, weekends, missed practices, and injuries, there are just not enough days to play every match. With only eight members on a team you must play twenty-eight matches for a complete round robin tournament. The second problem is that you spend all of your practice time in competition, which forces you to neglect the other important phases of practice. There is also the possibility that an upset during the intra-squad competition could result in a lineup that does not reflect your players' true abilities. The last and most serious complication is that your players may be so tired from playing for position in practice that they cannot perform well when the season begins.

What can you do to avoid these problems? Do not commit yourself to complete a round robin tournament as the criteria for the team's lineup. Assume the responsibility of deciding yourself who will play each position. A pecking order is usually established on tennis teams, and players know how good they are and who they can beat. Therefore, the coach can arrange only the matches among players of similar ability or when there is some uncertainty about a given position. It does very little good for the number one player to play the number eight player for position, so why waste practice time letting them play. If you must play a round robin, allow plenty of time for completion before the first match. If you do not finish in time, you can do it after the season starts. Never place yourself in a position of having one match to be the only factor in determining a player's position for the season. Positions on a team should be determined by performance over a long period of time, not on what happened one day out of six months. Once the lineup has been established, it should remain stable for the season. There may be some changes as players improve or consistently defeat someone higher in the lineup, but the business of players constantly challenging each other after the schedule has begun can be time consuming, tiring, and unsettling to the team morale.

FREE PLAY

There may be times when the players on a tennis team should be free just to play for fun, but these times are limited. The whole idea of playing tennis is to play for fun, but structured play during practice can be fun. If that is not enough, there is plenty of time on weekends, at night, during holiday breaks, and during the summer for free play. If this advice sounds rather dogmatic, remember that you are coaching a varsity athletic team, not an intramural, recreation, or church league team. It is doubtful that coaches in other sports allow their players much free time during practices.

STRATEGY SESSIONS

Most tennis coaches integrate any comments they have on strategy into on-the-court work rather than making those comments in a classroom type lecture. There may be times when it is appropriate for the coach to call all of his players together to discuss a match or some phase of the game.

The best time to have a group strategy meeting is immediately before a practice. Players can then put into practice the ideas just discussed.

WEIGHT TRAINING

Tennis players are not known as very conscientious workers when it comes to lifting weights. They just want to play the game. Coaches frequently do not know enough about weight training to incorporate it into their programs. There are definite, tangible results possible from an organized strength building program, and most tennis players could benefit from a regimen designed for their individual needs. Weight training programs are more effective in the fall semester or early during the spring semester because there is more time for the players to work with the weights than during the regular season. If weight work is done during the season, the goal should be to maintain levels of strength previously achieved. This can be done with a few minutes of work two or three times a week.

The type of program will vary with the individual and should be directed toward development of general muscular fitness. Tennis players will be particularly interested in increasing strength in the wrists, forearms, shoulders, and legs. Exercises which may be helpful in these areas are curls, push-ups, pull-ups, rope jumping, and leg presses. Some weight training can be done at the tennis courts without special equipment. Swinging weighted rackets, two rackets simultaneously, or rackets with covers are effective exercises.

If you are not well enough informed about weight training to install a program, consult a physical education teacher or athletic trainer. With knowledge about the goals you want to achieve in terms of increasing muscular fitness and with information about your particular athletes, he should be able to advise you on how to start a program.

RUNNING

As with the weight program, a running program should be directed toward specific goals. Most of the hard work can be done early in the year or semester, but it is common for high school and college coaches to conclude practice sessions with sprints or laps. Sprints seem to be more useful to the tennis player because the game requires starting, stopping, quick bursts of speed, running a few steps at a time, and changing directions. Running laps and cross country running may help build strength in the legs and certainly help to build pulmonary fitness, but leg strength can be increased in ways already mentioned and lung capacity is not that important in tennis. If you want to put running into your conditioning program, try sprints of ten to forty yards; wave drills in which players move forward, backward, or laterally at your command; or up-and-back drills in which players run forward at the sound of the first command, backward on the second sound, forward on the third, etc. You can design your own continuity conditioning drills by combining weight training, calisthenics, and running into five, ten, or fifteen minute continuous movement periods.

OTHER CONSIDERATIONS

Remember to take these factors into consideration before organizing practices:

1. **The number of players on your team.** The larger the number, the more detailed your planning must be. Have something for everybody to do at all times.

2. **The abilities of your players.** At the high school level, spend more time teaching fundamentals and less time playing matches. Use drills that are consistent with the talent of your players.

3. **The physical condition of your players.** Get them into shape before the bulk of court work begins so you can concentrate on strokes and game situations when the time comes. Give them a rest after difficult matches and do very light work the day before a match or tournament.

4. **The amount of time and space available.** These factors are related to the number of players on the team, but use space efficiently. There will usually be recreational tennis players waiting to use any courts not in use by the team. Allow others to use the courts as long as they do not interfere with what you are doing.

5. **The time of year in relation to your schedule of matches.** Organize your practice program so that your team is fresh and at its peak when interscholastic or intercollegiate competition begins or when the conference tournament is played. Do not burn them out early.

6. **The specific purposes for a practice session.** Have goals in mind you want to reach in every practice. Your players should leave the courts feeling that they have accomplished something.

Now that you have some ideas about what can go into a tennis practice, you must consider the alternatives and design your own program. A typical workout consists of a warm-up period followed by drills, a period of singles or doubles play, and conditioning exercises. A sample practice schedule is given on the next page. (Players are numbered 1 through 8; courts are lettered A through D.)

3:30	Stretching exercises	All players	Court A
3:35	Groundstroke drills	#1 and #3 #2 and #4 #5 and #7 #6 and #8	Court A Court B Court C Court D
3:50	Drills for the serve and service return	#1, #2, #3, #4 #5, #6, #7, #8	Court A Court B
4:05	Drills for the net game Singles play	#1 and #2 #3 and #4 #5 vs. #7 #6 vs. #8	Court A Court B Court C Court D
4:20	Doubles play	#1 and #2 vs. #3 and #4	Court A
5:00	Ten minutes of conditioning drills	All players	Courts A and B

Figure 6-8

SCOUTING

Most tennis coaches are too involved with their own player's games to have the time or interest to scout future opponents. But if you know something about your team's opponents, you can help prepare your players to compete with them. Since tennis teams usually see each other more than once a season and since most players represent a school for more than one year, it is possible to develop informative postmatch scouting reports.

You will not have time nor should you take the time to make scouting reports yourself. It is better to have each player evaluate the opponent he or she played. Here are some advantages of postmatch, player-prepared scouting reports:

1. They can be used by the player in later matches if the same opponent is played.
2. They can be used the next year against returning opponents.

203

3.   Scouting reports force your players to be conscious of the opponents' style of play.

4.   The reports encourage some players to evaluate their own styles more closely.

5.   They consume less time than a report prepared by the coach on each opponent.

6.   The reports may stimulate a higher degree of interest among some of your players.

The scouting report form should be short, simple, and easy to read. Although each coach can prepare a form that is best for his situation, certain basic information must be included. That information consists of the opponent's name and school, the date of the match, the type of surface played on, and the weather conditions. The first section is followed by information concerning each of the opponent's strokes, his strongest shots, weakest shots, unusual shots, quickness, strength, and endurance. The report concludes with comments on the opponent's honesty in making calls and his style of play, and an overall evaluation of his game.

Elaborate scouting reports should be avoided. Most players would rather play the game than analyze it. They should prepare the reports as soon after a match as possible, while the shots and situations are still fresh in their minds. After a match away from home, the reports can be completed during the trip back. For home matches, the players can take the forms home and return them at practice the next day.

How can the information be used best? First, the files should be stored in the coach's office and made accessible to every player. The team members should be encouraged to come in on their own to read about future opponents. Two players who have faced a mutual opponent might compare notes, or the coach might review a report with an individual player, possibly making additions and modifications. The reports can also be discussed at team meetings. This will help promote team unity and give less experienced or observant players an opportunity to listen to the observations made by their teammates.

Coaches should not expect a wealth of new information from the reports. If each player can observe and record a single strength, weakness, or characteristic of an opponent (or himself), the report will be worth the effort. The benefits from postmatch scouting are more subjective than objective, and are more difficult to measure. The reward may come months or even years later.

The form shown in this chapter (Figure 6-9) was designed for relatively experienced players. For younger, less analytic players, a multiple choice type of questionnaire can be developed. For example, "What was

```
                    SCOUTING SUMMARY
Player  Brenda Marcus                    School  Barbe

Date of Match    5-5            Reported by  Emily Harold

Results:  Harold              (beat)    Marcus
                               lost to
Score   6-3, 6-4              Type of Court  Laykold

Weather   Mild, Windy                        (RH) - LH

Attitude  Very Competitive; Serious

Forehand  Likes to use Topspin

Backhand  Two-handed; Likes Crosscourt

First Serve  Flat, Hard

Second Serve  Weak, Flat

Net Game  Good with Volleys; Strong, But
          Inconsistent Overhead

Best Shot  FH

Weakest Shot  Second Serve

Unusual Shots  —

Quickness  Nothing Special     Strength  Average

Endurance  ?                   Speed  Slow

Calls  Honest

Style of Play  Aggressive

Comments  —
```

Figure 6–9

your opponent's style of play, (1) serve and volley, (2) retriever-pusher, (3) unorthodox, (4) no special style?"[3]

PUBLICITY

If you don't remember anything else about publicizing high school and college tennis programs, remember this: if you—the coach—do not push tennis with the media, no one will. It would be nice if newspaper re-

[3] Jim Brown, "Post-Match Scouting in Tennis," *Scholastic Coach*, 43, no. 7 (March, 1974), 74.

porters and radio-TV announcers would come to you for match results, story lines, quotes, and information about your team, but it just doesn't happen very often. Writers and sportscasters are going to cover the major sports like baseball, basketball, and football, which are usually the sports they know best. So if you want publicity to draw spectators, to keep the name of your school before the public, to help you with recruiting, and in general to promote tennis—get ready to do it yourself. Here's how.

If you have any writing ability, learn to write news stories. Sportswriters may be more likely to run your stories if you do some of the work for them. Even if your story is not perfect, it will give the writer something to work with instead of a list of scores. Indicate who or what the story is about, when it happens, and where it takes place in the first paragraph. First paragraphs seldom run more than one sentence. Limit subsequent paragraphs to three or four sentences each. Keep the most important parts of the story near the top of the article. Close with information about the next match, tournament, or event. Then give a complete resume of match results, if that is what you are writing about, after the last paragraph. If you are not sure about what to do, watch the sports pages and follow the style you see there. Just change the names and scores. If you have absolutely no talent for writing, don't try. Just be ready to give complete, accurate results and information when you call reporters.

Get to know sports reporters in your community. They will give publicity to somebody they know, like, and trust. If a stranger calls in a story, it may or may not make the news. If a friend or acquaintance needs help, he or she will probably get it.

Find out what the sports desk hours are at local outlets and report your scores during times when you know your friends will be there. The five to eight o'clock period in the afternoon seems to be a universally bad time to get in touch with reporters. Later in the evenings and early to mid-morning are good times to call. Know what other sports events are on the schedule and avoid conflicts with bigger stories when possible. Television and radio stations need plenty of time to prepare copy and there is a lot of competition for very little air time. When you call in a story, keep it short. They do not have time to run long stories.

Be fair, complete, and reliable with publicity information. Don't just call your favorite paper, station, or reporter. Call or write to all of them in your area, and time it so that no one source of information gets to break a story sooner than the others. You may have to learn what each publication's policy is regarding simultaneous submissions. Give all the information they will take, then let each writer or announcer do the editing. Submit your stories regularly, not when you think about it or only when your team wins. Prompt reporting is even more important for out-of-town matches. Most places will let you call collect if you arrange things before you leave on a trip. If you do not call in the results before leaving on your return trip, make arrangements for someone at the host school to do so.

Matches and tournaments can be publicized around your high school or college in a variety of ways. Work closely with the school paper's sports editor and, at the college level, the sports information director (SID). Provide as much information as you can. Talk to the SID about making up schedule cards or brochures describing the tennis program. Wallet size schedules can have a picture on one side the dates of matches with an advertisement on the other. Brochures can include pictures, schedules, vital information of players, school records, conference records, names of former lettermen and champions, a biographical sketch of the coach, and publicity about the school. If the sports editor or SID needs leads for tennis stories, your players' backgrounds, summer circuit results, rankings, academic achievements, and plans after graduation are ideas to start with. The foreign player angle at the college level opens many areas of interest to tennis fans. Why did they come to your school? How were they recruited? What adjustment problems do they have?

Attract people to matches and tournaments by flooding the campus and community with posters, leaflets, signs, banners, and bumper stickers. Get team members to hand out or post leaflets the day before a match. Organize booster clubs on and off campus. These supporters can not only attend matches and take a special interest in the players, they can also help at home matches as linespersons, umpires, score keepers, and ball persons. Publicize home matches on billboards, bulletin boards, and marquees (Figure 6-10). If you coach at a college, invite area high school players to all home matches. Give them a special place to watch matches. See that they get to know your players.

High school and college teams, even good ones, can go unnoticed unless you become a tennis promoter. Not every high school has a newspaper and not every college has a sports information director, so you may have to do a lot more than coach your team. Whatever the situation, do not assume that if your team wins, the publicity will take care of itself. You take care of it.

INJURIES

As if responsibilities such as recruiting, scheduling, ordering, organizing practices, scouting, and publicizing the tennis team are not enough, you may also be the team trainer. Most tennis injuries do not involve serious emergencies, so coaches who have some information about taking care of common ailments can give reasonably good treatment and advice about medical care. Keep a first aid kit at the courts during practices as well as

Figure 6–10 A bank marquee is one example of using public signs to publicize tennis events.

matches. Blisters, sprains, pulled muscles (strains), cramps, shin splints, and tennis elbows are the problems you are most likely to encounter.

BLISTERS

Beginners and people who have not played for a while are probably going to have blisters on the racket hand and on the feet, in that order. A blister is an accumulation of fluid between the top two layers of skin. Blisters are caused by irritation; in this case, irritation between the racket and the hand, and between the foot and the sock, shoe, or court.

There are ways to reduce the possibility and frequency of blisters. Play for short periods of time when beginning a practice session and gradually increase the amount of playing time as your skin becomes tougher. Playing tennis for two or three hours the first day out is a sure way to get blisters. Make sure that the racket grip is the right size. Rackets with grips that are too large or too small tend to slip on impact and that increases the amount of friction. Keep the racket handle as dry as possible. The more it slips, the more irritation to the hand will occur. Wear a tennis glove or tape on the areas of the hand most likely to blister. You may lose a sense of touch wearing a glove, but it can be removed after your hand toughens. Cutting out the finger tips of the glove can restore the feel between hand and racket. Avoid blisters on the feet by putting powder in the shoes or socks, wearing two pairs of socks, and wearing shoes that fit.

If you get a blister and have to continue playing, clean the area with alcohol or soap and water, sterilize a needle (burn it with a lighted match), and make an opening in the skin so that the fluid can drain. Then place a bandage over the entire area. Some players can play with the pain caused by blisters and others cannot. If you or your players keep on playing, have first aid supplies nearby, because the areas on the hands and feet likely to blister are difficult to bandage, and the bandages will come off as a result of movement and perspiration. Vaseline applications can reduce the friction. In some cases, the top layer of skin can be removed, but this should only be done by a trainer or physician. If you do not have to play tennis for several days, leave the blister as it is. The fluid buildup is a natural protective reaction for the irritated skin below. The skin will heal and the fluid will be reabsorbed if the area is protected long enough.

SPRAINS

A sprain is an injury to a joint which usually damages blood vessels, ligaments, and tendons. The injury is frequently caused by forcing a joint beyond the normal range of motion. In tennis, the most common sprains occur in the ankles. The symptoms are swelling, tenderness, discoloration, and pain, especially upon motion or when weight is placed on the joint. An ankle can be sprained and fractured at the same time. The degree of pain should not be the only factor in trying to determine whether or not a break has occurred. Sprains can hurt as much as breaks.

Remember "I-C-E" for first aid of sprains. The "I" is for ice—twenty minutes on and twenty off during the twenty four hours after the injury. The purpose is to reduce the flow of fluid into the area by constricting blood vessels. The "C" stands for compression—applying pressure to the affected part, also to control swelling. Compression is difficult unless you have the right supplies, so it may not be possible without medical help. "E" means to elevate the leg or any other part that has been sprained.

Do not return to the courts too soon after a sprain. Sprained joints may be more susceptible to subsequent sprains. When the injured player does resume play, the ankle may be taped for support.

STRAINS

Strains are tears in muscle tissue and connective tissue. They are also called pulled muscles and muscle tears. They can be caused by overexertion, sudden movement, fatigue, and not warming up properly. Pulled muscles in the legs, back, and wrist are common in tennis players. The symptoms are pain when the muscles are exercised, general soreness, and muscle spasms. Most trainers now use the method of applying ice packs every twenty minutes for the first day after a muscle has been injured. If the athlete continues to play, heat to increase circulation may help before competition and ice would again be helpful immediately after playing.

Trainers, therapists, and physicians can treat pulled muscles by more sophisticated methods than you can as a coach. If the injury is serious enough, get help from a specialist.

CRAMPS

Heat cramps are involuntary contractions of muscles and can be caused by a variety of factors. Fatigue, overexertion, and an electrolyte imbalance seem to trigger cramps in many tennis players. Conditioning programs could probably eliminate some of the cramps caused by fatigue and overexertion. The electrolyte imbalance can be avoided by maintaining a balance between potassium, sodium, and water. The idea is to replace all three in proper proportions during and after competition. Loading up with salt before a match probably won't help. Eating bananas might.

Pressure on the cramped muscle may help it return to its normal condition. Something called "acupinch" may also help. Regardless of where the cramp is, some trainers grab the area between the upper lip and nose and exert a forceful pinch. It hurts, but it also makes the cramp subside in many cases. Don't ask why.

SHIN SPLINTS

A shin splint is a rather vague term referring to pain in the front part of the lower leg. There are a lot of things that could go wrong down there, but it is safe to say that shin splints involve inflammation of tendons and muscles in that area. They can be caused by running on hard surfaces, poor conditioning, poor running technique, or congenital problems. Poor arch supports can also cause or compound the problem.

Tennis players are likely to suffer from shin splints early in the season, especially if they practice on hard courts. The treatment involves taping and elevating the arch, running in proper shoes, resting, and applying ice.

Fill a cup with water and freeze it. Then rub the affected area with the ice for seven to ten minutes. That should cut down on the inflammation. The best advice is to try to avoid shin splints by sound conditioning and practice periods which allow players to gradually adjust to new surfaces.

TENNIS ELBOW

Tennis elbow is an inflammation of the tissue around the end of the bone in the upper arm at the elbow. Tendonitis is probably a more accurate description of the condition. Bone fragments could cause the pain, as could the constant impact of the ball on the racket (producing stress in the forearm muscles), improper technique on certain strokes, weak muscles, and the use of a racket not suited for the player. The primary symptom is severe pain in the elbow area. The pain may occur only on certain shots or in certain positions of the arm, but if the injury is serious enough, there may be pain to the touch and even pain when the player shakes hands or brushes his teeth.

No single method of treatment is effective for everyone, so see a physician or trainer if it is a serious problem. If not, try ice packs for twenty minutes, two or three times a day. Aspirin may relieve the pain temporarily, and rest is a more permanent alternative. Elbow braces and constricting bands around the forearm work for some people. Even changing rackets can help, if the new racket either absorbs more of the pressure or shifts it to another part of your arm.

DEVELOPING PROFESSIONALLY

Whether you are a coach, teacher, program director, or player, there are many ways to increase your knowledge of the sport and to improve your instructional and administrative skills. There are national, regional, state, and local tennis organizations you can join. There are tennis and coaching publications which contain news, advertisements for products and services, and instructional articles. Besides holding memberships in professional organizations and keeping up with tennis literature, you can participate in a variety of activities which will help your game or the games of your team members and students.

ORGANIZATIONS

The United States Tennis Association (U.S.T.A.) defines itself as "a nationwide, noncommercial membership organization devoted to the development of tennis as a means of healthful recreation and physical fitness and to the maintenance of high standards of amateurism, fair play, and sportsmanship." The association's main office is in New York, and there are seventeen sections throughout the United States. Officials and members in each section promote and govern a variety of activities in their area. Where a section encompasses more than one state, there may be state associations also. Within this structure there are almost one hundred committees dealing with subjects such as rules, rankings, facilities, and education. These committees work with thousands of volunteers at the regional level. Following are some of the programs administered by the U.S.T.A.

Players who join the U.S.T.A. will probably benefit most from the tournaments, publications, and junior development programs. There are tournaments for amateurs and professionals, men and women, and for children and adults. Members of the organization can receive the official publication, *Tennis USA*, as part of their membership package. The junior development program ranges from services designed for schools, parks, and recreation centers to tournaments which provide outstanding players the opportunity to earn state, regional, and national rankings and recognition.

The Education and Research Center is located in Princeton, New Jersey, and is especially helpful to teachers, coaches, and club professionals. By writing to the center, you can get information on subjects such as group instruction, coaching, program planning, publications, facilities, lighting, and teaching workshops. The center also maintains a national film library, film service, and index on all tennis films. There are also sectional and regional film libraries with films available to the public.

The U.S.T.A. sponsors workshops and clinics throughout the country in conjunction with other organizations and agencies. A National Tennis Teachers Conference is held each year during the U.S. Open tournament. Other conferences are conducted with the President's Council on Physical Fitness and the Sports and Tennis Industry's National Buying Shows in Florida and California.

Below are the addresses for the main office of the U.S.T.A. and for the Education and Research Center:

United States Tennis Association
51 East 42nd Street
New York, N.Y.   10017

United States Tennis Association
Education and Research Center
729 Alexander Road
Princeton, New Jersey   08540

The United States Professional Tennis Association (U.S.P.T.A.) is an organization composed primarily of teaching professionals. There are seventeen geographical divisions which are managed by a board of officers. Committees are appointed at the national and regional levels to supervise activities such as budgets, awards, testing, education, ethics, publicity, and tournaments. To become a member, a person must submit a membership application, successfully complete written and practical examinations covering material on tennis instruction, pro shop management, and administration of programs, and pay membership dues.

Some of the benefits of joining the U.S.P.T.A. are

1. being associated with a professional organization;
2. participating in insurance programs;
3. competing in the organization's tournaments;
4. using the U.S.P.T.A. Job Bureau;
5. having access to a film library
6. receiving *Tennis Magazine*, a monthly newsletter, and a yearly directory.

The American Alliance for Health, Physical Education, Recreation, and Dance (A.A.H.P.E.R.D.) is an organization with headquarters in Washington, D.C., whose membership consists primarily of health and physical education teachers and coaches. This organization is also divided into regional and state divisions. Members can affiliate themselves with any of seven associations within the Alliance. Many tennis coaches belong to the National Association for Sport and Physcial Education (N.A.S.P.E.) and to the National Association for Girls and Women in Sports (N.A.G.W.S.), which are two of the seven associations. A.A.H.P.E.R.D., N.A.S.P.E., and N.A.G.W.S. distribute literature, conduct research, promote physical fitness, sponsor conventions, conferences, and workshops, and cooperate with other organizations such as the U.S.T.A. in advancing sport and physical education related activities.

PUBLICATIONS

Magazines containing tennis related material are usually directed toward one of three groups: tennis players and fans, tennis coaches and teachers, and persons with commercial tennis interests.

Tennis Magazine and *World Tennis* are two of the more widely circulated magazines for players and fans. These publications have news stories, tournament results, features, editorial comment, columns, schedules, and instructional articles. Each is a monthly publication. Both come with memberships in the U.S.P.T.A. and the U.S.T.A., respectively.

Athletic Journal, Coach and Athlete, Scholastic Coach, and *The Coaching Clinic* are not tennis magazines, but are general coaching magazines which have articles related to tennis teaching and coaching. These articles usually appear in issues published during the January to June period.

Tennis Industry and *Tennis Trade* are tennis business magazines, and have information for the teaching professional, tennis shop owner, and club manager. The articles are specifically written to help the professional become a more effective business person.

Too many books have been written recently to give a complete list or review, but some of them stand out as being particularly helpful for either players or the teacher-coach group. Players should read these:

- *Tennis, Anyone?*—Dick Gould
- *The Inner Game of Tennis*—Tim Gallwey
- *Tennis Without Lessons*—Jim Brown
- *Inside Tennis*—Jim Leighton
- *Tennis: The Bassett System*—Glenn Bassett
- *Tennis for the Future*—Vic Braden and Bill Bruns
- *The Compleat Pocket Tennis Strategist*—Donald Sonneman
- *Use Your Head in Tennis*—Bob Harman
- *The Game of Singles in Tennis*—William Talbert and Bruce Old
- *The Game of Doubles in Tennis*—William Talbert and Bruce Old
- *The Code*—Nick Powell
- *Tennis Drills for Self Improvement*—Steve Kraft (ed.)
- *Tennis Equipment*—Steve Fiott

Teachers and coaches would learn something by reading:

- *Advantage Tennis: Racket Work, Tactics, and Logic*—John Barnaby
- *Teaching and Coaching Tennis*—John Kenfield
- *Tennis for the Player, Teacher and Coach*—Chet and Bill Murphy
- *Tennis: Teaching, Coaching, and Directing Programs*—Jim Brown

- *Complete Book of Championship Tennis Drills*—Bill Murphy
- *Tennis*—Elaine Mason
- *The Tennis Workbook*—Eve Kraft
- *Advanced Tennis for Coaches, Teachers, and Players*—Gundars Tilmanis

ACTIVITIES

There are additional ways to become a better player, teacher, or coach:

1. Join or organize local tennis organizations or groups which promote tennis, hold clinics, and conduct competition.
2. Participate in or observe local, state, regional, and national tournaments.
3. Attend tennis camps.
4. Take private or group lessons.
5. Attend workshops, clinics, and conferences for teachers and coaches.
6. Become an active U.S.T.A. member by serving on committees or running for offices.
7. Join booster groups for high school and college teams.
8. Contribute money and time to tennis support groups.
9. Play tennis regularly for fun and fitness.
10. Recruit others to participate in the sport.

REVIEW QUESTIONS

1. What information should a high school coach obtain from players at the first fall team meeting?

2. How could a college coach go about looking for high school players good enough to be considered for a college team?

3. What factors should be considered in making a high school or college schedule?

4. How can a coach save money on racket stringing for team members?

5.   List eight possible practice activities.

6.   Design a practice schedule for twelve high school players (six boys and six girls), four courts, and two hours.

7.   Figure out how many tennis balls should be ordered to field a team of eight players for a two month season with ten dual matches (six singles, three doubles) and an average of four practice days a week.

8.   How can a coach increase the amount of publicity a team receives?

9.   Give a one sentence first aid suggestion for each of the following cases:

    a.   blister on the index finger of the racket hand,

    b.   sprained ankle,

    c.   pulled muscle in the lower back,

    d.   cramp in the thigh,

    e.   shin splint,

    f.   tennis elbow.

10.   How can a player reduce the possibility of getting a blister?

11.   What services are provided by the United States Tennis Association Education and Research Center that would benefit a high school or college coach?

12.   What are some of the benefits of joining the United States Professional Tennis Association?

13.   List five magazines containing tennis related articles.

14.   List the names of five tennis authors and the books they have written.

Chapter 7

Competition

ORGANIZING AND DIRECTING COMPETITION

Before a tennis competition such as a tournament can be held, many decisions must be made. These decisions may be made by the tennis administrator such as a coach, club pro, camp sports director, or recreation coordinator, or a tournament steering committee may be formed to consider recommendations and to make the necessary decisions.

Among the decisions which must be considered in the early planning stage is which kind of tournament to conduct. The most common forms are the single elimination, the single elimination with a consolation bracket, the round robin, the ladder, and the pyramid. The single elimination format is used when there is a large number of participants present at one site and not much time available to complete the competition. Round robins, ladders, and pyramids are used when continuous competition over a period of weeks or months is the objective. Each of these forms of competition will be discussed in detail later in this chapter.

The tournament director or committee must also make some early decisions about money. How much money will be needed for the tournament? Where will the money come from? Will the players be charged entry fees? If so, how much? Will tennis balls be supplied by tournament officials or by the players? How many and what type of awards must be purchased?

A decision must be made regarding facilities. Are there enough courts available to accommodate the number of players expected to enter the tournament? Are the courts in good enough condition to conduct formal competition? Are there additional courts available within a reasonable distance of the primary tournament site should they be needed?

The committee has to decide who is eligible to compete in this event. Will the tournament be open to people of all ages or will there be divisions for juniors, adults, junior veterans, and seniors? Is the competition to be for men, women, or both? Will participants have to be affiliated with a club, organization, or school to be eligible? Will entries be restricted to residents of a city, state, or region? Will the tournament be open to players of all levels, or will there be divisions for novices and advanced players?

In addition to the general format of competition, the specific form that individual matches will take must be determined. Will play be restricted to singles, or will there be doubles and mixed doubles? Will matches consist of pro sets, two out of three sets, three out of five sets, or some other arrangement? If tie-breakers are to be used, which method would be appropriate? Will there be a forfeit time allowed to participants? If so, how long? How many events will a player be allowed to enter?

How much time will be necessary to complete the tournament? Will the tournament schedule interfere with any other tennis activities planned for the courts? Will there be other athletic, social, business, or educational events which may conflict with the dates planned for the tournament?

Finally, are there enough people who are qualified and willing to conduct the tournament? It is not difficult to find lots of people who would enjoy hosting or participating in a tennis event. It is very difficult to find these people when the work of planning and conducting competition begins. So, once the preliminary decisions regarding the tournament have been made, volunteer workers must be recruited, coordinated, and supervised. Besides the tournament steering committee, there may be a need to organize others into committees to help coordinate various efforts. The people on these committees should be enlisted and told about their responsibilities as much as six months prior to a tournament in which there will be a large number of participants. This is especially true of the open single elimination tournament with many out of town players. Junior age division events also need special preparation and involvement of much of the tennis community. Here are possible committee titles and suggestions for those who serve on the committees.

TOURNAMENT COMMITTEE

This committee has responsibilities in addition to deciding on the type of tournament, funding, facilities, and eligibility. If the tournament is to be sanctioned by the United States Tennis Association or any other organization, the committee should make a request for sanctioning and for playing dates. These requests must be made prior to yearly deadlines already established by each sanctioning organization. If local sponsorship by a club, civic group, or school is necessary, the tournament steering committee should seek such support a year to six months before the tournament is tentatively scheduled.

REGISTRATION

The registration committee is responsible for registering participants when they first arrive at a tournament, and the same group can also be asked to prepare and distribute entry blanks. Entry blanks should be distributed a month to three weeks before the date of the tournament, and players should return the forms at least one week before the event begins. An entry blank should contain rules and information about the tournament, a schedule of events, space for vital information about the entrant, a list of events in which the player may indicate his plans for participation, the address to which the entry form and fees may be mailed, and a statement releasing the tournament officials from responsibility for damages, losses, or injuries sustained during the tournament.

Registration of players usually begins the day before a tournament starts and continues until all players have reported in and doubles entries have closed. Registration tables should be placed at a central location near the courts. Specific instructions should be given to the registration workers about their duties and the times they are expected to be at the tables. Players will have been notified to report to the registration area when they arrive. The registrars should have some system of recording the names of players who have checked in. Entry fees may also be collected and doubles entries accepted at the registration site. Finally, workers may be asked to give the registering players information about housing, and to tell them where the brackets have been posted.

COMPETITION

A competition committee may be established for the purpose of seeing that matches are played on schedule and according to the rules. A tournament referee heads the committee and is the principal authority in matters related to play for the tournament as a whole. Umpires and linespersons may also serve on this committee. Umpires oversee individual matches by introducing players to the audience, keeping score, repeating linespersons' calls, and generally seeing that a given match proceeds normally. Linespersons are assigned to watch specific boundary lines on the court and to make calls of "out" or "fault" when necessary. These officials may also be responsible for calling foot faults on the server.

One of the greatest services a junior tournament director can provide is to see that conduct rules are established and enforced. The conduct of many spoiled, undisciplined tournament players is disgusting. If the rules regarding their behavior are made clear at the beginning of competiton and rigidly enforced with penalty points, disqualifications, and notification of parents, there will be fewer problems. It is unfortunate that tournament directors, pros, and coaches have to handle discipline problems that parents should have taken care of, but they do.

TENNIS BALLS

This committee may seem to have rather limited responsibilities, but some tournament directors assign one or two persons with the tasks of pricing and purchasing tennis balls for the event. Enough balls should be purchased to provide new ones for each match played, and if possible, new balls should be given to players who play a third set. It is better to overorder balls than to risk not having enough to complete a tournament. Some dealers may allow for the unused balls to be returned and the money refunded. This committee may collect used balls after matches have been completed, and then sell the balls or distribute them in some other manner.

TRANSPORTATION

For junior tournaments and some open events, a transportation committee may be needed. This group of people can be responsible for transporting players among various court sites or for getting players from the courts to private homes, motels, or dormitories. Station wagons and vans can be used by this committee more effectively than city buses because there are seldom more than three or four players to be moved from one place to another at a time. Departure times from sites should be posted at the courts. The transportation committee must work closely with the housing committee.

HOUSING

Many tournaments for junior players still provide housing in private homes for participants. The person who serves as the committee director must be one who can persuade others to house players, one who is very efficient in handling details, and one who is willing to do as much or more work than anyone else involved with the tournament. An experienced housing committee chairperson has given these suggestions for others who accept the same responsibility:

1. Begin compiling a list of persons willing to serve as hosts at least two months before the tournament begins.
2. When requests for housing are received, send a letter to the person making the request stating the provisions of being housed and giving the names and addresses of the hosts. Try to arrange all housing at least one week before the starting date.

221

3.   Do not allow arrangements to be made by calling the housing director or committee members.

4.   See that arrangements are made for the hosts and visitors to meet when the players arrive for registration.

5.   Maintain a card file containing the names and vital information for all players who will be housed.

6.   Save all material for future reference.

PUBLICITY

The people on the publicity committee are responsible for all public information about the tournament before, during, and after the event. They should get to know members of the press personally and provide them with stories or ideas about every phase of the tournament. During the tournament a copy of the bracket with winners' names circled should be provided to reporters. Publicity committee members may also call in results to newspapers in cities represented by players in the tournament. All news releases and other printed matter related to the tournament should be kept for future use.

ENTERTAINMENT

Some tournaments provide junior players with free tickets to theaters, bowling lanes, and miniature golf courses. Cookouts, beach parties, and dances are also popular forms of entertainment for younger players. However, keep in mind that players will be on or around the courts all day, and that competition may not be completed until well into the evening. Many well-intentioned plans for entertainment have not materialized because the participants of the tournament were not able to attend or were too tired. The trend is toward fewer extratournament entertainment activities.

AWARDS

Awards such a trophies, plaques, and ribbons are usually presented to first and second place finishers in each division. A sportsmanship award is also frequently awarded. The people responsible for ordering trophies or other items should allow for a two-or three-week delivery time. The committee chairperson or tournament director should have the awards before the tournament begins. Local businesses may be willing to sponsor awards.

After all of these arrangements have been made, there must be at least one person who knows the mechanics of structuring the various kinds of tournaments previously mentioned. That person may be the tournament dirctor, the umpire, or someone else. If you are a coach, teacher, or program director, you will probably be the one expected to do the work of drawing up the tournament pairings. Here are descriptions and procedures for organizing and directing various kinds of competition.

SINGLE ELIMINATION

The basic idea of the single elimination tournament is that players' names are drawn and placed on lines in a tournament bracket. Matches are played between players whose names appear on connected bracket lines. Winners of those matches advance to another round of competition, and losers are eliminated from the tournament. There are many contingencies which will be discussed in the step-by-step description of how to draw up this type of tournament. Single elimination tournaments are probably the most common method used to determine tennis championships. The advantages of this format are its familiarity among players, its simplicity, and the short amount of time needed to complete play. The primary disadvantage is that approximately half the participants get to play only one match in each division they enter. Following are instructions for setting up a single elimination bracket.

Step #1 Determine the number of participants. Entry blanks or sign up sheets will have been distributed and returned by a stipulated date. The tournament may be open to as many people who care to enter or the field may be limited to a certain number of players.

Step #2 Determine the number of lines needed to arrange first round matches, draw up the bracket sheet, and number the lines in the first vertical column. The number of lines will be 2, 4, 8, 16, 32, 64 or 128, depending on the number of participants. The next highest power of two above the number of participants will be the number of first round bracket lines needed. For example, if twelve people enter the tournament, a sixteen line bracket will be used. If there are twenty-eight entries, a thirty-two line bracket is necessary. Brackets may be constructed manually, or printed brackets may be available from sporting goods companies.

Step #3 Determine the number of first round byes and place them in the bracket. If the number of entries does not equal an exact power of two, some players will not have to play a first round match. By receiving a bye (not having to play in that round), a player advances to the next round. This system ensures that the number of players in the next round will equal an exact power of two, thus eliminating the need for byes after round one.

To determine the number of byes, subtract the number of entries from the number of lines in the bracket. For example, if there are twenty-five players entered in a tournament, the bracket will have thirty-two lines. There would be seven first round byes. If the event is sanctioned by the United States Tennis Association, there are specific guidelines to follow in placing the byes. These guidelines are given in that organization's literature. Other organizations such as school athletic conferences may have their own set of rules for placing byes in the bracket. Figures 7-1 and 7-2 illustrate two methods of placing byes in a thirty-two line bracket. In the first bracket (Figure 7-1), there are twenty-eight entries and four byes. The byes are separated by placement in each of the four quarters of the bracket.

In the second bracket (Figure 7-2), there are twenty-seven entries and five byes. The byes are placed on every other line beginning with the second line up from the bottom and the second line down from the top. The larger uneven number of byes (three, in this case) is placed in the bottom half of the bracket.

Step #4   Determine the number of rounds to be played. A round is a stage in the bracket through which players must advance. In an eight line bracket, there will be three rounds; in a sixteen line bracket, four rounds; in a thirty-two line bracket, five rounds; in a sixty-four line bracket, six rounds; and in a bracket of one hundred and twenty-eight lines, seven rounds. With this information, a player can tell how many matches must be won to reach a certain level in the event.

Step #5   Determine the total number of matches to be played in the tournament. That number will be one less than the total number of participants. Knowing how many matches will be played will help you in scheduling matches.

Step #6   Determine the number of first round matches. This number can be calculated by subtracting the number of byes from the number of participants in the tournament and dividing the result by two. For example, if seven players enter the tournament, there will be one bye. One from seven equals six; six divided by two equals three first round matches. This information is also necessary before scheduling can begin.

Step #7   Determine the number and names of seeded players. Seeded players are those whose past record indicates that they will be the best players in the tournament. By seeding, or placing their names in the bracket rather than drawing the names of all players, you can avoid the possibility

Figure 7-1 Placement of four byes * in separate bracket quarters in a field of twenty-eight players.

Figure 7–2 Placement of five byes * from bottom and top of bracket respectively in a field of twenty-seven players.

of the best competitors facing each other early in the tournament. If seeds receive byes, others have the opportunity to play against opponents of similar ability before meeting the best players. Seeding also makes it more likely that outstanding players will be competing in the later rounds of the tournament, which is desirable for attracting spectators. The U.S.T.A. stipulates that in events which it sponsors, no more than one out of every four players entered in the tournament may be seeded. Fewer than that number may be seeded, or no players at all may be seeded.

Step #8 Determine where the seeded players will be placed and write their names on the appropriate lines. There is more than one way this can be done. If the tournament is informal, the director may use any system that is fair and that has been agreed upon by the participants. If the event is controlled by school or conference rules, they must be followed. If the tournament is sanctioned by the U.S.T.A., the instructions are very specific. In the bracket shown in Figure 7-3, a coin flip is used to determine the placement of four seeded players in a thirty-two line bracket. A coin is flipped to decide whether the number one seed goes on line one or line thirty-two. The number two seed is placed on the line not filled. Another coin is tossed to determine whether the seeded player goes to line nine or line twenty-four. The fourth seed is placed on the line not filled by the third seed. Figures 7-4 and 7-5 show where seeded players should be placed in sixteen and eight line brackets, respectively.

Allow players, especially adult weekend tournament players, as much time between matches as you can. You only have to give them fifteen minutes, but the quality of play will be much better and the chance of injuries and defaults much less if they can get adequate rest after a match. In some tournaments, the players are so tired by the time they reach the semis and finals, they play worse than in earlier rounds. Figure out a way to keep players busier during the early rounds when they are fresh so they can pace themselves to go at full speed in the most important matches.

Step #9 Draw for the remaining positions and place the players' names on the bracket lines. As each name is drawn, it is written on the first open line starting from the top of the bracket. If names of two players from the same school or city are drawn to play each other in a first round match, the tournament director may place the second name on the first open line in the bottom half of the bracket.

Figure 7–3 Placement of the names of four seeded players in a thirty-two line bracket as determined by a coin toss.

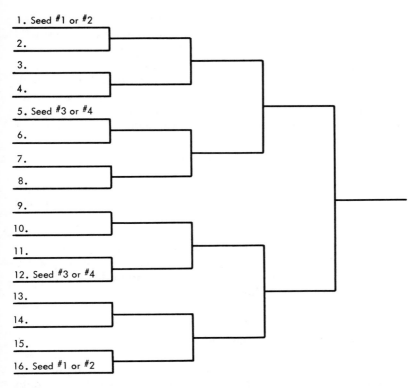

1. Seed #1 or #2
2.
3.
4.
5. Seed #3 or #4
6.
7.
8.
9.
10.
11.
12. Seed #3 or #4
13.
14.
15.
16. Seed #1 or #2

Figure 7—4 Placement of the names of four seeded players in a sixteen line bracket as determined by a coin toss.

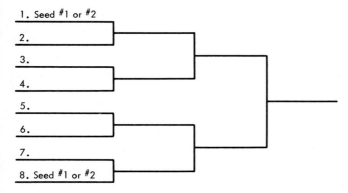

1. Seed #1 or #2
2.
3.
4.
5.
6.
7.
8. Seed #1 or #2

Figure 7—5 Placement of the names of two seeded players in an eight line bracket as determined by a coin toss.

Step #10   Write in days, times, and court assignments. This information should be inserted into the space between the names of the two players who are to compete against each other. Information for all first and second round matches should be posted, as well as information regarding days, times, and court assignment for matches in subsequent rounds. The scheduling of matches in later rounds may be done as the first round matches are completed or at the end of the first and second days of play.

All of the preparatory work on the bracket should be completed at least twenty-four hours before the tournament begins. Figure 7-6 shows a thirty-two line bracket filled out and ready for the tournament to begin.

Step #11   Begin play. As the players arrive at the courts, give court assignments, match balls, and instructions for reporting scores and returning used balls.

Step #12   As matches are completed, record scores, collect used balls, and tell the players when and where their next matches will be played. Names of winning players are written on the appropriate line in the next round, and scores are written below the lines.

Step #13   Determine time and court assignments for any matches not already scheduled and write the assignments on the bracket.

Step #14   Record scores and collect used balls as the remaining matches are completed. Figure 7-7 illustrates a thirty-two line bracket as it would appear after the tournament had been completed.

SINGLE ELIMINATION WITH A CONSOLATION BRACKET

The single elimination tournament with a consolation or losers' bracket ensures that each participant will play at least two matches. This format is especially useful when there are sixteen entries or less. The method of placing names and byes is the same as for the straight single elimination tournament. Players who lose in the first round of championship competition move into a separate bracket which is then played out from the start as a completely different tournament. The winners advance and the losers are eliminated. A consolation champion is determined.

There are two ways to draw up the brackets. The first method is to post a completely separate draw sheet for the consolation participants. As players lose first round matches in championship play, insert their names in the consolation bracket from top to bottom as they appeared on the original bracket. This method is shown in Figure 7-8.

Another way to establish the pairings for the losers' bracket is to con-

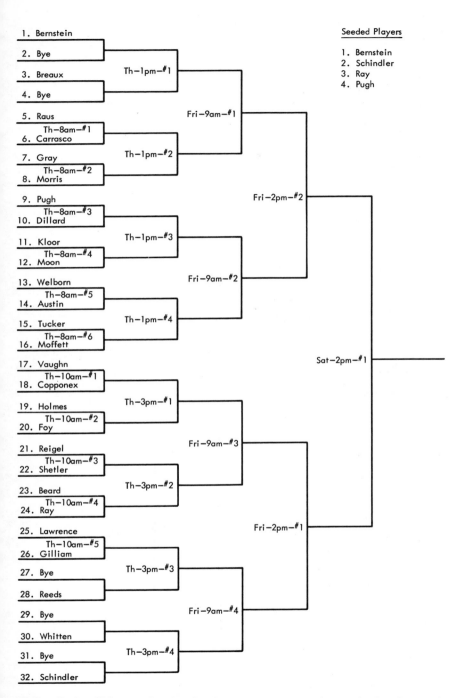

Seeded Players

1. Bernstein
2. Schindler
3. Ray
4. Pugh

Figure 7-6 Thirty-two line bracket for twenty-seven entries as the bracket would appear prior to the beginning of play.

231

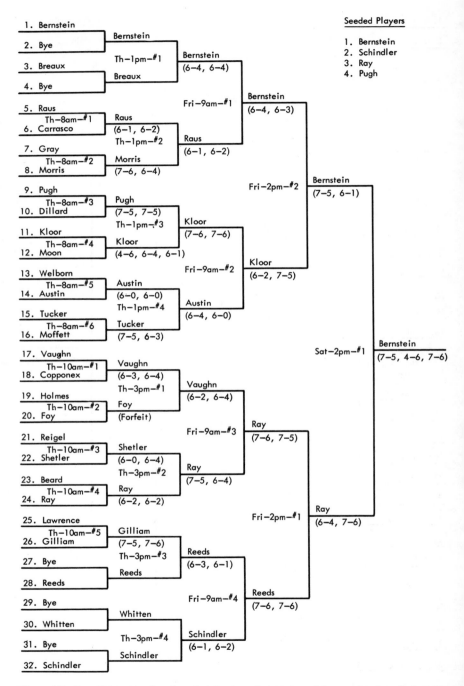

Figure 7-7 Thirty-two line bracket for twenty-seven entries as the bracket would appear after completion of play.

Figure 7–8 Single elimination tournament with a separate consolation bracket.

struct the bracket adjacent and to the left of the championship draw. As first round matches are completed, the names of winners move into the right (championship) side of the bracket while the names of losers move to the left side. This arrangement is illustrated in Figure 7-9. Days, times, and court assignments must be inserted just as in any other type of bracket.

ROUND ROBIN

In a round robin tournament, every player or team plays every other player or team once. The winner of the competition is the player or team finishing play with the best win-loss record. This form of competition is especially suitable for interscholastic competition and city tennis leagues. As with the single elimination tournament, decisions must be made regarding

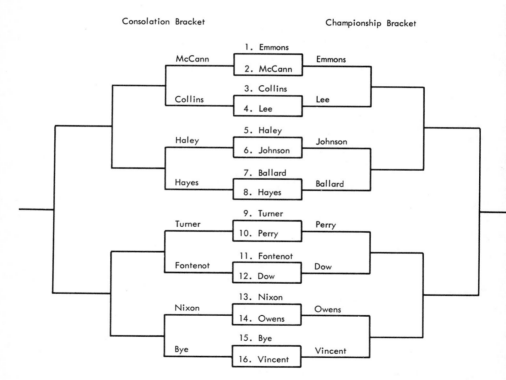

Figure 7-9   Single elmination tournament with an adjacent consolation bracket.

the format of competition, eligibility, entry fees, provisions for balls, etc. Here is a step-by-step procedure for scheduling and conducting matches in a round robin tournament.

Step #1   Determine the number of participants.

Step #2   Determine the total number of matches to be played. This can be done by multiplying the number of participants by one less than the number of participants and dividing the result by two. For example, if there are ten entries, ten multiplied by nine equals ninety; ninety divided by two equals forty-five. There will be forty-five matches played in a single round robin tournament with ten entries. If a formula will help you to remember how to establish the total number of matches, the formula is $\dfrac{N (N - 1)}{2}$, with N representing the number of participants.

Step #3   Assign a number to each player or team and list the numbers and names at the top of the schedule sheet.

Step #4   Determine the arrangement matches to be played. If there is an even number of participants, list their corresponding numbers in two vertical columns as shown in Figure 7-10. The numbers will be separated by the "vs." abbreviation. The numbers represent the names of first round opponents.

To arrange pairings for the second round, leave the number "1" stationary and rotate all other numbers one place in a counter-clockwise motion. Continue the rotation, moving the numbers one place for each subsequent round of play until the original arrangement of numbers has been reached. A completed round robin arrangement of pairings for an even number of players is shown in Figure 7-11.

If there is an odd number of players, place the word "Bye" in the

Team Names

1.	Aces	5.	Pushers
2.	Racketeers	6.	Netters
3.	Foot Faulters	7.	Slammers
4.	Rockets	8.	Letters

1	vs.	8
2	vs.	7
3	vs.	6
4	vs.	5

Figure 7–10 First round pairings in a round robin tournament with an even number of participants.

Team Names

1. Aces	5. Pushers
2. Racketeers	6. Netters
3. Foot Faulters	7. Slammers
4. Rockets	8. Letters

First Round

1	vs.	8
2	vs.	7
3	vs.	6
4	vs.	5

Second Round

1	vs.	7
8	vs.	6
2	vs.	5
3	vs.	4

Third Round

1	vs.	6
7	vs.	5
8	vs.	4
2	vs.	3

Fourth Round

1	vs.	5
6	vs.	4
7	vs.	3
8	vs.	2

Fifth Round

1	vs.	4
5	vs.	3
6	vs.	2
7	vs.	8

Sixth Round

1	vs.	3
4	vs.	2
5	vs.	8
6	vs.	7

Seventh Round

1	vs.	2
3	vs.	8
4	vs.	7
5	vs.	6

Figure 7–11 Completed round robin arrangement of pairings for an even number of participants.

Team Names

1. Lake Charles	5. Moss Bluff
2. Sulphur	6. Iowa
3. West Lake	7. Vinton
4. Maplewood	

First Round

Bye	vs.	7
1	vs.	6
2	vs.	5
3	vs.	4

Second Round

Bye	vs.	6
7	vs.	5
1	vs.	4
2	vs.	3

Third Round

Bye	vs.	5
6	vs.	4
7	vs.	3
1	vs.	2

Fourth Round

Bye	vs.	4
5	vs.	3
6	vs.	2
7	vs.	1

Fifth Round

Bye	vs.	3
4	vs.	2
5	vs.	1
6	vs.	7

Sixth Round

Bye	vs.	2
3	vs.	1
4	vs.	7
5	vs.	6

Seventh Round

Bye	vs.	1
2	vs.	7
3	vs.	6
4	vs.	5

Figure 7–12 Completed round robin arrangement of pairings for an odd number of participants.

upper left corner of the vertical listing of players' numbers. As the numbers are rotated for each round of play, the "Bye" remains stationary. Players or teams whose numbers appear opposite the "Bye" have an open date. A completed round robin arrangement of pairings for an odd number of entries is illustrated in Figure 7-12.

Step #5 Determine and write in days, times, and court assignments for each match. If these factors create an advantage for a player or team, rearrange the order of matches in each round in a way that will negate the possible advantage. A sample round robin schedule is shown in Figure 7-13.

Step #6 Begin play. The only thing left to do is the day to day supervision of competition. Someone must be designated to see that play runs smoothly, to record results, to maintain league standings, and to see the tournament through to the end.

Player's Names

1. Savoy   5. Bond
2. Powell   6. Adams
3. Gary   7. Cotten
4. LeBato   8. Porter

First Round

1	vs.	8	Mon – June 1st – 6:00 – Court #1
2	vs.	7	Mon – June 1st – 6:00 – Court #2
3	vs.	6	Mon – June 1st – 8:00 – Court #1
4	vs.	5	Mon – June 1st – 8:00 – Court #2

Second Round

1	vs.	7	Wed – June 3rd – 6:00 – Court #1
8	vs.	6	Wed – June 3rd – 6:00 – Court #2
2	vs.	5	Wed – June 3rd – 8:00 – Court #1
3	vs.	4	Wed – June 3rd – 8:00 – Court #2

Third Round

1	vs.	6	Fri – June 5th – 6:00 – Court #1
7	vs.	5	Fri – June 5th – 6:00 – Court #2
8	vs.	4	Fri – June 5th – 8:00 – Court #1
2	vs.	3	Fri – June 5th – 8:00 – Court #2

* Fourth Round

7	vs.	3	Mon – June 8th – 6:00 – Court #1
8	vs.	2	Mon – June 8th – 6:00 – Court #2
6	vs.	4	Mon – June 8th – 8:00 – Court #1
1	vs.	5	Mon – June 8th – 8:00 – Court #2

Fifth Round

1	vs.	4	Wed – June 10th – 6:00 – Court #1
5	vs.	3	Wed – June 10th – 6:00 – Court #2
6	vs.	2	Wed – June 10th – 8:00 – Court #1
7	vs.	8	Wed – June 10th – 8:00 – Court #2

Sixth Round

1	vs.	3	Fri – June 12th – 6:00 – Court #1
4	vs.	2	Fri – June 12th – 6:00 – Court #2
5	vs.	8	Fri – June 12th – 8:00 – Court #1
6	vs.	7	Fri – June 12th – 8:00 – Court #2

Seventh Round

1	vs.	2	Mon – June 15th – 6:00 – Court #1
3	vs.	8	Mon – June 15th – 6:00 – Court #2
4	vs.	7	Mon – June 15th – 8:00 – Court #1
5	vs.	6	Mon – June 15th – 8:00 – Court #2

* The numbers in this round have been rearranged so that
  Player #1 is scheduled at a later time and on a different
  court than usual.

Figure 7–13   Sample round robin schedule for eight players.

LADDER

A ladder tournament is one in which the names of players are listed vertically and numbered consecutively from the top to the bottom of the list. The positions of the players may be initially determined by chance or may be listed according to ability. A participant may challenge another player who is ranked one or two positions above the challenger. If the challenger wins the match, he changes places with the defeated player. Players should not be allowed to challenge the same person twice within a short period of time, and no player should be required to play more than one match per week or other stipulated period of time. Results of challenge matches must be reported within a specified period of time, and the tournament director must post all changes in ranking. A central listing of names and telephone numbers should also be posted at the playing site. The ladder tournament can continue for an indefinite length of time.

PYRAMID

The pyramid tournament is similar to the ladder format in that players may challenge other players to matches, and competition may continue over a long period of time. Names of players are placed on rows of the pyramid by chance or by design. The pyramid may have any number of horizontal rows, depending on the number of participants. The bottom row, for example, might have six names on it. The next row above would have five names; the third row from the bottom, four names, etc. A player may challenge anyone on his or her row. The player who wins may then challenge a player on the row above. If the challenger wins that match, he or she changes places on the pyramid with the defeated players.[1]

KING OR QUEEN OF THE COURT

This form of competition requires that you have an even number of players and enough courts to accommodate all players. Singles or doubles can be played. The director assigns courts to all players at random. They begin playing, counting by points or games, and continue until the director says to stop. At that time, the teams or players who are ahead move up one court and those who are losing move down one court. The player(s) who are winning on court one stay there and those who are losing on the last court remain on that court. In case of a tie when you say stop, one more point or

[1] Brown, *Tennis*, 116–135.

game is played. As many changes can be made as you want to make, but it is best to allow opponents to play each other at least ten minutes before a rotation. The two teams or players who finish the competition on court one are the champions. This format can be used in physical education classes, junior development groups, clinics, and in club competition.

DUAL MATCHES

Matches between two schools involving a set number of singles and doubles are easy to arrange and conduct if you are willing to give attention to details. When you are arranging the schedule for the coming season, you will have already exchanged letters with other coaches to establish dates, times, places, and type of competition (pro sets, two out of three sets, number of matches to be played, etc.). A few days before each match, call or write the opposing coach to reconfirm the date and time and to give him information about dressing facilities. The day before the match, let your players know who will be playing, what their respective positions will be, and what time they should be at the courts.

On the day of the match, you or someone you designate should be responsible for getting the following supplies to the courts: enough new tennis balls for each match to be played, towels, scoreboards, a first aid kit, water containers, and score sheets if they are to be used.

It is appropriate for you and your players to introduce yourselves to the visiting team and for you to introduce all players to the spectators. See that new balls are given to each pair of singles participants and give them instructions about special ground rules, tie-breakers, third set balls, and to whom to report scores and return the balls after the match. Once the match begins, there is nothing you can do except try to keep up with all the matches simultaneously and to see that the crowd does not interfere with play. Some conferences allow coaches to talk to their players when they change ends of the court, but others do not. Find out what is proper in your area. You should roam throughout the match and try to watch each of your players for part of his match. Your attention will give you more insight into each player's game and it will be encouraging to your team members to know that you are keeping up with their progress. This is especially true for the players in lower line-up positions. There is nothing wrong with asking the score as long as you ask at a time when play or concentration on the next point is not interfered with. Let your players know before the match that you will be asking for their scores periodically.

Once the singles matches have been completed, you or the umpire should record each score. Try to speak to your players privately after a match. If they win, congratulate them. If they lose, be positive, but ask them how the match went. After a reasonable rest period, get the doubles matches started by calling for the players by their names. Make sure that your players do not wander off while waiting for doubles competition to begin. When the doubles matches have been played, again record the scores and collect the used balls. Unless your players have to be somewhere else, ask them to stay at the courts until all matches have been completed. The team is playing a match and each player should remain to watch his teammates compete. You may want to have a team meeting after the match. Before leaving, make sure that the visiting team has a place to shower and dress.

LEAGUES

Tennis leagues consist of team competition, dual matches, and a round robin schedule. In order for them to work well, several ingredients must be present. The ingredients are one director, several team captains, lots of players, available courts, good publicity, team sponsors, and an acceptable format for competition.

Most people like the idea of participating in a tennis league, but few have the interest or time to make the idea workable. Someone has to take charge. That person can be a coach, a club pro, a tennis association officer, or anyone else who has the time, leadership ability, and tennis contacts to get people involved. In addition to a director, there have to be enough leaders to serve as team captains. These should be people who can hold a group together and get team members to matches on a regular basis.

There obviously have to be enough players interested in league competition. Teams can be composed of at least three members and as many as ten to fifteen. In some communities, there are small groups of people who prefer to play only with their tennis friends. The idea of playing outsiders does not appeal to them, so leagues may not be appropriate. In other places, players are eager for new competition or would like to be guaranteed a time and place to play regularly. These places are ideal for leagues.

Even if the league idea is popular where you live, some decisions have to be made about who will make up the teams. The easy answer is that everyone should have the opportunity to participate, but it isn't that simple. Is this going to be a men's league, women's league, or a mixed league? All three ways have been used, but each community has to decide what is best for its players. How old do these people have to be? If you decide that only adults can play, what is the minimum age? If you make it eighteen, what about the fifteen year old junior champion who can beat ninety per cent of the adults? Well, let him play. Then you get a call from a thirteen year old's parents who want to know why their child is excluded. Again, each situation is different, so it is hard to recommend the right course of action. What you can do is make your decisions regarding eligibility based on sound reasons. Then be ready to give those reasons if you have to defend your policy. How good do these players have to be? The alternatives are to have an "A" league, a "B" league, or a league in which players on each team compete by position. With the latter system, good players meet each other at the top of the lineup and weaker players play the lower positions.

If you have a league director, enough people to serve as team captains, and enough players to fill the rosters, make sure you have enough courts available for matches. The possibilities include club courts, public courts, and school courts, but getting them when you want them may be difficult. Club courts might be used if club members form some of the teams. Even if they do, other members may resent their court time being occupied by the league, so be diplomatic in requesting private court use. Public courts can be used if you get permission from the city or county recreation authority in the area. One way to do that is to have the city or county as a co-sponsor of the league. Recreation directors like to show how many people participate in public activities, so leagues can bolster their statistical reports. If the city does not go along with co-sponsorship, you may have problems. Some authorities do not like the idea of public courts being used by private groups. That might open the possibility of other requests for the courts, so the objection is understandable. School courts are the third option, but they are primarily for the use of faculty, staff, and students. Those groups could be involved in the league unless school is out of session when you want the courts. Even then, permission to use those facilities is necessary. Wherever you play, try to have enough courts in one place to accommodate the number of players who will be participating in matches. At least three courts at each site is almost a necessity.

Now you have decided who is going to run this thing, who is going to help run it, who the players will be, and where matches will be played. The next problem is how to publicize the league to attract players. The league director usually has to take this responsibility. He or she will have to prepare a news release and contact clubs, schools, towns, independent groups, businesses, radio and television stations, and newspapers to let people know there is going to be a league. This news release should contain information about the league idea, when and where the organizational meeting is to be held, and who to contact for more information. At the meeting, the director can explain the details of the proposal. A deadline should then be set for teams wishing to enter. At that point, a judgment has to be made about the feasibility of pursuing the idea. If interest is limited, either increase recruiting efforts or scrub the idea.

The teams will usually come from the groups already mentioned. They may represent tennis clubs, schools, communities or suburbs, apartment complexes, civic groups, independents, and businesses. The sponsors do not have to provide money unless they want to. The reasons for having sponsors is to attract people who have something in common and see each other regularly. If sponsors are not used, all interested players' names can be placed into a pool and drafted by team captains. This will only work in communities where everybody knows everybody else.

The last ingredient is a format for competition, which means a lot of details must be spelled out very specifically to avoid problems. Here are the details:

1.   **Scheduling**—The spring and fall seasons are best in most parts of the country because of bad weather and low interest in the winter and heavy tournament schedules in the summer. If indoor facilities are available, winter leagues can be good. Check on other community activities before deciding which days of the week to play. Avoid conflicts with church, school, and cultural events. Do not ask teams to play more than once a week. Try to finish league competition within eight weeks. Interest will diminish toward the end, especially among those teams that are losing.

2.   **Team composition**—There are almost limitless possibilities. Men's, women's, and mixed teams can be arranged for singles only, doubles only, six singles and three doubles, four singles and two doubles, two singles and one doubles, and many other combinations.

3.   **Individual match and team scoring**—Most people like the two out of three set method with tie breakers at six-six. The team that wins the most individual matches gets a team victory. Some leagues count each individual match toward a team total which is carried into the next match. If a team wins three matches to two, the winner has permanently won three points on the season's total and the loser gets two points. With each subsequent match, point totals are added to the previous balance. The team which accummulates the most points is the league champion, or the top finishers qualify for the playoffs.

4.   **Tennis balls**—Make some kind of arrangement about who will provide the balls and what kind will be used. A home team can be designated and made responsible for the balls. A list of acceptable balls should be given to each team captain.

5.   **Forfeits**—Establish a forfeit time (fifteen minutes is common) and a policy about players' positions when one does not show up. Either that player's match is forfeited and all other players stay at the same position, or everybody moves up a notch and the last position in the lineup is forfeited. Both methods are used, but everyone should understand the ground rules before the league begins.

6.   Substitutes—If substitutes or alternates are used, the league director should approve them. If not, some teams will use "ringers" to strengthen their lineups. Additions to rosters should also be cleared with the director.

7.   Makeups—For matches that are completely rained out, leave dates at the end of the schedule for makeups. If a match is partially rained out, make a rule about what constitutes a completed match. The choices are to state that all matches must be completed for the team to get credit for a win or that a majority of matches must be completed. In leagues which use a total point system of scoring, all matches completed before the rain or other bad weather can count toward a grand total. Other matches must be finished at a later date.

8.   Reporting scores—Assign team captains the responsibility of recording scores and reporting them to you, if you are the director. The director calls in results to the media and keeps records.

Leagues can be fun, but only if you and a few others do the work and make the decisions. If any of the ingredients are missing, look for other forms of competition.

Regardless of the kind of competition, once the semi-finals and finals are reached, take the trouble to stage the match. Give the players involved all the recognition they deserve and all the attention you can provide. Publicize the matches in newspapers and on radio and television. Get ball boys and ball girls to work at the tournament site. Don't let anyone play on adjacent courts. Umpire the match and get linespersons, if available. Reaching the final rounds of a tournament is a big achievement for many people. Treat them like champions.

REVIEW QUESTIONS

1.   Discuss the following factors as they relate to planning tournament competition:

a. money	**d.** tennis balls
b. facilities	**e.** entry blanks
c. eligibility	**f.** awards

2.   What is a single elimination tournament?

3.   How is the number of byes determined in a single elimination tournament?

4.   How many matches will be played in a single elimination tournament with fifteen entries? with thirty-two entries and a third place match between semi-finals losers?

5.   How is the number of first round matches in a single elimination tournament determined? Why is that information important?

6.   How many bracket lines are needed in a single elimination tournament with twenty-four entries? nine entries? sixty-three entries?

7.   What is the maximum number of seeds allowable in a tournament with thirty-two entries? eight entries?

8.   How many matches will be played in a single elimination tournament with a consolation bracket if sixteen players enter?

9.   How many matches will be played in a round robin tournament with five entries? ten? fifteen?

10.   What are some of the responsibilities of a coach conducting a dual match?

11.   What are the ingredients necessary to conduct a successful tennis league?

Chapter 8

Drills

Use drills that are directly related to tennis playing skills. Too much emphasis has been placed on interesting, intricate, and impressive looking routines and activities that may or may not help a player improve. Some drills only enable the player to do the drills better. Tennis players can learn best by participating in specifically designed leadup activities, repeatedly practicing strokes, and by playing tennis.

SERVES

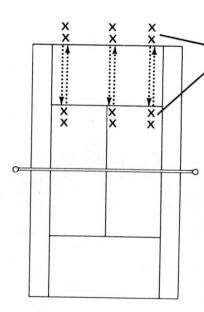

Players form lines facing each other; play catch with tennis ball.

Figure 8–1 Baseball Throw

1. BASEBALL THROW (Beginners—Two to Twenty Players)

This drill is simply a game of catch with a tennis ball. Beginning players line up in two or more groups facing each other or facing the teacher at a distance of about twenty feet. Each player throws to another in an overhand motion, then goes to the end of the line. The teacher observes each player, and makes necessary corrections in the throwing motion. The better the form in throwing, the easier the serve will be to learn. The two motions are almost the same.

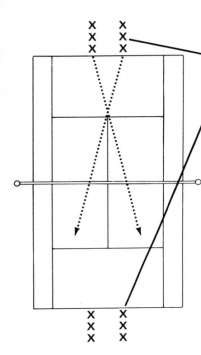

Players on each side of the net take turns using the baseball throwing motion to toss balls crosscourt into the proper service court.

Figure 8–2   Throw Into Service Court

2. THROW INTO SERVICE COURT (Beginners—Two to Twenty Players)

To follow up the baseball throw drill, the players are positioned behind the service line or behind the baseline. The drill consists of using the baseball throwing motion to throw the tennis ball into the proper service court. Players may rotate after every throw or series of throws. When all of the balls have been retrieved by players on the opposite side of the net, these players return the balls by throwing them into the proper court.

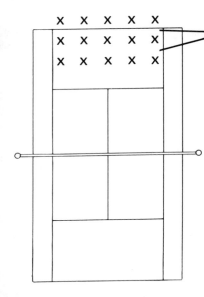

Players spread out; face same direction; practice service toss.

Figure 8–3   Toss and Catch

3. TOSS AND CATCH (Beginners—Two to Twenty Players)

Players are positioned anywhere on the court, but facing the same direction and with enough space to move freely. Either on signal or working individually, each player goes through the preliminary service motion, but catches the toss instead of continuing the motion. The purpose of the drill is to practice the toss. The instructor moves through the group as the toss is practiced.

247

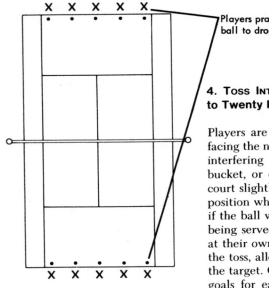

Players practice the service toss by allowing the ball to drop into a target.

4. Toss Into Basket (Beginners—Two to Twenty Players)

Players are stationed along the baseline, facing the net, with enough room to avoid interfering with each other. A basket, bucket, or other target is placed on the court slightly in front of the baseline in a position where the service toss would fall if the ball was allowed to drop instead of being served. On a command or working at their own pace, the beginners practice the toss, allowing the ball to drop toward the target. Competition among players or goals for each individual may be established for motivational purposes.

Figure 8–4   Toss Into Basket

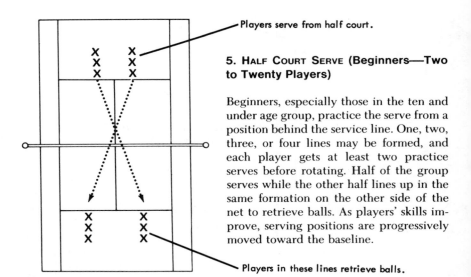

Players serve from half court.

5. Half Court Serve (Beginners—Two to Twenty Players)

Beginners, especially those in the ten and under age group, practice the serve from a position behind the service line. One, two, three, or four lines may be formed, and each player gets at least two practice serves before rotating. Half of the group serves while the other half lines up in the same formation on the other side of the net to retrieve balls. As players' skills improve, serving positions are progressively moved toward the baseline.

Players in these lines retrieve balls.

Figure 8–5   Half Court Serve

6. Serve Into Fence (Beginners—Two to Forty Players)

If groups are too large for the available space, or if the number of balls does not allow for actual serving practice, have the players face the fences or walls surrounding the court at a distance of ten to twelve feet. The players serve into the fence as the instructor moves through the group to observe and correct swings. Allow for adequate space between the players to avoid accidents.

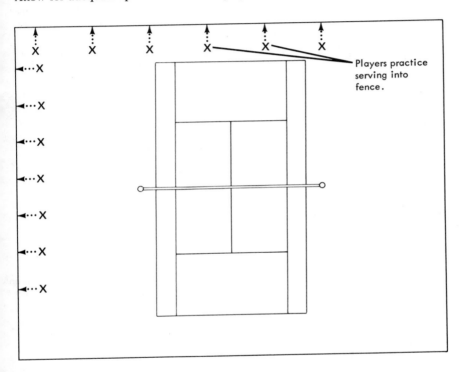

Figure 8-6   Serve Into Fence

7. Suspended Ball (Beginners—Two to Four Players)

A tennis ball is attached to a length of cord, wire, or string, and suspended from a ceiling or from an apparatus extending out from a fence. The ball should be suspended at a point where contact should be made on the serve, and it should be possible to adjust the height of the ball according to the player's height and reach. Players practice the service motion and hit the suspended ball at the proper height. Several players can participate in the drill simultaneously if there are enough suspended balls, but the teacher should be in a position to observe and make corrections when necessary.

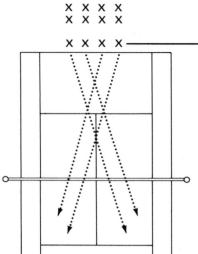

X X X X
X X X X

X X X X —————————— Competing players serve two balls, then go to end of line.

8. Serving Contest (Beginners and Intermediates—Four to Twenty Players)

Players are divided into two or more teams. Team members then take positions behind the baseline, ready to serve in turn. As many as four players can serve simultaneously, and several courts can be used at the same time. When a signal is given, teams compete to see how many serves can be hit into the service courts. Winners can be determined by time limits or by the team reaching a certain number of "in" serves first. At least one person per court is needed to count the serves that are good.

X —————————— Instructor or player counts "in" serves.

Figure 8–7   Serving Contest

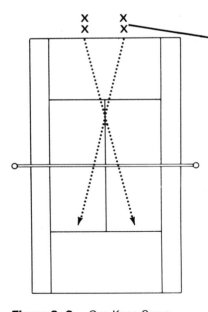

X   X
X   X

Players serve from the baseline with one knee on the court. This position forces the server to use topspin.

9. One Knee Serve (Intermediates and Advanced—One to Four Players)

In order to develop the technique of putting topspin on the serve, players get down on one knee and serve from a position behind the baseline. The low position of the racket at the peak of the swing forces the server to put topspin on the ball in order for it to clear the net and fall into the service court.

Figure 8–8   One Knee Serve

250

10. Serve From Fence (Intermediates and Advanced—Two to Eight Players)

In order to overload the muscles used in the serve, the players practice serving from a position well behind the baseline or from the fence. After practicing the serve from this distance over a period of time, the player should have more power from the normal serving position.

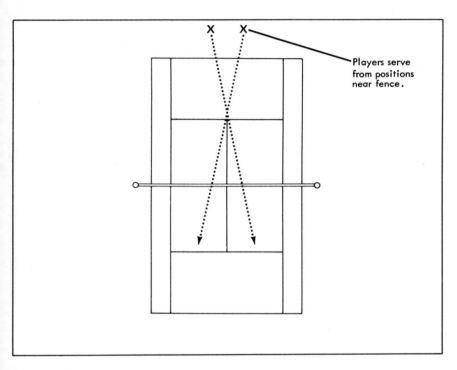

Players serve from positions near fence.

Figure 8–9   Serve From Fence

11. Deep, Topspin Serve (Advanced—Two to Eight Players)

Place a temporary net or wall beside the regular net. The temporary net should be at least twice the height of the regulation net. Players must serve over the temporary net, using an exaggerated topspin action. The server should also place the ball deeply into the opponent's service court. Overlearning the topspin serve will help on second serve situations, in doubles competition, and when the server needs time to follow his serve to the net.

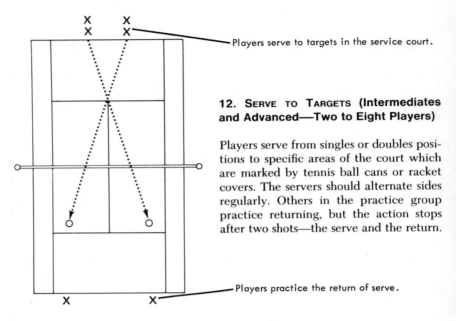

Players serve to targets in the service court.

12. SERVE TO TARGETS (Intermediates and Advanced—Two to Eight Players)

Players serve from singles or doubles positions to specific areas of the court which are marked by tennis ball cans or racket covers. The servers should alternate sides regularly. Others in the practice group practice returning, but the action stops after two shots—the serve and the return.

Players practice the return of serve.

Figure 8–10   Serve to Targets

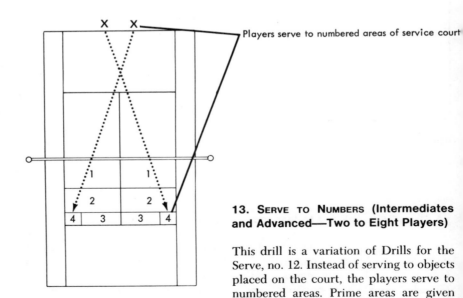

Players serve to numbered areas of service court

13. SERVE TO NUMBERS (Intermediates and Advanced—Two to Eight Players)

This drill is a variation of Drills for the Serve, no. 12. Instead of serving to objects placed on the court, the players serve to numbered areas. Prime areas are given higher numbers, so that score may be kept for intrateam competition.

Figure 8–11   Serve to Numbers

GROUNDSTROKES

1. UPS AND DOWNS (Beginners—Two to Twenty Players)

Players hold their rackets with the Eastern forehand grip and dribble a tennis ball against the court. Goals of 25, 50, or 100 "downs" may be used to stimulate interest. Players then turn the palm up and practice air dribbles or "ups." Variation: *Shadow Downs.* In this drill, "downs" are practiced, but a second ball is placed on the court. Players attempt to dribble one ball on the shadow of the second ball.

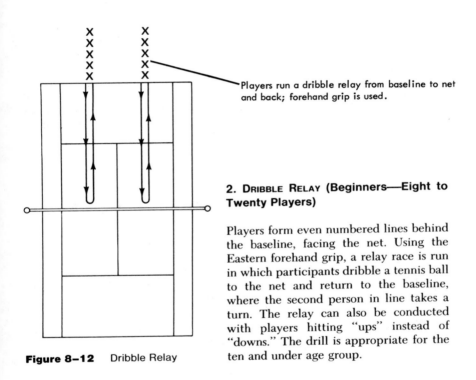

Players run a dribble relay from baseline to net and back; forehand grip is used.

2. DRIBBLE RELAY (Beginners—Eight to Twenty Players)

Players form even numbered lines behind the baseline, facing the net. Using the Eastern forehand grip, a relay race is run in which participants dribble a tennis ball to the net and return to the baseline, where the second person in line takes a turn. The relay can also be conducted with players hitting "ups" instead of "downs." The drill is appropriate for the ten and under age group.

Figure 8–12   Dribble Relay

3. PROGRESSION DRILL (Beginners—Two to Twenty Players)

This is a series of drills leading to the forehand stroke. Step #1: The player drops a ball and catches it with the other hand, using a forehand swing motion. Step #2: The player drops the ball and hits it with an open hand to a partner or to the teacher. Step #3: The player drops the ball and hits it with a forehand stroke, choking up on the racket. Step #4: The player drops the ball and hits it with a forehand stroke, holding the racket at the grip.

4. FOOTPRINTS (Beginners—Two to Ten Players)

The instructor prepares paper outlines of feet. The outlines are placed in positions to indicate where the feet should be moved in preparing to hit a forehand or backhand shot. The players then simulate the movement necessary to hit those shots, stepping on the paper outlines. At first, the drill may be performed individually in order for the beginners to become accustomed to the pattern of movement. Then the entire group may follow the lead of the instructor in practicing the footwork.

5. READY, PIVOT, STEP, SWING (Beginners—Two to Twenty Players)

This is a footwork drill directed by the teacher, who faces the group. The instructor either says the words: Ready, Pivot, Step, and Swing, or One, Two, Three, Four. The players assume the ready position on the "Ready" command; pivot so that the side is to the net on the word "Pivot;" step forward slightly (into the ball) on "Step;" and go through with the swing on the last command. Although this drill is effective with beginners of almost any age, the instructor should be careful not to teach a mechanical, stiff preparation for groundstrokes. Once the concept of preparation is learned, the drill should be modified to include movements to either side of the court.

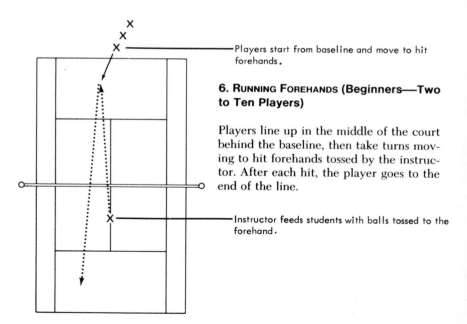

Players start from baseline and move to hit forehands.

6. RUNNING FOREHANDS (Beginners—Two to Ten Players)

Players line up in the middle of the court behind the baseline, then take turns moving to hit forehands tossed by the instructor. After each hit, the player goes to the end of the line.

Instructor feeds students with balls tossed to the forehand.

Figure 8–13   Running Forehands

7. RUNNING BACKHANDS (Beginners—Two to Ten Players)

This is the same drill as "Running Forehands," except that the balls are tossed to the backhand side.

8. TOSS TO FOREHAND (Beginners—Two to Ten Players)

The title explains the drill. The instructor tosses soft bouncers to the forehand side of the student. The student practices preparation and stroking the ball, aiming for the teacher. If large groups are involved, players find a partner, spread out on the court, and take turns tossing and hitting. Some students may be used to retrieve balls. Competition can consist of the total number of balls hit into the proper area by two or more groups.

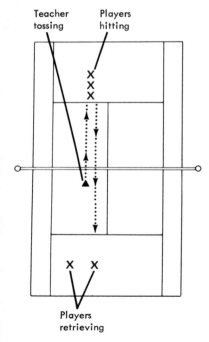

Figure 8–14a   Toss to Forehand

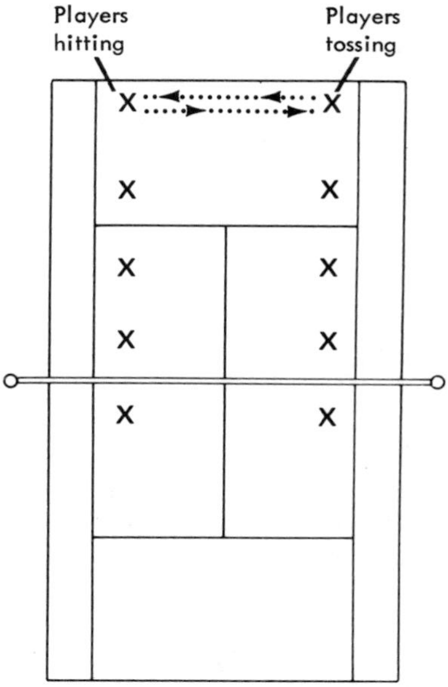

Figure 8–14b

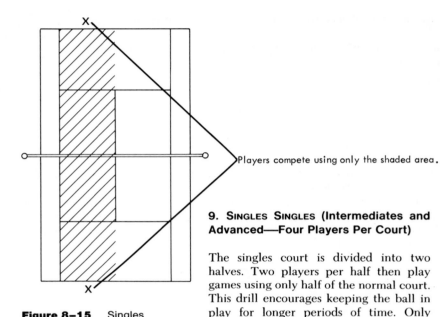

Players compete using only the shaded area.

Figure 8-15 Singles Singles

9. SINGLES SINGLES (Intermediates and Advanced—Four Players Per Court)

The singles court is divided into two halves. Two players per half then play games using only half of the normal court. This drill encourages keeping the ball in play for longer periods of time. Only groundstrokes are allowed.

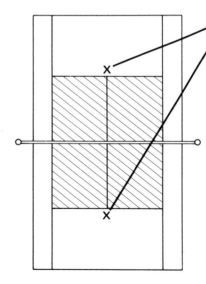

Players play regular games, but ball must be hit into area marked by diagonal lines.

Figure 8-16 Short Game

10. SHORT GAME (Intermediates and Advanced—Two, Three, or Four Players)

Participants play singles, doubles, or two against one, but with these rules: (1) the normal service lines become baselines; (2) serve by dropping the ball and putting it into play; (3) volleys and smashes are illegal. Emphasis is on ball control, angles, and dropshots.

11. WALL STROKES (Intermediates and Advanced—One or Two Players)

A player practices forehand and backhand strokes by hitting against a wall or backboard. The player should stand at a distance from the wall comparable to the distance from the baseline to the net. Shots should be directed to a point over a line on the wall indicating the height of a net.

12. ALTERNATING WALL STROKES

Two players alternate hitting groundstrokes against the wall, counting the number of consecutive hits or competing against each other by counting the number of misses.

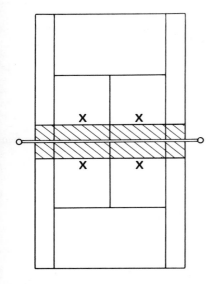

Players compete against each other, keeping score as usual, but only shots falling into the marked area are in play.

13. DROP SHOT GAME (Intermediates and Advanced—Two to Four Players)

The players play games as in the "Short Game" drill, but now no shots may land beyond a chalk line approximately six feet from and parallel to the net. Two, three, or four players may compete. If there is an odd number of players, they should rotate so that each person gets the opportunity to play alone against the other two.

Figure 8–17   Drop Shot Game

14. SLOW POINT GAME (Intermediates and Advanced—Two to Four Players)

Two, three, or four players play regular games, but only groundstrokes may be used. Serves are put into play by dropping the ball and hitting it into the proper service court. Groundstrokes may be placed, but the idea is to keep the ball in play until someone makes an error rather than putting shots away. Players may not hit volleys or overhead smashes.

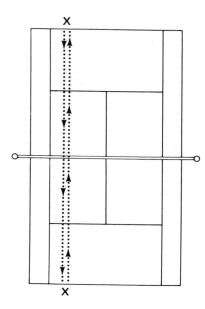

Figure 8-18   Down-the-Line
Warmup

Players warmup by hitting groundstrokes down the line; change sides after 5-10 minutes.

15. DOWN-THE-LINE WARMUP (Advanced —Two Players)

Two players on opposite ends of the court move slightly to one side of the center mark. The ball is put into play, and the players hit all shots down the line on that side of the court. All shots should be played on one bounce. After hitting down the line for five to ten minutes, the players change sides (not ends), hitting down the opposite side lines for the same time period.

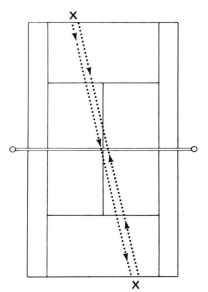

Figure 8-19   One-on-One
Crosscourt

Players use 5-10 minute warmup hitting crosscourt groundstrokes.

16. ONE-ON-ONE CROSSCOURT (Advanced —Two Players)

Two players line up on opposite ends of the court in positions to warm up with crosscourt groundstrokes. Shots should be placed deeply, crosscourt, and played on the first bounce. The players should change sides after five minutes.

17. TWO-ON-ONE CROSSCOURT (Advanced—Three Players)

Players A and B take positions on the same baseline. Player C takes a position on the opposite side of the net behind an alley. A puts the ball in play down the line. C responds with a crosscourt shot, and moves along his baseline to prepare for another crosscourt shot. B returns the first crosscourt shot with another down-the-line placement, which is returned again by Player C. A and B will remain in their respective areas; C will move from side to side. Each player should get a five minute turn at each position.

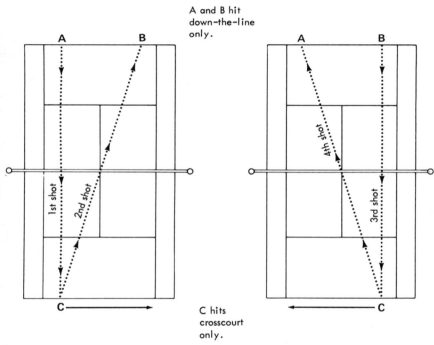

A and B hit down-the-line only.

C hits crosscourt only.

Figure 8–20a   Two-on-One Crosscourt

Figure 8–20b

18. Down-the-Line Crosscourt Combination (Advanced—Two Players)

One player puts the ball into play, hitting down the line. After he hits, he moves to the opposite side of the court to prepare to hit a second down-the-line shot. This player will continue to hit all shots down the line as long as the ball is in play. On receiving the first shot, a second player hits his groundstroke crosscourt, then moves to the opposite side to prepare to hit another. The second player will hit only crosscourt shots. If the players can keep the ball in play, the drill should last at least five minutes.

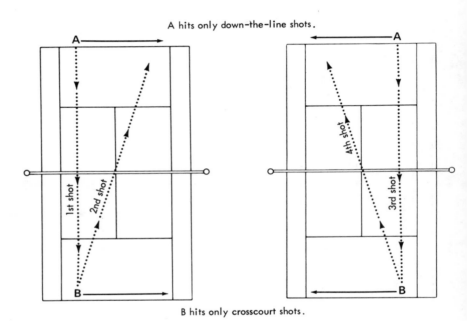

A hits only down-the-line shots.

B hits only crosscourt shots.

Figure 8–21a Down-the-Line Crosscourt Combination

Figure 8–21b

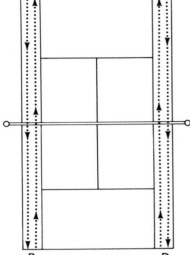

Figure 8–22 Alleys Only

A vs. B and C vs. D practice groundstrokes by hitting to alleys.

19. ALLEYS ONLY (Advanced—Two Players per Alley)

Players take positions on opposite ends of the court behind the baseline. After putting the ball into play, both players attempt to hit all groundstrokes so that they fall into the opponent's alley. Score may be kept by counting the number of shots falling into the alley. For example, the first player to score twenty points wins the game. The remainder of the court may be used by other players.

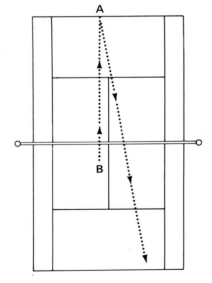

Figure 8–23 Half Volley Attack

Player A hits attacking shot off the half volley forehand.

Player B or coach drives shots at feet of Player A.

20. HALF VOLLEY ATTACK (Advanced—Two Players)

The tournament tennis player must learn to turn the deeply hit half volley into an attacking shot of his own. The coach stands at the net with a basket of balls, and drives shots at the player's feet. The player stands on the baseline, steps into every shot driven at him, and half volleys a forehand. The purpose is to condition the player to make attacking shots out of what are normally defensive shots.

261

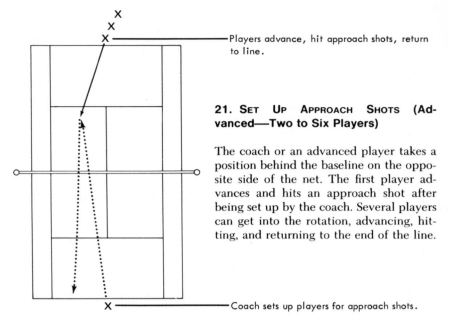

Players advance, hit approach shots, return to line.

21. SET UP APPROACH SHOTS (Advanced—Two to Six Players)

The coach or an advanced player takes a position behind the baseline on the opposite side of the net. The first player advances and hits an approach shot after being set up by the coach. Several players can get into the rotation, advancing, hitting, and returning to the end of the line.

Coach sets up players for approach shots.

Figure 8–24   Set Up Approach Shots

22. RUNNING GROUNDSTROKES (Advanced—Two Players)

The coach stands in the forecourt with a basket of balls, and the player starts the drill standing in the middle of the opposite court at the baseline. The coach alternately hits balls to each corner of the singles court, forcing the player to hit forehand and backhand groundstroke returns while running. At least 25 and as many

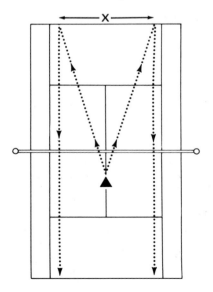

Player moves alternately to each corner, hitting forehand and backhand ground strokes.

Coach hits or throws balls to corners of the singles court.

Figure 8–25   Running Groundstrokes

as 100 balls can be hit consecutively, depending on the physical condition of the player. Although only one player at a time may participate in the drill, a second player can be used to retrieve balls and take a turn hitting while the first player rests.

VOLLEYS

1. Reach and Catch (Beginners—One to Four Players)

This drill can be used as the first step in the progression for teaching the volley to beginners. The player stands near the net in the ready position. The teacher stands on the opposite side of the net and either tosses or softly hits shots to either side of the player. The player reaches out and "catches" or stops the ball with the racket. Although no attempt is made to actually make a return volley, some balls may cross the net. Once the beginner can consistently stop the ball with the racket strings, the teacher can begin to teach the volleying motion.

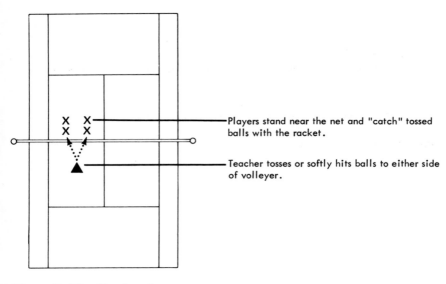

Players stand near the net and "catch" tossed balls with the racket.

Teacher tosses or softly hits balls to either side of volleyer.

Figure 8–26   Reach and Catch

2. Toss to Volley (Beginners—Two to Ten Players)

The instructor tosses or hits balls to the player standing two or three steps from the net. Instead of just stopping the ball with the racket as in the *Reach and Catch* drill, the beginner volleys the ball in the direction of the teacher. If large groups are being taught, the partner method of tossing and volleying may be used. After the forehand volley is practiced, balls should be tossed to the backhand side. As the student becomes more comfortable at the net, balls may be tossed or hit to either side of the player.

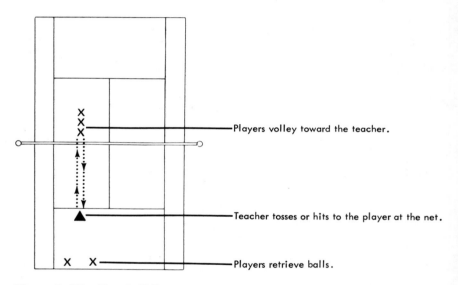

Figure 8–27   Toss to Volley

3. VOLLEY FROM FENCE (Beginners and Intermediates—Two to Twenty Players)

In order to teach the short backswing required for volleys, the player is positioned with his back near the fence or wall surrounding the court. The instructor hits or tosses balls, and the player is forced to return with a short backswing volley. If the group is large, players may be paired so that each has one turn tossing and one turn volleying.

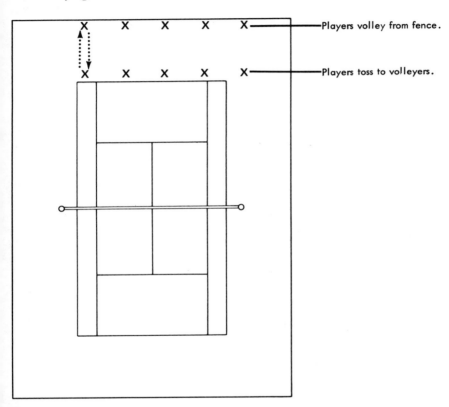

Figure 8–28   Volley From Fence

4. VOLLEY FROM GATE (Beginners and Intermediates—Two to Six Players)

In order to teach the short backswing and the forward motion necessary for volleys, the player is positioned in the space normally occupied by a closed gate. The coach hits or tosses balls, and the player is forced to step forward, using a short backswing to volley the ball. If he touches the fence with the racket, he is either not stepping forward or taking too long a backswing.

5. CROSSCOURT SET-UPS (Beginners and Intermediates—Two to Eight Players)

As the player learns when to come to the net and how to hit the volley, he can begin to place the ball to various spots on the court. In this drill, the instructor hits medium paced shots down the line to the player at the net, who volleys the ball crosscourt to the open area. The drill should be repeated on the opposite side of the court so the player can practice forehand and backhand crosscourt volleys. A rotation can be used in which a player hits and moves to the other side of the court or to the end of the line while other players move into the volleying position.

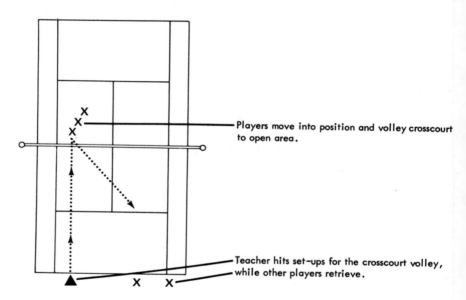

Players move into position and volley crosscourt to open area.

Teacher hits set-ups for the crosscourt volley, while other players retrieve.

Figure 8—29 Crosscourt Set-ups

6. UMPIRING DRILL (Intermediates and Advanced—One or Two Players)

Some players have difficulty in knowing which shots are going in and which ones are going to be out. Misjudgment frequently occurs when high, hard shots are hit toward a man at the net. In this drill, a coach or advanced player has a basket of balls and stands on one baseline. A second player is positioned in an area where he would normally hit volleys. The coach hit shots in his direction, but rather than volleying, the player at net simply calls balls "in" or "out" before they hit the court. Each team member gets the same number of calls if score is kept.

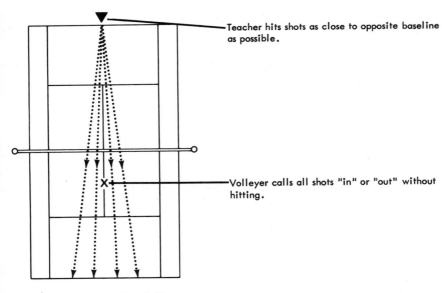

Teacher hits shots as close to opposite baseline as possible.

Volleyer calls all shots "in" or "out" without hitting.

Figure 8–30   Umpiring Drill

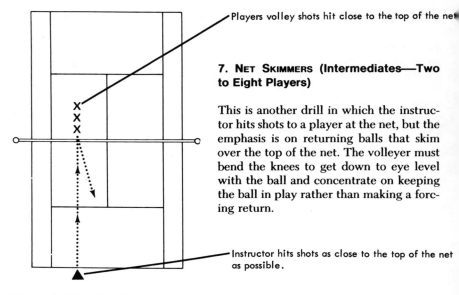

Players volley shots hit close to the top of the net

7. NET SKIMMERS (Intermediates—Two to Eight Players)

This is another drill in which the instructor hits shots to a player at the net, but the emphasis is on returning balls that skim over the top of the net. The volleyer must bend the knees to get down to eye level with the ball and concentrate on keeping the ball in play rather than making a forcing return.

Instructor hits shots as close to the top of the net as possible.

Figure 8–31 Net Skimmers

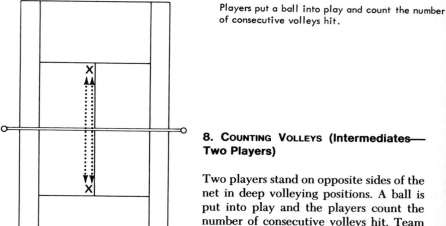

Players put a ball into play and count the number of consecutive volleys hit.

8. COUNTING VOLLEYS (Intermediates—Two Players)

Two players stand on opposite sides of the net in deep volleying positions. A ball is put into play and the players count the number of consecutive volleys hit. Team or individual records may be established to stimulate interest in the drill. Doubles teams may also compete against each other, but the emphasis is on keeping the ball in play rather than hitting winners.

Figure 8–32 Counting Volleys

9. WALL VOLLEY (Advanced—One or Two Players)

In this drill, a player counts the number of times he can volley against a wall or board without missing. To stimulate team competition, each player's score is recorded and compared to others. Variation: *Alternating Wall Volley.* Two players alternate hitting volleys against a wall. Competition may be between the two players or between two-player teams.

10. VOLLEY THROUGH THE RING (Advanced—Two Players)

A ring or hoop is mounted and placed two to three feet above the net. Two players attempt to volley through the ring, practicing ball control volleys. Score may be kept between individuals or doubles teams. The players may line up directly opposite each other or at crosscourt angles.

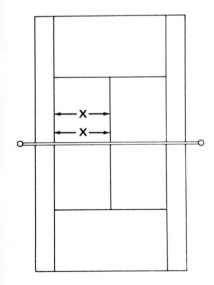

Figure 8–33 Side-to-Side

Players move from center line to sideline touching racket to court ten or more times.

11. SIDE-TO-SIDE (Advanced—One to Six Players)

The player stands in a volleying position near the net, halfway between the center line and the singles sideline. When given a signal, he moves laterally as fast as possible to the right, touches the singles sideline with the racket, then moves to the left and touches the center line with the racket. He completes ten touches (or any number determined by the teacher or coach) before stopping. Several players can do the drill simultaneously by forming a line parallel to the sideline behind the first player. The drill is effective for conditioning and for improving lateral mobility.

269

12. TWO-ON-ONE VOLLEY (Intermediates and Advanced—Three Players)

Two players are positioned near a basket of balls on the baseline. A third player takes a position across the net ready to hit volleys. The baseline players alternate hitting two balls each to the net man in a rapid-fire type drill. No attempt is made to return the volleys. The players rotate after each basket of balls. Other players may be used to pick up balls. Variation: *Two-on-One Volley Rally*. With tournament players, the drill may be varied so that balls are kept in play as long as possible. The baseline players practice groundstrokes and passing shots, while the net player works on deep volleys.

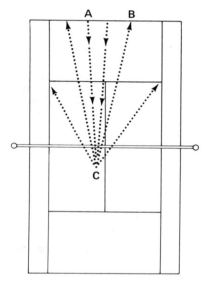

Players A and B feed Player C with groundstrokes.

Player C puts away volleys.

Figure 8–34   Two-on-One Volley

270

13. HALFCOURT ONE-ON-ONE (Advanced—Two Players)

One player stands at the net halfway between the center line and the singles side-line. Another player stands at the opposite baseline between the same two lines. A ball is put into play; beginning with the third shot, the player on the baseline tries to pass the player at the net, who defends the halfcourt area in which he is standing. Shots which land beyond the halfcourt boundaries described are out. Score can be kept by counting the number of misses or by keeping score as in a regular game.

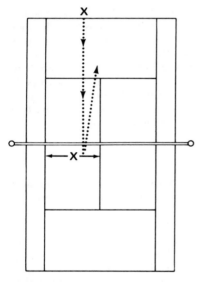

Player attempts passing shots.

Volleyer defends area from center line to singles sideline.

Figure 8–35   Halfcourt
One-on-One

14. ADVANCING VOLLEYS (Advanced—Two Players)

Two players stand on opposite ends of the court facing each other. A ball is put into play. With each shot that is hit the player who hits the shot moves one step forward until players are firing at almost point blank range. When a shot is missed, both players must return to the baseline. The drill begins as a ground-stroke drill, but as the players move toward the net, it becomes a volley drill.

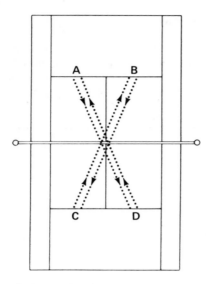

Figure 8–36 Crosscourt Volleys

Players A vs. D and B vs. C keep crosscourt volleys in play as long as possible.

15. Crosscourt Volleys (Advanced—Two or Four Players)

Two or four players take positions just behind the service lines opposite each other in crosscourt alignments. The players practice crosscourt volleys by keeping the ball in play as long as possible. Score may be kept. The players should change positions periodically. The drill may be conducted with four players by keeping two balls in play simultaneously.

16. Team Volleys (Intermediates and Advanced—Six to Twelve Players)

Two teams line up, both in single file on opposite sides of the net and about ten to fifteen feet from it. A ball is put into play and each player hits one volley, then goes to the end of his or her line. The team that misses ten volleys first loses. The coach serves as referee on questionable shots.

Players hit one volley and go to the end of the line.

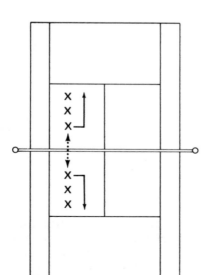

Figure 8–37 Team Volleys

17. KNOW YOUR PARTNER (Intermediates and Advanced—Two Players)

In order for new doubles partners to get to know each other's moves, range, and capabilities, place the partners in volleying positions. A third person drives shots down the middle of the court within the reach of both players. Each partner must learn to react not only to the shot, but also to what his partner will do in a given situation.

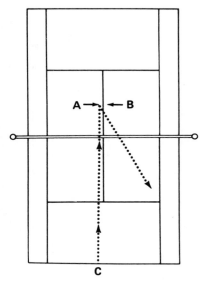

Doubles partners volley shots hit down the middle.

C drives shots down the middle of the court.

Figure 8-38   Know Your Partner

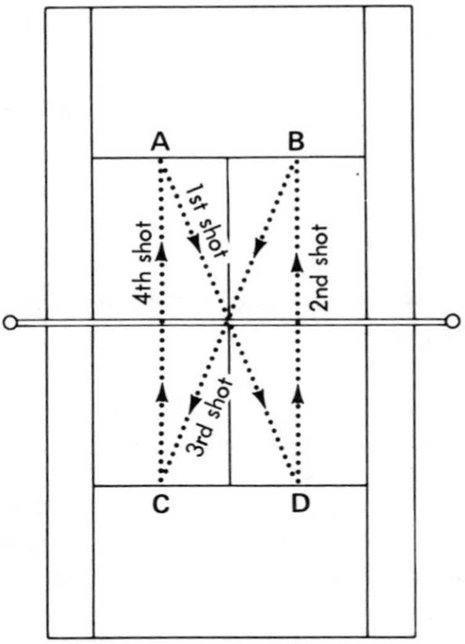

Players keep volleys in play; A to D to B to C to A, etc.

18. ALTERNATING VOLLEYS (Advanced—Four Players)

Four players take positions just behind the service lines opposite each other in cross-court alignments. The players practice volleys, but must hit in this order: Player A to Player D to Player B to Player C, back to Player A, etc. The order in which volleys are hit should be changed frequently so that the players practice volleying in different directions.

Figure 8-39   Alternating Volleys

COMBINATION DRILLS

1. SERVE, RUSH, AND VOLLEY (Advanced—Two to Eight Players)

This is a three shot drill. Player A serves and rushes the net, Player B returns the serve, and Player A hits a crosscourt volley. The same drill can be structured for doubles situations by adding a net player, a receiver's partner, and moving the server closer to the alley.

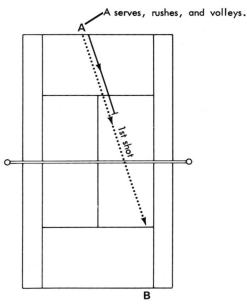

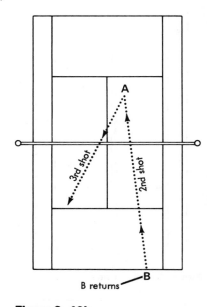

Figure 8–40a   Serve, Rush, and Volley

Figure 8–40b

Player serves and moves to a volleying position while coach times his approach to that position.

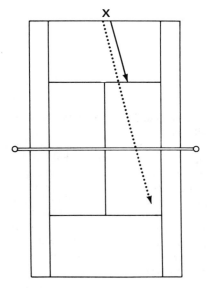

Figure 8–41   Stop Watch Drill

2. STOP WATCH DRILL (Advanced—Two to Eight Players)

This drill is a variation of the *Serve, Rush, and Volley* drill. The player serves and moves in to a volleying position. The coach records the time it takes for the server to reach the volleying position. The purpose of the drill is to make the player conscious of getting good court position, but this should not be done at the expense of losing body control. The velocity of the serve must also be taken into account; fast serves give the server less time to rush, while slow serves give him more time.

3. APPROACH AND VOLLEY (Intermediates and Advanced—Two to Eight Players)

The player takes a position in the middle of the court at the baseline. The coach hits shots that fall short enough in the service courts so that the player can move in to hit an approach shot. After the approach shot, the coach returns the ball with a set-up which the attacking player puts away with a volley.

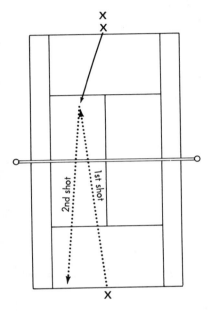

Players start at baseline; move in to hit approach shot and volley.

Coach hits set-up for approach shot.

Figure 8–42a   Approach and Volley

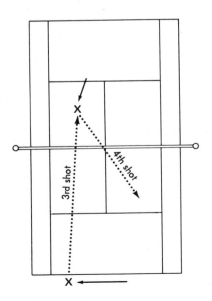

Player moves in behind approach shot for put-away volley.

Coach moves to return with a set-up volley.

Figure 8–42b

4. SERVE, APPROACH, AND VOLLEY (Intermediates and Advanced—Two to Eight Players)

This drill is an extension of the drill previously described (Figure 8-42a & b). Instead of beginning with an approach set-up by the coach, the player serves the ball. The complete sequence is: (1) player serves; (2) coach returns with an approach set-up; (3) player hits down-the-line approach shot; (4) coach returns down the same line; (5) player hits crosscourt volley.

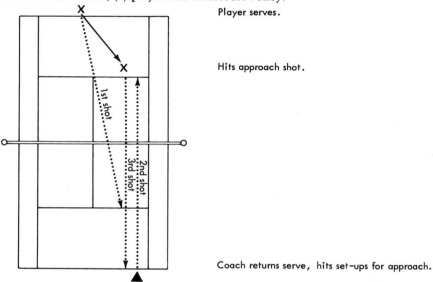

Player serves.

Hits approach shot.

Coach returns serve, hits set-ups for approach.

Figure 8–43a　Serve, Approach, and Volley

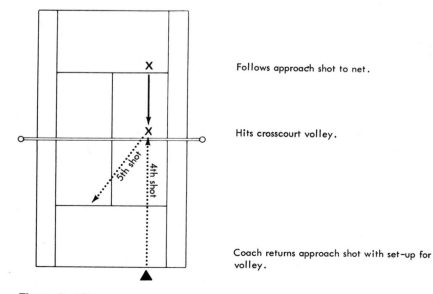

Follows approach shot to net.

Hits crosscourt volley.

Coach returns approach shot with set-up for volley.

Figure 8–43b

5. SERVICE RETURN ATTACK (Intermediates and Advanced—Two Players)

Two players play games or sets, but the server is not allowed to come to the net following the serve. The player returning the serve attempts to hit forcing returns so that he can take the net. After the first two shots, either player may move in to a volleying position. The purpose of the drill is to develop a player's ability to hit forcing shots against a nonattacking server.

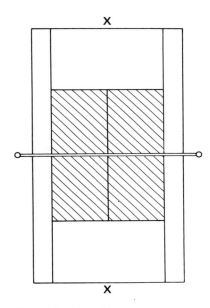

Figure 8–44 Attack

Players hit groundstrokes until one shot falls into marked area; opponent responds with approach shot; point is played out.

6. ATTACK (Advanced—Two, Three, or Four Players)

Two players begin hitting groundstrokes from baseline positions. When either player hits a shot which falls into the opponent's service court area, the opponent responds with an approach shot, and rushes the net. From that position, the point is played out under game conditions.

7. GET TO THE NET (Advanced—Four Players)

Two doubles teams play a twenty-one point game. The serve changes every time the score equals a multiple of five. A team that wins an exchange when both partners have taken a position inside the service line receives two points. If either partner is behind the service line, only one point is earned. The purpose of this drill is to stimulate doubles partners to attack and take positions at the net.

8. RECEIVER'S ADVANTAGE (Intermediates and Advanced-Two or Four Players)

Players or doubles teams play five-point games. However, the server or serving team gets only one-half point on each exchange won while the receiving player or team gets one point. The difference offsets the advantage usually held by the server.

277

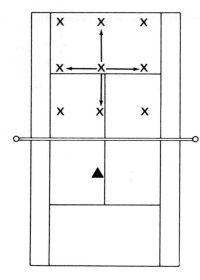

Players move in the direction indicated by the coach.

Coach motions, indicating forward, backward or lateral movement.

Figure 8—45   Wave Drill

9. WAVE DRILL (Beginners, Intermediates, Advanced—Two to Twenty Players)

This is a footwork drill in which players are positioned in rows, facing the net, with room to maneuver. The instructor indicates either forward, backward, or lateral movement by waving his hand. As he motions, the players move in the direction indicated, and they carry their rackets as if preparing to hit a shot. The drill may be used to develop footwork and as a conditioning drill.

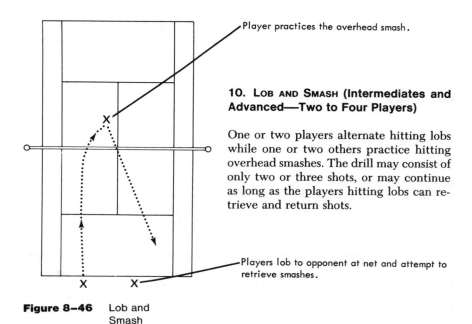

Player practices the overhead smash.

10. LOB AND SMASH (Intermediates and Advanced—Two to Four Players)

One or two players alternate hitting lobs while one or two others practice hitting overhead smashes. The drill may consist of only two or three shots, or may continue as long as the players hitting lobs can retrieve and return shots.

Players lob to opponent at net and attempt to retrieve smashes.

Figure 8—46   Lob and Smash

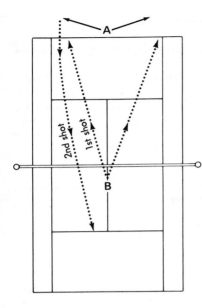

Figure 8–47 Defensive Lobs

Player A retrieves deep drives; returns with high, deep, defensive lob.

Player B or coach drives shots deeply to either forehand or backhand.

11. DEFENSIVE LOBS (Advanced—Two to Six Players)

The coach or teacher stands at the net with a basket of balls. The player assumes a position in the middle of the baseline on the opposite side of the net. The coach drives shots deep to either corner, and the player attempts to chase the shots down, return shots with a high, deep, defensive lob, and return to a central position on the baseline. This drill consists of only two shots.

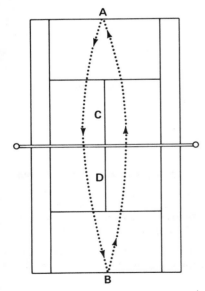

Figure 8–48 Over the Net Player

Players A and B hit lobs only, attempting to clear net man. Players C and D smash any lobs hit short.

12. OVER THE NET PLAYER (Intermediates and Advanced—Four Players)

Two players keep the ball in play hitting only lobs. Two other players are placed near the net on opposite sides. Any lob which goes short is smashed by one of the net players. The player hitting the smash must avoid hitting at the net player opposite him. Score may be kept by counting the number of lobs which clear the players at the net.

13. SERVE, LOB, AND COVER (Advanced—Three Players)

This is a drill for doubles players to practice the serve, the return of serve with a lob, and a third shot which may be a smash or another lob. Here is the sequence of shots: (1) One player serves and moves into a volleying position; (2) The player returning the serve lobs down the line; the third shot is either an overhead smash by the server's partner at the net or a return lob by the server covering for his partner. The drill stops after three shots. The server should alternate sides, and the players should rotate among positions. A fourth player may be added to the drill as the service returner's partner, and the point may be played out.

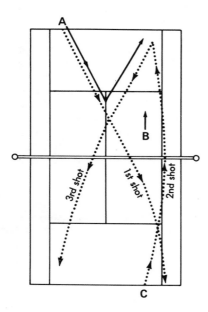

Player A serves, moves to the net and retreats to cover the deep lob.

Player B smashes any short lobs off the return of serve.

Player C returns serve with a lob.

Figure 8–49   Serve, Lob, and Cover

14. VARIATIONS (Beginners, Intermediates, and Advanced—Two to Four Players)

There are many variations of the traditional methods of scoring and positioning of players to begin play. Here are some of them which may be used as drills:

 1. **No Ad Sets.** Scoring is conventional, except that when the score reaches deuce, the receiver has the choice of courts and the player who wins the next point wins the game.

 2. **VASSS Simplied Scoring System.** Twenty-one point games; serve changes every five points; players change sides after five, fifteen, and twenty-five points.

3. **Tie Breakers.** Players practice nine- or twelve-point tie breakers without playing regular games to get used to the pressure created by tie breakers in six-six sets.

4. **Two On One.** Two players are matched against one; partners defend doubles court, while opponent defends singles court.

5. **15–30 Games.** Many coaches feel that the fourth point in a game is the most crucial one; in this variation, play begins with the score at 15–30, and the game is played out from that point.[1]

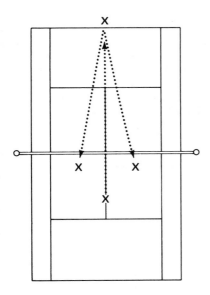

Baseline player practices groundstrokes.

Volleyers and feeder keep ball in play with controlled volleys.

Figure 8–50   Three Against One Monster

15. THREE AGAINST ONE MONSTER (Intermediates and Advanced—Four Players or Three Players and a Coach)

Two players take positions at the net with a third player (or coach) behind them with a basket of balls. This player feeds shots to a fourth player on the opposite baseline. The baseline player works on groundstrokes; the other three keep the ball in play with controlled volleys. As soon as a ball goes out of play, the player or coach with the basket puts another ball into play. Players rotate to the right or left after each turn.

[1] Brown, *Tennis,* 151-168.

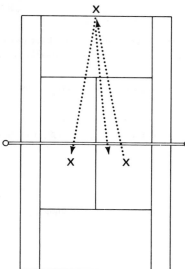

Baseline player works on groundstrokes.

Net players keep ball in play with controlled volleys.

16. Two Against One (Intermediates and Advanced—Three Players)

Two players at the net keep the ball in play with controlled volleys against one player at the baseline who works on groundstrokes. Players rotate after a specified time period or after a certain number of balls have been played.

Figure 8–51 Two Against One

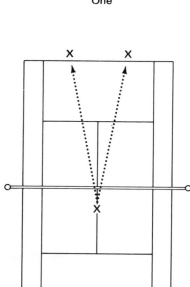

Baseline players hit controlled groundstrokes.

Net player practices put-away and controlled volleys.

17. One Against Two (Intermediates and Advanced—Three Players)

One player at the net practices controlled and put-away volleys against two players on the opposite baseline. The two at the baseline hit controlled groundstrokes to give the volleyer practice.

Figure 8–52 One Against Two

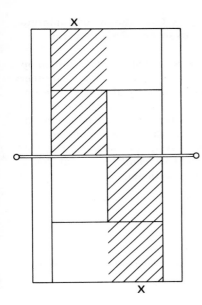

Figure 8-53   Crosscourt
Singles

Players compete using only crosscourt areas and shots.

18. CROSSCOURT SINGLES (Advanced— Two Players)

Two players play games using only the crosscourt areas of respective singles courts. The players can stay on the same sides of the court the entire match or change from left to right with each point or game. This drill is helpful in developing crosscourt patterns with the forehand or backhand.

Baseline players practice serves.

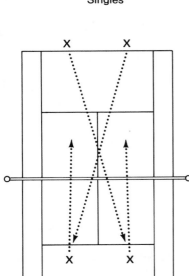

19. CLOSE UP RETURNS (Intermediates and Advanced—Four Players)

Two players practice the serve while two others practice returning serves from positions well inside the baseline. The "close up" positions force the receivers to react quickly to the ball.

Receivers return serves from positions near the service line.

Figure 8-54   Close Up
Returns

283

20. SHADOW DRILL (Beginners, Intermediates, Advanced—Four Players)

Two players per half court line up on opposite sides of the net facing each other. One player is designated as the leader. That player moves in any direction while the other player tries to go in the same direction at the same time. After thirty seconds the players reverse roles. This drill can be used for court movement, quickness, and conditioning.

These two players move in any direction.

These players try to move in the same direction.

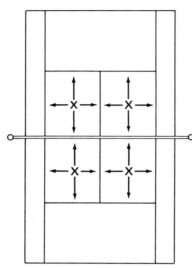

Figure 8-55   Shadow Drill

Baseline player tries to hit passing shot.

Net player puts ball into play and defends the court.

21. PASSING SHOTS (Intermediates and Advanced—Two Players)

A player at the net puts a ball into play to an opponent on the opposite baseline. The ball has to be placed easily to either the forehand or backhand side. The player at the baseline then tries to pass the net player and the point is played out from there. Five points wins the game, then the players change places.

Figure 8-56   Passing Shots

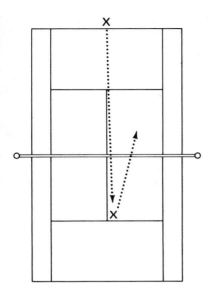

Baseline player puts ball into play with an easy, shallow shot.

Service line player tries to hit drop shot, but may hit any other shot.

Figure 8–57   Drop Shots

22. DROP SHOTS (Intermediates and Advanced—Two Players)

One player stands at the baseline, drops a ball, and hits a shallow, easy shot to the opponent positioned on the opposite service line. The player at the service line may hit a drop shot, but may also hit any other shot if the baseline player charges the net too soon. The point is then played out, and the first player to win five points wins the game. The purpose is to practice hitting drop shots, to learn to disguise the shot, and to learn how to anticipate the shot.

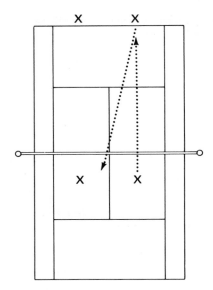

Doubles partners at baseline try to hit low, down the middle shot.

Partners at net put ball into play, then play the point out.

Figure 8–58 Doubles Passing Shots

23. DOUBLES PASSING SHOTS (Intermediates and Advanced—Four Players)

Two doubles partners take positions at the net and put an easy shot into play against two partners on the baseline. The baseline players practice hitting low and down the middle, but may use any other shot. The point is played out after the ball is put into play.

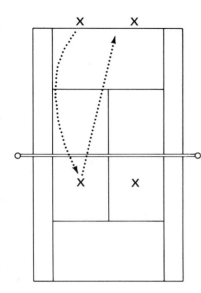

Baseline partners lob to opponents, then play the point out.

Players at net try to win with smashes.

24. DOUBLES LOBS AND SMASHES (Intermediates and Advanced—Four Players)

Two doubles partners take positions on the baseline and put the ball into play with a lob to two players at the net. The point is then played out. The first team to win five points wins the game, then positions are changed.

Figure 8–59   Doubles Lobs and Smashes

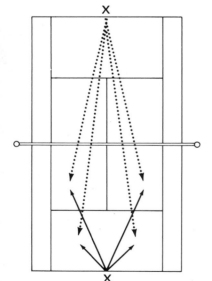

Player with basket of balls hits to any part of court.

25. TWO MINUTE DRILL (Intermediates and Advanced—Two Players)

One player stands at the baseline with a basket of balls. He begins hitting balls to any part of the opposite court while the second player gets everything within reach in a two minute period. As soon as one shot is hit, another ball is put into play. The drill can be expanded to longer time periods. Other players can serve as timers, hitters, and ball retrievers while waiting their turns.

Retriever gets every shot for two minutes.

Figure 8–60   Two Minute Drill

References

BARNABY, JOHN M. *Advantage Tennis: Racket Work, Tactics, and Logic.* Boston: Allyn and Bacon, Inc., 1975.

BONNETTE, LOUIS, AND JIM BROWN, "Publicizing a Collegiate Tennis Program," *Tennis Trade,* 3, no. 3 (March, 1974), p. 20.

BROWN, ARLENE, AND JIM BROWN, "A Woman's Guide to Beginning Tennis," *The Woman,* 10, no. 2 (June, 1975), p. 110.

BROWN, JIM, "Coaching Without a Background," *Scholastic Coach,* 40, no. 6 (February, 1971), p. 42.

————, "Do-It-Yourself Tennis Clinic," *The Coaching Clinic,* 11, no. 1 (January, 1973), p. 9.

————, "Fixing a Faulty Forehand," *Tennis USA,* 40, no. 11 (November, 1977), p. 37.

————, "Flaw Finish: #1, The Service," *Scholastic Coach,* 43, no. 9 (May, 1974), p. 44.

————, "Flaw Finish: #2, The Forehand," *Scholastic Coach,* 44, no. 6 (February, 1975), p. 28.

————, "Flaw Finish: #3, The Backhand," *Scholastic Coach,* 44, no. 7 (March, 1975), p. 8.

————, "Flaw Finish: #4, The Overhead Smash," *Scholastic Coach,* 44, no. 9 (April, 1975), p. 15.

————, "Flaw Finish: #5, The Volley," *Scholastic Coach,* 45, no. 7 (February, 1976), p. 64.

————, "How to Go From Doorstep to Dominance in College Tennis," *Tennis Trade,* 2, no. 7 (July, 1973), p. 34.

————, "Newcomers to Tennis Instruction are Often Oldtimers," *Tennis Trade,* 2, no. 4 (April, 1973), p. 32.

————, "Post-Match Scouting in Tennis," *Scholastic Coach,* 43, no. 7 (March, 1974), p. 74.

————, "Psychological Factors in Teaching Tennis to Pre-Teens," *Scholastic Coach,* 41, no. 8 (April, 1972), p. 104.

————, "Recruiting College Tennis Players," *Coach and Athlete*, 32, no. 11 (June, 1970), p. 30.

————, "Seven Cardinal Sins of High School Tennis Players," *Scholastic Coach*, 41, no. 7 (March, 1972), p. 68.

————, *Tennis: Teaching, Coaching, and Directing Programs*. Englewood Cliffs, New Jersey: Prentice-Hall, Inc., 1976.

————, *Tennis Without Lessons*. Englewood Cliffs, New Jersey: Prentice-Hall, Inc., 1978.

————, "Thinking Lefthanded," *Scholastic Coach*, 42, no. 7 (March, 1973), p. 68.

CHAMBERLAIN, BRIAN, AND JIM BROWN, "Anticipation and the Intermediate Tennis Player," *Athletic Journal*, 51, no. 9 (May, 1972), p. 38.

GALLWEY, W. TIMOTHY, *The Inner Game of Tennis*. New York: Random House, 1974.

GOULD, DICK, *Tennis, Anyone?* (2nd ed.). Palo Alto, California: National Press Books, 1971.

KENFIELD, JOHN, *Teaching and Coaching Tennis*. Dubuque, Iowa: Wm. C. Brown Company Publishers, 1964.

MASON, ELAINE, *Tennis*. Boston: Allyn and Bacon, Inc., 1974.

MURPHY, BILL, *Complete Book of Championship Tennis Drills*. West Nyack, New York: Parker Publishing Company, 1975.

MURPHY, CHET, AND BILL MURPHY, *Tennis for the Player, Teacher and Coach*. Philadelphia: W. B. Saunders Company, 1975.

Index